Mother Nature's
Daughters

T0048305

ALSO BY PAULA vW. DAIL
AND FROM McFARLAND

*Hard Living in America's Heartland: Rural Poverty
in the 21st Century Midwest* (2015)

Women and Poverty in 21st Century America (2012)

Mother Nature's Daughters

21st Century Women Farmers

PAULA vW. DÁIL

McFarland & Company, Inc., Publishers
Jefferson, North Carolina

LIBRARY OF CONGRESS CATALOGUING-IN-PUBLICATION DATA

Names: Dáil, Paula vW., author.
Title: Mother nature's daughters : 21st century women farmers /
  Paula vW. Dáil.
Description: Jefferson, North Carolina : McFarland & Company, Inc.,
  Publishers, 2016. | Includes bibliographical references and index.
Identifiers: LCCN 2016041154 | ISBN 9780786497829 (softcover :
  acid free paper) ∞
Subjects: LCSH: Women farmers—United States. | Farm life—United
  States.
Classification: LCC S521.5.A2 D35 2016 | DDC 630.82—dc23
LC record available at https://lccn.loc.gov/2016041154

BRITISH LIBRARY CATALOGUING DATA ARE AVAILABLE

ISBN (print) 978-0-7864-9782-9
ISBN (ebook) 978-1-4766-2722-9

Front cover: Sonia Kendrick proudly shows off carrots harvested
from her first crop as an urban farmer in Cedar Rapids; the farming
effort is part of the Feed Iowa First initiative Sonia founded
(photograph by Terra Firma Anthony Masterson Productions); In
order to not overeat, which cows are prone to do, all 150 of Sadie
Zimmer's cows at Otter Creek Organic Farm must take turns in the
barn feed stations during the winter (courtesy Sadie Zimmer).

Printed in the United States of America

McFarland & Company, Inc., Publishers
  Box 611, Jefferson, North Carolina 28640
  www.mcfarlandpub.com

This book is dedicated to the amazing women farmers
who are working hard to put good food on our tables.
I wish I could be more like you.
It is also dedicated to women everywhere who,
like women farmers, live their lives their way,
on their terms.

Acknowledgments

This book would not exist without the awesomely remarkable women farmers who were willing to share their stories. They are all very busy people, and I am deeply honored that they felt this project was worthy enough of their time that they were willing to talk with me.

Katilyn Peck is a dedicated, committed assistant who stepped up to do whatever needed doing as this book came together. As we worked through several versions of the manuscript she was generous with her praise, never hesitated to express her concerns, and always offered good insights. She is the colleague every writer wishes for, and I am very thankful to have.

Heather Kurek at Springs Printing deserves a special shout-out for always making my poor planning her emergency. She would say she was just doing her job; I would say she made it possible for me to do mine.

My husband, Bill Ladewig, has been a terrific partner in this endeavor. He thrashed out ideas with me during the entire time I was writing this book, and I knew he would always tell me what he thought rather than what he thought I wanted to hear. As an award-winning writer himself, I trust his opinion on everything I write. We don't always agree, and I don't always take his advice, but I deeply appreciate his willingness to cast a critical eye over my work and offer an opinion. Most of all, I am profoundly grateful that he is willing to live with a dedicated writer who doesn't cook or do laundry.

Table of Contents

Preface

Only three things will kill a farmer: being struck by lightning, rolling the tractor in a ditch, and old age.

—Bill Bryson

June Hartline was generally regarded as a tough old broad. Most people guessed her age at between 60 and 80 years old, and she wasn't telling. June was as wide as she was tall, and those who knew her made a purposeful effort to stay on her good side because she never met a problem she couldn't solve, and sometimes her solution didn't meet with widespread enthusiasm.

My first encounter with June occurred soon after the county magistrate suspended her driver's license for a year. June's solution to losing her chief means of transportation was to leave her truck parked on the farm and drive her New Holland 682 horsepower tractor, with the high capacity John Deere 785 manure spreader attached, into town to run her errands. Technically this wasn't illegal because a tractor is farm equipment, not personal transportation, and at that time driving one on public roads did not require a driver's license.

June's livelihood involved crop farming about 300 acres and running a 200 head beef cattle operation just outside of town. She kept several robust one ton bulls for breeding purposes and sold their semen as an additional source of income. I met her when my editor at the local newspaper assigned me to cover a breaking story about a dust-up at the county airport, which was situated adjacent to June's pastures.

The issue involved Boxer Radke, the newly hired airport manager. Boxer had allowed several stunt pilots to rent hangars to store their planes and use local air space to practice their craft, which involved dive bombing June's prize bulls. When this occurred, the bulls went berserk, broke through the pasture gates and took off down the nearby interstate highway, creating a serious traffic hazard and endangering public safety. Running

1

loose on a heavily traveled highway wasn't good for the bulls either. The local sheriff, who didn't want to tangle with June if he could avoid it, always apologized before reminding her that he was sworn to uphold the law and his only choice was to issue her a citation for failing to control her livestock.

After the third citation, which carried a hefty fine, June drove her manure spreader over to the airport, parked it on the runway, and threatened Boxer's manhood if he didn't stop the stunt flyers immediately. Boxer took June's threat very seriously, called the county board chairman and demanded he convene an emergency meeting of the five-member airport commission, which oversaw airport operations.

The meeting was held at the airport. I arrived to find June and her support crowd milling around inside and outside the airport office. The airport commissioners were standing around looking as unsettled as I imagined General Custer's troops must've been as they prepared to face down Chief Crazy Horse in the Battle of the Little Big Horn. Clearly the commissioners were outnumbered, and to the extent June's reputation preceded her, they were outsmarted—and they knew it. Intending to claim their right to fly in public airspace, the stunt pilots also came to the meeting. However, when they realized what they were up against, they left.

As was often the case, I was asked to take the minutes of the commission meeting, since I would be reporting on the story anyway. I was seated at the front of the room, next to the commission chairman, and facing the crowd. The chairman, mistakenly as it turned out, thought it wise to begin by allowing June to speak her mind, and invited her to explain her perception of the problem. At that point he lost control of the meeting.

June, who hadn't bothered to change out of her work clothes which, on this humid August afternoon, carried the thick, pungent aroma of a recently reloaded manure spreader, stomped her way around the attendees and up to the front of the room. Without missing a beat, she proceeded to describe, in very graphic detail, the reproductive behavior of a bull. When necessary to make her point, she compared this activity to the same behavior in human males.

The commission members sat stone-faced silent, squirming in their seats and staring at the floor. Boxer looked as if he were going to be sick and June's support system was not making much effort to hide their amusement. Trying to maintain a minimal level of journalistic professionalism by not laughing out loud, I jammed my fist into my mouth.

June asked the local veterinarian to provide supporting testimony.

Doc A, as he was affectionately known, affirmed that a bull's reproductive system doesn't work as well as it should when the bull is upset. He went on to explain the semen extraction process with greater precision than I felt was really required in these circumstances. Doc stressed that while he had full confidence in his professional ability to perform the procedure, he wouldn't want to try it on a recently disturbed 2000 pound bull. To emphasize his point, Doc popped out his four front teeth. "Continual stress can cause a bull to become permanently sterile," he lisped, adding that this would negatively impact June's bottom line, and also his own, since he didn't perform the procedure for free. He ended his presentation by snapping his teeth back into his mouth.

The chairman said he was sorry about all this, but didn't know what the commissioners could do about it. "Stop the goddamned planes, or I'll take care of the problem myself," June hollered out from the back of the room, using additional body language to make it perfectly clear that she was finished discussing the issue and the meeting was over. Boxer took June's threat personally, panicked, and called the sheriff. The commissioners were the first out the door, before the meeting was formally adjourned. Later that day the commission chair contacted me, sheepishly requesting that I not report all the details of what had occurred at the meeting. "Depends on how many newspapers we need to sell next week," I replied, realizing how much I was enjoying this story.

By month's end Boxer was seeking other employment and the commission had refunded the pilots' hangar rent and told them to move on. Because of continual complaints about June spilling manure all over the city streets every time she went into town, the mayor pressured the magistrate, who was up for re-election, to vacate her sentence and restore her driving privileges. He reluctantly complied, citing environmental impact concerns.

Once her bulls were happily grazing in the pastures and June had retired her manure spreader in favor of her driving truck things settled down. "There's peace in the valley once again ... until somebody else crosses her," the sheriff told me when I called to inquire about any further incidents involving June and law enforcement officials. After we hung up I found myself in awe of how one woman was able to hold an entire county hostage to her wishes, and I couldn't help admiring June's remarkable ability to control her environment by manipulating whatever situation she found herself in to achieve her desired outcome, using any means necessary, to get the job done.

June Hartline was one of the first woman farmers I ever met. While

I've never forgotten her, she isn't the only woman farmer who really impressed me, because every woman farmer I've ever met has impressed me. I have envied each of them for their remarkable self-assurance, abundant courage, creative problem-solving abilities, and personal resolve to live life on their own terms, regardless of the economic or social costs these terms imposed. I've not met many women like them, and I carried that thought with me for a long time before I became serious about writing this book.

A few years later, while writing *Women and Poverty in 21st Century America,* I developed a clear picture of the food issues facing the poor and how ingenious poor women can be when having to cope with these challenges. Then, while I was writing *Hard Living in America's Heartland: Rural Poverty in the 21st Century Midwest,* I began seeing a lot of bumper stickers saying "Want to Eat? Support Women Farmers" and discovered that women now own nearly half the nation's farmland. I also discovered that many women farmers live at or below the poverty line, and even those who manage seven figure farm enterprises live modestly and fold most of their profits back into the farm operation. While none of the women like their sparse and unpredictable economic circumstances, they love being farmers too much to quit farming just to earn more money. Personal satisfaction and making a positive contribution to their communities, not chasing after the almighty dollar, is the driving force in their lives. I deeply admired this level of personal freedom and resolve to configure their lives into what they want them to be rather than seeking to become what society might expect women to be. "These are brave women leading very courageous lives," I said to anyone who would listen. I found that most people hadn't thought about women farmers in that context and were captivated by the notion of a woman voluntarily taking on a "man's job."

At the same time, on a fairly routine basis, I was encountering women farmers in places like the hardware store, Farm and Fleet stores, and the local farmers' market and roadside farm stands. I began chatting with them about farming in general and their own farm work in particular. The common theme in every one of these conversations was the fact that not only were these women leading amazing lives, they were also making heroic efforts to improve the quality of the food supply while living in poverty themselves. They were, I thought, a book-worthy group.

But this wasn't the whole picture. As a career poverty researcher I was intrigued by both the similarities and the differences between women farmers specifically and women in poverty generally. These seemed to revolve around three issues:

First, women farmers love what they are doing, and they work for themselves. Poor women generally are either unemployed, seeking and unable to find employment, or underemployed. Worse, the jobs available to them are the ones no one else wants, because the work is nasty and the pay is minimal. These women work for bosses who don't necessarily have their best interest at heart and are subject to discrimination and sexual and other harassment by their employers. If they want to keep their job, these women often feel powerless to stop any of this.

Second, women who farm have made a conscious lifestyle choice and are willing to accept the economic consequences of this choice. They have not been, as is true with most poor women, born into or thrust into poverty by circumstances far beyond their control. There is a big difference between choosing how one wants to live and being forced to accept a life one doesn't want and can't do anything to change.

Third, women farmers are organized and have a voice in the political arena where policy decisions affecting them are made. Most poor women have no political voice at all. As a result, women farmers have a sense of political power other poor women can't claim and have no means to access.

These issues have always fueled my deep and abiding interest in women's struggles and in all the ways women work for greater social responsibility and even-handed social justice, often under very trying circumstances. I decided documenting the lives of women farmers would make an important contribution to the body of knowledge about all the ways women struggle to survive in the world and work hard to make the world better. Once having made that determination, the rest was amazingly easy.

Almost immediately I discovered that the existing literature on women farmers is surprisingly sparse, particularly considering how many of them there are. I'm not sure why this is, but the void fueled my desire to push forward, and since I was not constrained by a large body of existing research, it was clear I could structure this book in any of several ways. I wanted to include women who were engaged in various kinds of farming operations, and it was not difficult to identify several who were willing to share their stories. To the contrary, once word got out that I was writing this book, women farmers seemed to find me, with one exception: The Cistercian nuns who farm land belonging to Our Lady of the Mississippi Cistercian Abbey in Iowa. They are a cloistered religious community that does not interact with the wider world and strictly limits their public presence. I doubted they would have any particular interest in this book and certainly would have no reason to allow me to interview them. Nevertheless, I really wanted to talk with them, because they represent a farming lifestyle that several orders of nuns have been engaged in for hundreds of years and is built upon a value system driven by ancient scripture and commitment to the principles behind good farming practices. With this in mind, I knew the farming sisters had something very valuable to say on the topic and wanted to include them. I felt sure my ten years in Catholic girls' boarding school might help, because it gave me the vocabulary to converse comfortably with nuns, and they with me, but I couldn't figure out how to begin a conversation.

In early spring, I happened to sit next to a Franciscan Sister of Perpetual Adoration at the special screening of a DVD on women and farming being held at the Sinsinawa Dominican Motherhouse not too far from the abbey. We began chatting and it turned out Sister Kristin knew Mother Rebecca Stramoski, the abbess of Our Lady of the Mississippi Abbey, and agreed to intervene on my behalf. Several weeks later, Sister Gail Fitzpatrick, former abbess of the Cistercian community, sent me an email asking several specific questions about the project. After receiving my answers, Sister Gail said she would reflect on them, present the idea to the community and offer them the opportunity to dialogue about their participation, then get back to me. In late August, she sent me another email, inviting me to come to the abbey, but asking that I wait a month because they were busy with a timber harvest.

When the day of my appointment with Sister Gail arrived I was greeted by one of the most delightful and interesting religious women I have ever encountered. She had invited some other sisters to join us, and we had a wonderful conversation that opened the door to many more. I came away profoundly grateful for the time we spent together—and honored that the sisters felt the book project was worthy of their time, and thus were willing to allow me to visit.

Ultimately, the biggest challenge was getting the women who did agree to participate in the book to talk about their lives in deeper ways that went beyond the good deal they'd just gotten on a used combine. They all were curious about the book project and most were willing to be interviewed, but none believed what they were doing as women farmers was "that interesting." Convincing them otherwise took effort.

The most difficult decision I had to make was who, among the many fascinating, hard-working women farmers I encountered, to include in the book, because I wanted to include them all. After doing several interviews, it became apparent that the women were tending to fall into categories that would make good book chapters, and I decided to include the stories that best fit these topics. Thus, after an introduction that focuses on the history of women's relationship with land and growing things, subsequent chapters explore women's unique connection with land and growing food; farming for the love of God; farming to make a living; farming as political action; farming to heal a broken soul; food politics and women farmers getting organized; and farming simply because this is what a woman farmer wants to do.

I have never enjoyed writing a book as much as I enjoyed writing this one. I loved the topic and the characters that play leading roles in the story of women and the land. I met so many strong, vital, interesting women who, without even knowing it, are living out the essential feminist life in all its glory, and I likely would not have encountered any of them under other circumstances. I am profoundly grateful for the time we spent together, and I hope I have told their stories as well as they deserve to be told.

Introduction:
The Dirtier My Clothes—
The Better My Day
A Brief History of Woman Farmers

The test for whether or not a woman can do a job should not be the arrangement of her chromosomes.

—Bella Abzug

FARM HAND WANTED—Must have experience and live on property. Pay negotiable. If interested stop by the Mueller farm.

—Job notice posted in central Illinois grain elevator office

I discovered this job notice, scribbled in pencil on a half sheet of lined notebook paper and hanging by one thumbtack on a large bulletin board. I'd come across it when I stopped for directions in some flatland town so similar to all the other rural towns in the farm belt that I can't even remember its name. The note was strategically placed among advertisements for quick and easy artificial insemination services using prize bull semen; cheap manure, delivered free; a quarter horse for stud; notice of an emergency Grange meeting the next day; and an open invitation to attend a Saturday night barn dance featuring half-price beer, live music and karaoke.

Grain elevators define the skyline in farm country. These giant, aluminum tin cans rising ten, twelve, or more stories can be seen from great distances. They serve as, among other things, important landmarks, as in "turn right at the grain elevator," that many rural communities depend upon. One sure thing about rural life is that crop farmers routinely hang out at the grain elevator, either to do business, catch up on the local gossip, or both. The office bulletin boards provide valuable free advertising, as well as being a sure source of information about anything going on that everyone should know about.

I'd stopped in at this particular elevator on a blistering hot, hazy summer day because I was looking for directions to an apparently unmarked township road I'd found impossible to distinguish from all the other unmarked township roads in this particular county. I passed the time while waiting for someone to come into the office by reading the notices, randomly piled at least three deep on the bulletin board.

A few minutes later, the burly elevator operator, wearing bib overalls, a John Deere hat that had seen better days several years ago, and a Pioneer Seed Company plastic name tag that identified him as Lloyd, walked through the back door. Having heard me wonder aloud about who'd gotten the farm hand job, Lloyd's first words were that he didn't think I had the necessary qualifications for farm work. "You gotta be able to drive a 650 horespower John Deere tractor, run a combine, and operate a post-hole digger and bale hay. Helps if you can program a GPS to plant straight rows, milk cows, castrate pigs, and bale hay, and other stuff," he told me, adding that it didn't look to him like I knew how to do those things. I decided to follow this conversation wherever it went, and promptly admitted that he was right about all those things, but I was sure I could learn to operate the farm machinery. I chose to ignore the pig castration requirement.

"I suppose it's pretty long hours," I said. "Long as it takes," Lloyd told me. "How about medical and dental?" I asked. "Doc Wilson don't charge much to fix you up if you get hurt, and the new dentist over in Colfax replaces teeth pretty reasonable," he answered, apparently oblivious to the fact that there's a lot more to health and dental care than getting stitched up or fixing teeth a horse just kicked out. Wanting to appear seriously interested, I asked whether the job was still available. "Nope," Lloyd answered.

I had to pump Lloyd for further information and was quite surprised to learn that the farm hand Homer Mueller chose was a local girl. She had graduated from the state agricultural college the previous spring and was looking to gain more hands-on farming experience. She'd also won this year's tractor pulling championship at the county fair which, in Homer's eyes, I was told, was a particularly valuable qualification none of the other applicants could claim.

When I expressed genuine surprise at Homer Muller's hiring decision Lloyd said that the girl "was the best qualified—and real hard worker." No further explanation was forthcoming. I'd just spent several long hours driving across roads so overheated steam rose up from the blacktop, only to find myself in a place whose only distinction was seemingly endless, flat miles of wilted cornfields begging for rain. Now, standing in a dusty grain office with sweat dripping down my back, I was having a very hard time envisioning why anyone, male or female, could possibly want a job working on a farm anywhere in this vicinity.

After Lloyd gave me directions to the road I'd already spent over an hour looking for, I turned around and headed 45 miles back in the direction I'd just come from. With many miles ahead of me, and the sun beating down through my windshield, I had plenty of time to wonder why any young woman, particularly one who could access all the opportunities college graduation provides, would want to become involved in farming.

"In my opinion, there is no career more rewarding than farming," says Zoey Brooks, a vivacious, bright-eyed, and articulate recent graduate of the University of Wisconsin–Madison's production agriculture program. She is serving as Wisconsin's 67th Alice in Dairyland[1] and clearly loving every minute of her year as the public face of Wisconsin agriculture. "Every day, every season, every year, you are able to see the fruits of your labor—literally. I want to be in a career where I am able to see my hard work pay off and when it comes to farming, while there are many unknowns, your efforts are visible," she explains enthusiastically.

Zoey's career decision to return to her family's farm after college was, for her, a no-brainer that reflects a sense of responsibility to both the past and the future. Her pioneering ancestors first began to till the land she was born and raised on in 1855. Six years passed before the Civil War broke out and threatened to tear our young nation apart, and another seven years before the Homestead Act would be legislated into law. The Brooks farm became operational a few short years after Wisconsin became a state, during an era when nearly all of the land west of the Appalachian mountain range was sparsely populated, wide-open prairie, for as far as the eye could see. "As the sixth generation on this farm, I feel a very keen sense of responsibility to keep it in the family and work to improve it for the next generation. I am eternally grateful to the generations who came before my own who also felt this responsibility and made the farm their lifestyle. I want to provide that opportunity to my own children and generations beyond."

That one family has managed to hold on to their farm for more than a century and a half, through the ups and downs of farming life, reflects an commitment to the land so deep that it has held strong, no matter what adversity has befallen the family or the farm economy over the years. Zoey agrees with this perception of her family as several generation, life-long farmers, but also sees her decision to return to the farm in broader terms. "Women have worked alongside their fathers, brothers, uncles, and husbands in this industry for a long time, but they haven't always taken the lead role in the operation. I hope to set an example and inspire other young women to consider a career in production agriculture. I am also grateful for the work ethic and knowledge I gained from growing up in production agriculture. These are things that are hard to attain anywhere else and are important attributes I want to afford future generations." She is also very clear that, for her, dressing up every day for a nine-to-five job sitting behind a desk holds no appeal whatever.

Some would say that, as a woman, Zoey is a pioneer in the agricultural enterprise, but this assumption would be misleading. While women have come a long way in the world of agriculture as a business endeavor, particularly as farming has moved away from small, single family operations to become a worldwide industry, they have always farmed. They just weren't officially called farmers; instead, they were referred to as farmer's wives. However, today, there is an official category in the agricultural census that allows women to identify themselves as farmers and, in 2012, 294,000 women, representing 14 percent of the nation's 2.1 million farmers did exactly that.[2] In some ways, this figure represents definite progress for women interested in pursuing careers in agriculture. In other ways, the number is not surprising, because farm wives have always been partners with their husbands in running all aspects of a farm operation. With this in mind, deciding to take on the responsibility for a farm of one's own would be the natural next step for any woman who is interested in pursuing a career choice that fosters independence, self-sufficiency, supreme self-confidence, pride and humility, and requires an array of unique personal abilities and skills.

Because the average independent, woman-operated farm nets a mere $4,484 in annual income, women who take up the hard work of farming have to be motivated by something much deeper than a simple desire to be their own boss.[3] Independent woman farmer Lyn Garling finds this income statistic "pitiful" and is convinced that women who pursue farming do not do it for the money. Since farming is a 24/7, 365 days per year job that, for women, can pay as little as $0.51 per hour, it appears that she is correct.

"It's in my blood and breath to be in cahoots with Mother Nature," explains Andrea Hazzard, the 39-year-old owner of Hazzard Free Farms. A farm operation her family began on the Illinois flatlands in 1847 is now, among other things, a heritage grain operation. "I'm restless and have a hard time being indoors ... and I'm fundamentally alienated from modern society.... I have always seen myself in a farming situation and as it is with all things, coincidental or magical, everything that I did before I became a farmer perfectly prepared me to become one now."

Petite, with strong hands, remarkable agility, and a big bundle of dreadlocks held back with a bandana, Andrea exudes great pride in her farming heritage, which began 13 years before the nation elected Abraham Lincoln, a man Illinois claims as their own, president of the United States. She talks of having learned to drive a tractor before she was old enough to drive a car, of knowing how to talk to a horse and mow a hayfield, and of having grown up in the wide open, outdoor spaces surrounding a four-square, prairie farmhouse. Although her eight-year-old sub-business of the larger farm operation has yet to operate in the black, she doesn't think about whether she can farm successfully. "Failure's just not an option," she explains, with firm conviction.

Zoey and Andrea both share a rich land heritage and proud pioneering tradition that continues to energize them today. They farm land originally acquired according to the conditions set forth by the Northwest Territorial legislature nearly two centuries ago, before proving up a land claim through homesteading was even possible. With their remarkable family history holding them up and pushing them forward, it's not difficult to grasp the depth of both women's commitment and self-assurance, or to understand what they mean when they say "farming is in my blood."

In the 21st century most, but not all, women farmers raise food rather than commodity crops or significant numbers of livestock. Women-owned farms tend to be smaller enterprises focused on sustainability for their families, their communities, and for the environment. In Andrea's case, an increased awareness of the missteps in the environment and how these were affecting people's health drove her specific interest in farming non-genetically modified heritage grains. "I started thinking too much... reading labels on my shampoo bottles, then the cleaning supplies and bread bags, yogurt cups and on and on. I couldn't stand it any longer ... the thought of plastic and chemical factories and mountaintop removal of mines and poisoned lands and dying oceans.... I decided food was going to be my path of action.... It is universal, it is ancient and it is one of the answers to the myriad of crises the human race faces, along with energy, health care, and climate change."

Women farmers like Andrea tend toward smaller operations, sell in smaller volume, and focus on different products than their male counterparts. They also claim an overall larger share of specialty crops and fiber-producing livestock. Additionally, the average age of a woman farmer is

60 years old, as compared to her male farmer counterpart, whose average age is about 58.[4] This statistic did not surprise me, because the women farmers I know appear healthier and considerably more robust than men farmers of similar age, who tend to "wear out" and start replacing knees, hips and other body parts much sooner. Perhaps the difference between them is at least partially accounted for by the fact that women who farm tend view their work as a healthy lifestyle choice, while for men, farming is a job and a way to earn a living.

Other changes the statistics describing women farmers identify, such as fewer beginners, more minorities, and increasing average age tend to mirror the changes in the agricultural sector generally, says Carolyn Sachs, professor of rural sociology and head of the Women's Studies Department at the Pennsylvania State University. She points out that between 1978 and 2007, the number of independent women farmers increased but, since 2007, has declined.[5] "I'm curious about why this change, and whether it matters. I'm also interested in whether raising different products from male farmers makes women farmers more vulnerable or more resilient during down markets," she says, adding that the answer to these questions "isn't at all clear."

Garling challenges several aspects of the national agricultural statistics, which are derived from the agricultural census conducted every five years. She cautions that looking to these data for answers about how, and why, women choose farming is fraught with difficulty and paints an incomplete picture of women farmers.[6] "Most women farmers receive loans from a special fund earmarked for socially disadvantaged farmers," she points out, "and some women farmers, particularly those running smaller operations, don't want to go there," she explains.

Labeling any woman who works in a male dominated field "socially disadvantaged" bespeaks an explosively negative attitude toward women that is surprising in 2015. It also reflects a residual social patriarchy both Sachs[7] and Sonya Salaman[8] have described as alive and well in rural areas as recently as twenty years ago. I tend toward believing this issue has been overstated and, because I have been unable to document it, would like to think it no longer exists. But, in reality, a rural patriarchy probably does exist, at least to some degree. Nevertheless, despite any label attached to women farmers, it is very unlikely that a descriptor, no matter how unflattering, has ever has been able to keep a woman who wants to farm from doing it.

Two other issues complicate efforts to obtain an accurate picture of how many women farm. One is that farming is no longer listed as an occupation on the regular census forms, so women who farm as a primary occupation won't be able to identify themselves. The other is that participation in the agricultural census, which occurs twice per decade, is voluntary and many farmers, both female and male, probably don't bother with it.

There is also the problem of how farming is defined when compiling the statistics on women farmers. "Farms can be very small, producing only $1000 in sales and income, including government payments, and still be counted as active farm operations[9] ... and there is no provision to reflect the entrepreneurial framework within which a lot of women farmers operate," Garling says. She goes on to explain that women in particular really want to understand the food system, and options that reflect that concern don't show up on the census forms. What Garling is suggesting is that women farm for reasons that expand in several directions that reach far beyond mainstream thinking about and understanding of contemporary agriculture, and the agricultural census hasn't caught up yet.

Within the broader picture of women in agricultural pursuits, not all are hands-on farmers. More women are assuming leadership positions in agri-businesses, innovating new food products and new methods of conservation, and managing complex farm operations, at the same time they are raising children and caring for their families. "Women are changing agri-business board rooms and rural landscapes," says Deputy U.S. Secretary of Agriculture Krysta Harden, who confidently asserts that "women are the past, present, and future of agriculture worldwide."[10] This is particularly true in third and fourth world, developing countries where agriculture is the only viable economic engine available.

Making the portrait of women in agriculture even more interesting is that, in today's world, women who farm come from all sorts of family, personal, and educational backgrounds. Not all grew up on farms, ever lived on a farm, or even lived in a small town, yet every one of them have decided to farm because they want to do it and, in their heart of hearts, believe they can do it. This one, very simple, fact propels women farmers straight to the top of the list of strong modern-day feminists who have challenged historical notions of women's work. These are women who, often in the face of extreme social pressure to assume more traditional social roles, have staked their claim to full rights of ownership over their own lives, and over their own choices ... and they don't waste time looking back.

Strong Women Make Hard Choices

"No one ever tells you about the financial risks involved [in farming] or that a piece of farm equipment can cost more than three times what you'd normally pay for a house."

—Kate Danner

Independent women farmers, perhaps more than women generally, know, in their bones, that a woman can do anything she wants to do. That they are doing what has traditionally been men's work at least as well as any man has done it doesn't escape their notice either. These are women who, without a male partner's help, have successfully penetrated a world formerly dominated almost exclusively by men. They have taken on the physically hard, forever challenging, financially risky, and endlessly demanding work of extracting a livelihood from the land—and are making it work.

These women do not have time for tanning booths nor are they the women the cosmetic industry depends upon. They don't spend exorbitant amounts of money on professional hair stylists, don't mind a little dirt under their fingernails, have never seriously considered a pedicure, don't aspire to making it into the annual *Sports Illustrated* swimsuit edition, and would do almost anything to avoid working behind a desk, or answering to a boss.

Farming women buy their clothes at Farm and Fleet, usually when they're there anyway, picking up screws, nails, tools or animal vaccines. They rely upon the nearest Walmart for household supplies, and can't remember the last time they drove anywhere in anything other than their dented-up, slightly rusty pickup truck with more than 100,000 hard miles on it whenever it was they last changed the oil. They are independent, smart, strong-minded, funny, and very charming women, entirely lacking in pretense, and overflowing with common sense. Most importantly, they expect that their male counterparts, and all others they do business with, to treat them as equals, and this assumption is at the forefront of all their interactions with the wider world.

"I've been doing this over 40 years and only had one loan officer ever refer to my gender when we were discussing an operating loan," cattle farmer Mary Dunn says. "I just sat there and stared at him until he got so uncomfortable he dropped it. I decided not to make an issue of it myself, but later I mentioned this to a couple of my friends, and it wasn't long before that bank changed loan officers."

Jewell Hairston, Virginia State University's dean of the School of Agriculture, believes "men may, or may not, have paved the way for women in agriculture."[11] Her point might reflect the regional differences between the Midwest's homesteading, pioneer history and the enduring traditions that governed the plantation culture of the Old South prior to the Civil War.

Regardless, Hairston stresses that women have to advocate for themselves and push forward in ways that involve acute political awareness. "You do have to be politically aware and active," says Kate Danner, vice-president of Longley Farms in Aldeo, Illinois. "If you're not at the table, you'll be on the menu, so you have to show up and be involved."[12]

Kate's point is supported by historian Jenny Barker Devine, who writes extensively about Iowa farm women's ongoing political activism and their own, feminist vision of farm life.[13] I've met many of these women personally, and have always admired their courage as well as their forthright ability to speak truth to power without blinking.

Nevertheless, farming's not for every woman. It's not even appealing to most women. But for women who do want to farm, there is no other life that even comes close to being as worthwhile or as satisfying. And while it isn't an easy life, most women succeed at farming for a myriad of reasons that begin, and end, with their being independent, strong-minded, confident, and endlessly hard working individuals. They bear the powerful legacy that comes with being Mother Nature's daughters, and everybody knows Mother Nature is an extremely effective teacher. More importantly, every daughter knows that if she wants to be successful in life, she should follow her mother's advice—a notion to which women farmers seem exquisitely attuned.

In the Beginning

"I've done everything else.... I might as well try homesteading."
—Pauline Shoemaker

"When in 1908 I heard about the homestead land one could get.... I thought, here is my chance."
—Louise Karlson

"Yes, we had rattlesnakes.... I killed them by myself. It didn't take much to kill a rattlesnake."
—Sara Isaacson Ingle

"I was only scared once...."
—Anna Nelson

Although traditionally farming has been regarded as men's work, in reality women have always nurtured deep connections with the land, if for no other reason than to grow food to feed their families. However, a woman owning land, with her own name, rather than her husband's or father's name, on the deed, was an entirely different matter.

In the United States, most women did not have an opportunity to own land outright until the first homestead legislation was enacted in1862. This legislation set the process for obtaining a land grant from the government into motion by allowing anyone who had never taken up arms against the United States (including freed slaves and women), was at least 21 years of age, or the head of a household, and could pay the $18.00 filing fee, to apply for a federal land grant.[14] These grants assigned ownership of 160 acre land parcels, surveyed from seemingly endless prairie stretching in all directions—westward, from the Appalachian Range, across the Great Plains and beyond the Rocky Mountains, all the way to the Pacific Ocean, and extending from south to north between the Mexican and Canadian borders.[15]

Though not often recognized as such, the 1862 Homestead Act, which afforded women rights of land ownership previously denied them, parallels suffrage as the most significant legislation ever enacted to advance women's social status and equality. Women who owned land in their own right enjoyed both personal and political power those who were landless were unable to achieve. However, because the legislation actually discriminated against married women, who were not allowed to take land in their own names unless they were heads of households, advancing women's rights probably was not foremost in the minds of the politicians who crafted the law, which evolved out of a complicated political environment.

Prior to the Civil War, the southern states had opposed homestead legislation, believing it would entice men away from the South and hasten the push westward. Southern politicians believed that an advancing western frontier would ultimately result in more free states that would, together, wield considerable political power, to the detriment of the South. Thus, they did not see settling the west as being in the South's best interests. Opposition rhetoric also focused on fear of a mass exodus of slaves (and white labor) that would occur if these individuals were permitted to claim large plots of free land in the far west, and would result in the demise of the southern plantation culture. Consequently, successfully shepherding the legislation through both houses of Congress was lengthy, a hard-fought battle.

As it became more obvious that civil war between the northern and southern states was inevitable, it should have been apparent that southern women would be running the plantations southern men left behind when they went to war. And, if their husbands died, surviving wives might attempt to claim ownership of these plantations by rights of inheritance. It would be hard to oppose this eventuality if the homestead legislation was enacted and allowed women to own land. Suddenly southern women would enjoy a level of social and economic power previously inaccessible to them, and it isn't difficult to understand how southern politicians, all of whom were male, would find this possibility an unacceptable personal and political risk.

There was also the matter, if the South seceded, of the new Confederacy of Southern States needing to form an army to oppose the Union, which was sure to balk at the idea of secession. Enacting homesteading legislation would offer southern men the opportunity to head west and claim land instead of volunteering to fight for the South in the Civil War and severely diminish the pool of eligible soldiers the Confederacy could draw upon.

Most non land-owning southern men would be very reluctant to forgo the chance for land ownership in favor of fighting a war many felt the South was very likely to lose. Bearing this in mind, Southern politicians must have known that war would result in the apocalyptic *Gone With the Wind* south Margaret Mitchell later described in her epic novel of the Civil War era.[16] Southern secession was bound to leave beloved family plantations throughout the south in shambles, with women being the only ones left to rescue and rebuild them.

Because the southern plantation culture, unlike the Midwestern frontier, was so heavily patriarchal, the reality was that there were not a lot of fearless, stubborn and manipulative southern women resembling the fictional southern powerhouse Scarlett O'Hara, who had emerged from deep in the heart of Mitchell's vivid imagination. Scarlett was a unique, one of a kind personality, and historical truth suggests that during this era it is unlikely there were many similar women available to rescue and rebuild the plantations. Most southern women of that era were chattel of their husbands, fathers, or brothers, thereby entirely unprepared and poorly suited to taking on the tasks associated with successful plantation management. However, it bears mentioning that while Mitchell was writing of the plantation south of the Civil War era, her heroine Scarlett embodied the spirited frontier woman who was helping to settle the west during the same time period.

Meanwhile, politically there had to be serious concerns among

Unionists about their own diminished strength as a nation if the South did secede. Indeed, as secessionists gained political traction, homestead legislation moved to the top of the Republican political agenda, finally opening the door for President Lincoln to sign it into law.

It was probably no accident that legislation's final version included a clause rendering anyone who had taken up arms against the government ineligible to receive a homestead land grant because this provision discouraged southern men from joining the Confederate Army to fight against the Union. This language was a clever political maneuver designed to help the Union prevail in a civil war if one were to occur. And, undoubtedly, Unionists saw homesteading as a way to increase their land mass and build political strength. As a result, they were unlikely to favor placing too many restrictions on who could take advantage of the opportunities the law provided.

Although legislatively unintentional, women were, nevertheless, direct beneficiaries of Union expansionism as expressed through the homesteading legislation. That the new land acquisition policy empowered women was an unintended effect that they, very wisely, took full advantage of when the opportunity was presented to them.

Nevertheless, obtaining land through homesteading was not designed to be an easy process. Upon receiving a land grant, the claimant was required to take up residency on the 160 acre parcel granted to him or her and commence making improvements sufficient to support the new owner. This generally involved, at minimum, building a shack sturdy enough to withstand the never-ending winds that continually blew across the flat prairie lands of the Great Plains, tilling enough acreage to plant crops or support livestock, and erecting border fencing. Once the homesteader had "proved up" his or her land, usually within five years, it was theirs forever, and there was no question that they had earned every inch of it.

While not all women who attempted homesteading on their own survived the experience, those who found the courage to try were supremely self-confident and determined. They left homes in the eastern United States, or immigrated to America from Europe and then set forth into an entirely unknowable future in unfamiliar, flatland surroundings where an unrelenting wind never, ever stops blowing. Some originally homesteaded with husbands, only to later find themselves widowed and alone, often with dependent children to provide and care for. Others acceded to the desires of their families to gain more land and homesteaded at the request of relatives who had already staked claims. Some women even took on the task of homesteading in later life and, somehow having managed to remain debt free, lived on their land until they died.

According to historian Elaine Lindgren, nearly all women who home-steaded had enough of a business head on their shoulders to view acquiring land as a speculative venture likely to bring a reasonable return on their investment. "Once title had been acquired, the claim became an asset to be sold at the market place or traded for something of equal value," Lindgren writes.[17]

Regardless of their reasons, women homesteaders were fearless adventurers cut from the same cloth as Christopher Columbus, Lewis and Clark, Daniel Boone, Zebulon Pike and Calamity Jane. They all set off into a vast unknown with nothing to fall back upon other than an unquenchable curiosity and a steadfast belief in their own ability to survive. Without a clear sense of what they were going up against, home-steading women turned their backs on traditional women's work and social expectations to forge a different life for themselves, according to their own wishes, on their own terms, in the lawless West. Opportunities to prepare for what they would encounter as they faced the vast, untamed prairie land stretching across the western frontier were rare—yet they went ahead and did it anyway.

While the homesteading era in American history marks a period of great personal advancement for women, it is also replete with stories of blizzards, prairie fires, death and other catastrophes. However, tragedy and continual struggle is only one part of the westward expansion story, and to dwell only on the hardships the pioneers encountered is to distort the experience of those women who were seeking to build an independent life for themselves. For single women in particular, homesteading was a grand experiment in finding out about themselves as individuals and discovering their strengths as businesswomen, farm and family managers, and as strong, courageous individuals capable of facing down the proverbial (and sometimes actual) wolf at the door. They prevailed over adversity and succeeded.

While some single women helped a male relative expand his acreage, this was the exception rather than the rule. When it did occur, the woman usually received fair compensation for her efforts. In other words, she hired on as a farmhand and, just like a man, was paid for her work. But many single women homesteaders preferred to stake and prove up their own claims themselves, and not in partnership with a man.

"Homesteading is not so much the story of how single women began to support themselves as farmers as it is a story of how single women began to further their fortunes through shrewd investment of time, labor, and money," explains Deborah Fink, writing about life in rural Nebraska in the late 19th century.[18] "When these women succeeded in proving up their homesteads, they almost invariably sold them, often to make money.... Although even a modest sum of cash could work to a woman's advantage in various ways, the one-time profit from the sale of a homestead did not afford a woman a lifetime of security in an economic system that rewarded her poorly in other contexts," Fink writes.[19]

Unlike single women, married women who homesteaded alongside their husbands could not claim ownership, even jointly, of the land they were helping to develop. These women held their life and family together with a powerful combination of grit, grace and courage, and along the way became equal partners with their husbands. They did whatever they had to do to survive and keep the land that they did not, themselves, own. As an added benefit, they were enjoying a level of autonomy never before available to them, but they could not claim rights of ownership to the land they lived on and cultivated.

"What was the work of a farm woman in those early days? ... Hers was the work of the Wife and Mother, the Helpmate of her husband, the Homemaker and the Home-helper," Kansas pioneer Clara Hildebrand wrote.[20] According to Hildebrand, a homesteading woman "shared her husband's work and interest in the garden, the orchard, the crops and animals of the farm; she worked in the garden and gathered its products. She knew just how each vineyard or tree in the young orchard was coming in. She shared in the hope for a beautiful crop as the field things sprouted and grew green and tall. Did a horse, dog, or other farm animal get badly gored, cut or wounded, hers was the task to cleanse the wound and take the stitches that drew the torn edges together."

Women played leading roles in American expansionism that were played out on the stage of an advancing western frontier, and were rarely assigned secondary or supporting roles in the American pioneer story.[21] Hard working, determined women broke through the western European male establishment that favored a land inheritance model designed to pass this valuable asset from oldest son to oldest son. That this happened by legislative accident doesn't really matter. It benefited women to have land rights in their own name written into law rather than simply existing as a common practice. Women saw an economic opportunity that would provide them greater autonomy and independence, so they tied back their hair, gathered their skirts about their ankles and went forth to firmly establishing themselves as vital partners in the new, post–Civil War America.

These early farming women were willing to gamble on their own ability to work with nature, and took advantage of an accidental loophole government policy had provided to them to achieve this goal. They were tough, practical, no nonsense individualists who believed they could farm land just as successfully as men had done, and proceeded to do it. From 1862 onward, farming and ranching women never looked back.[22]

Farming Over Here to Win Over There: The Women's Land Armies of World Wars I and II

Our Mother Earth has called us, for the nations we must feed,
We have rallied to her standard to produce our greatest need,
We will labor on her bosom and achieve that worthy deed,
As we go working on.
Chorus
Glory, glory, hallelujah,
Glory, glory, hallelujah,
Glory, glory, hallelujah,
As we go working on.
We are told by Herbert Hoover that the war by food is won,
So we're laboring at production from the dawn till set of sun
We have donned the khaki uniform to fight the mighty Hun,
As we go working on.
Chorus
We are going to whip the Kaiser and our hearts are unafraid,
We will help to win this wicked war with hoe and rake and spade,
Though our tasks be of the hardest, we will never be dismayed,
But still go working on.
Chorus
We have joined our hands for service with our sisters 'cross the sea,
We have forged a mighty weapon in our fight for liberty,
By the spirit of our labor in the Women's Land Army,
As we go working on.
Chorus
Anthem of the Women's Land Army by Myrtle Shepherd Francis (sung to the tune of the "Battle Hymn of the Republic")

Brutally hard-fought worldwide wars erupted twice in the 20th century. Each time every able-bodied man took up arms while, at the same time, women stepped up to do more of what they were already doing— growing food. For women the main difference between wartime and peacetime was that war meant women were needed to do the jobs both men and women had previously done. Women answered this call, and as armies of men marched across battlefields in foreign lands, armies of

women marched across the fertile fields of the homeland, growing the
food needed to feed the fighting troops in the front lines and the people
left behind at home. Victory would depend equally upon them both; however, the women on the home front were the first to figure this out.

In 1915, shortly after the outbreak of World War I, Emmeline
Pankhurst, a vocal, energetic, and politically astute British suffragette
became aware of the devastating toll an all-out war would take on England,
particularly the already tenuous food supply. Realizing that armed conflict
was becoming more certain, she issued a "Call to the Women" to rise to
the challenges facing Great Britain as war loomed on the near horizon.

Despite being a product of the fashionable, high-mannered Edwar-
dian era the stylishly elegant Mrs. Pankhurst was a force to be reckoned
with. She was also well attuned to the reality of necessity always being the
mother of invention. Not of a mind to be constrained by social customs
or in the habit of backing down from a challenge, she led thousands of
women through the streets of London in loud and enthusiastic support
for British women's right to serve the national cause. Her Right-to-Serve
idea quickly gripped women across all social classes and political persua-
sions, linked tightly together by their fears for the future of their beloved,
small island nation.

What British women sympathetic to the cause of women's wartime
service did not know was that the Right Honorable David Lloyd-George,
then ammunitions minister in His Majesty's government, and the passionate, volatile Mrs. Pankhurst had entered into a political marriage of
mutual benefit entirely unthinkable to anyone even remotely acquainted
with the two individuals involved. Mild-mannered, cautious and politically liberal, Lloyd-George was a pompous man who did not count the
determined Mrs. Pankhurst, who was not above using any means at her
disposal to make dramatic political statements, among his nearest and
dearest. He wasn't particularly fond of her militant followers either. Nevertheless, he was forced to forgo his negative views toward them all when
it was pointed out to him that men going off war would empty the mines
and factories of their labor force, leaving the farm fields fallow—and that
women were the only ones who could fill this void.

Making matters worse, England's longstanding practice of importing
food was quickly becoming an untenable solution to the challenge of feeding both the nation and the combat troops drafted to fight for the honor,
not to mention survival, of the British Empire. German submarines were
surrounding the island, clearly intending to starve England into rapid surrender. Unless something was done about this, Mrs. Pankhurst commu-

nicated to Lloyd-George, Great Britain, and her soldiers, risked starvation within weeks. Thousands of able-bodied women were standing at the ready, prepared to get to work immediately, an eager Mrs. Pankhurst told Lloyd-George. All he had to do was agree to train, and then pay, them as much as men were being paid to fight.

Lloyd-George, who was not accustomed to having a woman tell him what to do, knew in his heart of hearts that Emmeline was right. The fact that three million men had already exited the British labor force, severely weakening England's already fragile economy, had not escaped his notice either, and he knew he was cornered. As a result, the powerful David Lloyd-George had no choice but to listen to Emmeline. Pankhurst, and then do what she told him to do, whether he liked it or not. It is highly improbable that he found this an appealing situation, either personally or politically, but he wasn't a stupid man and, very wisely, as it turned out, did not dismiss her solution to England's dire need for able-bodied workers, or ignore the conditions she put forth for involving women in the war effort.

Meanwhile, the combination of a poor harvest and dramatically intensified German submarine and U-boat presence in both the North Sea and the English Channel forced His Majesty's government into a policy of widespread conscription. The flaw in this decision was the absence of formal plans for replacing the men removed from the workforce as a result. Ultimately it proved much easier for women to enter into factory and munitions work, to descend down into the mines, and to run the public transportation systems than to engage in farm work. But this wasn't because the women weren't willing to do it.

British farmers, believing the war wouldn't last long and that they would not be called to fight, weren't enthusiastic about hiring women as farm labor. The argument went something like this: women not trained in farm work were worse than useless and it took up too much of a farmer's precious time, better spent doing actual farm work, to train them. The unspoken message was that drafting farmers was a bad idea because they were irreplaceable. Farmer's wives, fearing that hiring women would force their husbands into war service, also strongly opposed hiring women as farm laborers.

The concerns about women working on farms were both politically driven and fear-based. No one was implying women were not smart enough to run a farm business, or saying things like "women aren't strong enough to hold onto a plow" or "women are too squeamish to take care of farm animals." Instead, the arguments focused on the political and eco-

nomic implications of a woman doing a man's job. This succeeded only
in diverting attention away from the more pressing concern, which was
the necessity of maintaining a viable and productive food system; it did
not solve the increasingly acute food shortage problem.

By the winter of 1916, England was very hungry. The numbers of
women demonstrating for the right to work on the farms increased dramatically, forcing the Minister of Agriculture, who opposed this solution,
to resign. A parliamentary coup resulted in Lloyd George being named
the new, wartime prime minister.

Likely remembering his earlier, often contentious conversations with
Mrs. Pankhurst, and his agreement with her to put women into full
wartime service, Lloyd George, both reluctantly and very wisely, made
protecting the nation's food supply a high priority. Not wanting to risk
getting on Emmeline's bad side, he pushed for rapid implementation of
new policies affecting the War Agricultural Committees, and put British
women front and center as an agricultural land labor force.

On the other side of the Atlantic, the outbreak of World War I found
American President Woodrow Wilson verbally quick to recognize that
"food will win the war and shape the peace that follows." However, Wilson
was much slower to understand that starvation, which was already becoming rampant in Europe, would lead to serious domestic unrest in the
United States, and that finding some way to feed both American and allied
fighting troops would have to become an immediate wartime priority.
Nevertheless, Wilson's prolonged neutrality regarding the war itself
resulted in painfully slow American efforts to develop a viable plan that
would ensure preservation of the nation's food system.

American suffragettes were much quicker to figure out that U.S.
involvement in the widening war in Europe was inevitable than President
Wilson was. Likely fearing the domino effect of Germany defeating the
European allies, which could result in German domination over America,
these women quickly realized that there was no point in fighting for the
right to vote if, at the end of the war, there was no sovereign American
nation remaining. They also knew a war would spin the domestic food
system into acute and immediate crisis, and were already far ahead of
Wilson in terms of a solution.

When Germany sank the Lusitania in 1915, taking 128 American lives
down with the ship, American reaction included activating the Women's
Section of the Navy League (WAVES) and establishing the National Service School to train women in service to their country. The Suffragettes
quickly fell wholeheartedly behind this effort and, seeing it as an oppor-

tunity to advance women's rights, persuaded wealthy women across the country to step up and pour their time, money and energy into the women's war effort. Ultimately, it was the New York City Standing Committee on Agriculture that drew together various options for using women to help save the food supply.

This odd coupling between the nation's largest city and widespread rural interests arose through the clever political maneuvering of Dr. Virginia Gildersleeve, chair of the Standing Committee on Agriculture of the New York City Mayor's Committee of Women on National Defense, and a dean at Barnard Women's College in Manhattan. Dean Glidersleeve, a robust, no-nonsense, politically astute middle-aged woman with a PhD in comparative English literature from Columbia University and a solid, well-established academic career, didn't even pretend any interest whatever in agriculture. However, she recognized a good opportunity when she saw one. Realizing that both her keen interest in women's war preparedness and her strong desire for college women to be active participants in any organized war mobilization effort could be effectively woven together for the common national interests, she stepped up to the challenge. "I knew very little about agriculture," she admitted, "but I did know something about organizing women."[23] She also knew all about the benefits of forging unusual political partnerships, and used her committee chairmanship to bring together the cause of women's rights and the imperative to win a world war. She began by considering all ideas presented to her, and the answer came from an unlikely person.

Even though Austria had aligned with Germany against America in World War I, an Austrian countess, married to an American architect, conceived a workable plan for women to save the food supply while the men were fighting the war. Camilla Hoyos Short requested a meeting with Dean Gildersleeve to propose a para-military-style "unit plan" whereby women who worked on the farms would live together in small, self-sufficient units, and be paid for their labor. This sorority-style living arrangement enabled the girls, most of whom were enrolled in the elite women's colleges, to live with one another in supportive environments while taking on farm labor tasks entirely unfamiliar to them, in places that were, for many, just as foreign as the far off lands where the men were fighting. Believing this idea was a stroke of genius, Dean Glidersleeve called in every political and practical resource at her disposal to carry it forward.

Even though many of the women who volunteered for land army service were so naïve they believed potatoes grew on trees, they were also adventure seeking, eager learners and, above all else, deeply patriotic. They quickly shed the prim and proper lifestyle demands of eastern establishment women and young ladies of "good breeding" to bond together in a determined sisterhood that eventually became the uniformed American Women's Land Army.

Despite over four million men having left farms and other agricultural pursuits to fight in Europe, creating a huge farm labor void, the U.S. Department of Agriculture, as well as many members of the Wilson administration, did not embrace the idea of women taking over farm responsibilities. Stubbornly unable to set aside their notions of what women "should" do, and failing to see the important role women could take in the war effort, male government officials expressed concerns that women were poorly suited for farm work. Some were so naïve they even went so far as to suggest that farm work would impair a young woman's future child-bearing ability.

This foolish, baseless male resistance aside, it is more likely that the men who opposed women doing farm work were really speaking to their own resistance to suffrage generally, and to their personal fears over the loss of control they believed men would suffer when women stepped out of their traditional social roles. These were likely the same men who opposed any new idea that would rock the boat of tradition and had spoken out forcefully against allowing women such simple freedoms as obtaining a library card.

Steadfastly believing that America had to farm over here in order to win over there, and that women would have to be the ones to step up to the challenge, Dean Gildersleeve and the WLA leadership refused to allow their critics to back them down. Instead, they ignored them and used their energy to move the idea forward. Soon they had created a fully functioning occupation force of soil sisters prepared to inhabit rural America and grow the food needed to feed the war effort both at home and abroad. They all were progressive-minded, politically astute and supremely clever women who saw an acute and vital national need and saw it as their patriotic duty to step up and address it. They launched a huge public relations campaign to face down their detractors, and in the process gave birth to the WLA. They were able to breathe enough life into this massive agricultural effort to keep it alive and thriving throughout the Great War.

"The creation of the Woman's Land Army of America in WWI enabled nearly 20,000 urban women to enter America's agricultural sector to work as ordinary wage laborers between 1917 and 1921. The active recruitment of urban women into a government-sanctioned, formally-organized, and (largely) female-managed workforce to labor in physically demanding tasks such as sowing and harvesting, was a revolutionary and—to some—a disconcerting idea, writes Rose Hayden-Smith, a former Food and Society Policy Fellow at the University of California–Santa Barbara.[24] "That these women were also young, college-educated, and lived in community with other like-minded women outside the authority of men challenged traditional stereotypes relating to women's roles and work all the more." They were also forming both proof of, and a perfect model for, women's ability to respond in time of national need. And, by 1918, 20,000 women were serving in 1000 separate WLA units in 21 Western, Midwestern, and Northeastern states.[25]

The WLA did not begin to dismantle until surviving soldiers returned from the war in need of jobs. "The patriotism that had drawn women into the land army ultimately forced them out," Hayden-Smith explains, adding that it was considered "unpatriotic" for women to hold jobs that the men returning from war needed. Nevertheless, it was probably not a coincidence that, within two years of World War I ending, the 19th Amendment was ratified, giving women the right to vote.

Unquestionably, women's exemplary service in the Women's Land Army, which saved the nation's food supply and helped win the war, gave the suffrage movement the final push it needed. It would have been nearly impossible to convincingly argue against the notion that women with hoes had not been just as instrumental in winning the Great War as men with guns had been, and thus, they, like men, deserved the right to vote—and those who still opposed suffrage were wise not to pick that fight.

It is difficult to imagine that women had to demand the right to serve their country in wartime. It's also impossible to know whether either Dr. Gildersleeve or Mrs. Pankhurst were aware of how important and far-reaching their efforts to provide women this opportunity would prove to be. However, they were smart women, and if I were to a guess, I would say they were very well aware of the broader implications of their efforts. Both clever, politically aware women who must have realized that they were opening the door to women everywhere being able to pursue independent lives in agricultural if they wanted to do it. However, with Dr. Gildersleeve living in New York City and Mrs. Pankhurst being a resident of London, and with no evidence that they knew one another, or coordinated their efforts, it is also possible they did not spend time wondering about how far their effective leadership would eventually reach. Regardless, they were both forward thinking, politically astute visionaries who, every day of their lives, carried with them a profound commitment to women's rights, no matter what form these might take. No wise man, or woman, would have bet against either one.

THE WOMEN'S LAND ARMY IN WORLD WAR II

Who Won the War?
It wasn't the WRENS who won the war
Whatever the WRENS may say
It was the Women's Land Army
They won it making hay
It wasn't the ATS who won the war
They never fired a gun
It was the Women's Land Army
Spreading cow muck by the ton
It wasn't the WAAFS who won the war
Though they said they did, and how,
It was the Women's Land Army
They even went to plough
It really was the land girls
Who won the war, you see
They heeded all those posters
And they DUG FOR VICTORY

—Anonymous

Twenty-three years after the end of World War I America was drawn into another global conflict. In the interim, World War I's girl with the hoe had given birth to World War II's Rosie the Riveter. That there was a new generation of women at the ready when war broke out again should not have been surprising since the women who had served in the original WLA had challenged women's traditional social roles in a myriad of ways. They knew they could do any job a man could do, including driving tractors, plowing fields, milking cows, or working in assembly plants—and they would naturally pass this confidence along to their daughters. They could not have known that these young women would be called upon, just as they had been, to help win another war; nevertheless, unknowingly they had prepared them well to do it.

Almost as soon as America entered World War II the Women's Land Army, which had already been mobilized in Australia and Great Britain, was resurrected in the United States. In this country, the WLA was part of the Emergency Farm Labor Program, which immediately trained and sent women farm laborers to agricultural areas having the greatest, most urgent, needs. Just as had happened in the First World War, many farmers, no matter how desperate they were, firmly opposed women working on their land. However, unlike World War I when the southern states did not accept WLA volunteers, and relatively few went to the Midwestern states, during World War II several hundred thousand women worked in both these regions. However, for reasons that have never been clear, the Great Plains and eastern Rocky Mountain region remained steadfast in their resistance to WLA-provided assistance. Both areas suffered serious agricultural losses as a result.

During the Second World War the need for farm labor joined the WLA together with several government agencies. The departments of agriculture and labor, the U.S. Women's Bureau, programs such as the Victory Farm volunteers, and the agricultural extension services of the land grant universities in each state all joined forces. However, even though the arguments against women's farm labor had gone stale by the end of World War I, in some corners of government stubborn, well entrenched opposition held steadfast. "Motherhood has not yet been classed as a nonessential industry," FBI Director J. Edgar Hoover wrote in *Women's Home Companion* magazine in 1944. "There is a small chance it will ever be. The mother of small children does not need to put on overalls to prove her patriotism…. Her patriotism consists in not letting quite understandable desires to escape for a few months from a household routine to earn a little money of her own tempt her to quit it."

Hoover was not alone in believing that absenteeism among mothers solved nothing in terms of the war effort. These male bureaucrats who, obviously, weren't mothers themselves, saw no value in hiring and paying another woman to do what mothers should be doing themselves, and ignored the important and needed skills these mothers possessed and the war effort desperately needed.

In reality, paying someone else to care for their children while mothers tended to the war effort wasn't how it always worked out. Young, able-bodied women placed their children in the care of older female relatives and left home to work for the war effort. These surrogate mothers saw their efforts as just as patriotic, and just as important to winning the war, as the efforts undertaken by the women who were working on the farms, in the factories, and as volunteer nurses in military hospitals nationwide. They understood that winning the war had to be a unified national effort and that everyone had a job to do. Many women willingly and lovingly took other women's children into their homes and raised them alongside their own children so their mothers could fill jobs supporting the war effort.[26]

Despite opposition, more than 5.5 million women quickly stepped

up to assist the nation's farmers. Even more women became defense workers. By 1942, in some companies, particularly within the aircraft industry,
96 percent of the paid employees were women. By the end of World War
II, more than 20 million women were in the American labor force.[27] These
women had quickly proven themselves precisely as capable as men, and
were successfully performing men's jobs just as well as men had always
done them.

Overall, the lives of World War II Women's Land Army farm workers
mirrored those of their World War I foremothers. World War II women
had joined the WLA for the same reasons their mothers' generation of
women had, knowing the job was temporary and would end when the
war did—and many of these women felt that unless there was a war on
women should be at home caring for their families. Nevertheless, by the
end of World War II, a surprising number of women had changed their
minds about needing to stay at home raising children and decided to
remain in the workforce. Additionally, large numbers of women who had
served in the WLA decided to remain in agricultural work and did not
return to full time homemaking, or to their pre-war employment. This
happened in part because, rather quickly after the war ended, post-World
War II prosperity took hold, allowing men to abandon their previous,
lower paying farm jobs for higher paying manufacturing work and opening the door for women who had previously done farm work to return to
it. Many women took advantage of this opportunity by signing on as members of the U.S. Crops Corps.[28]

Although the WLA never enjoyed the recognition brought forth by
the iconic Rosie the Riveter image, during World War II more than six
million non-farm women abandoned their traditional roles as housewives
and mothers to plant and harvest crops, milk cows, slaughter pigs, raise
livestock and otherwise keep the nation's agricultural supply lines moving.
This mass-scale effort cemented World War II as another watershed
moment in American women's struggle for equality. "Though short-lived,
the WLA was a catalyst for changing women's positions in agriculture and
society for later decades," historian Stephanie Carpenter writes.[29] The
WLA also opened the door to women's future in agriculture. It was an
organization run by women and for women, and very effectively provided
women everywhere an opportunity to prove they could farm successfully,
thus affording them another option for living their lives.

Members of the WLA were always viewed as "regular farm girls" and,
as a result, never received the recognition they earned, and remain entitled
to. Without begrudging combat veterans the honor they deserve, it is

important to recognize that they would not have been able to do what they did to save Great Britain, Australia or America during either world war without women back home growing the food that kept them alive while they did it.

VICTORY GARDENS

Mistress Mary, quite contrary, how does your garden grow?
With cockle shells and silver bells and fair maids all in a row.
Well, Mistress Mary's changed her plans—she's even learned to plow,
And tells the crowd she's very proud of her Victory Garden now.
—War song set to a popular nursery rhyme

Another solution to the persistent civilian food shortages in Europe and America during both world wars was to encourage women to plant victory gardens in their back yards. Expanding on the theme that "food will win the war," both England and America sent forth the message that "the kitchen is the key to victory." Rather than drawing from the national food supply farming produced, women who did not join the land armies were expected to do their part in the war effort by growing food to feed their own families at home. Propaganda from the National War Garden Commission and the Farm Security Administration included slogans such as "The Seeds of Victory Insure the Fruits of Peace," "Every War Garden is a Peace Plant" and "War Gardens for Victory—Grow Vitamins at Your Kitchen Door."

Clearly, food had become ammunition, and as a weapon of war, was as vitally important as the tanks and guns were. Realizing that a soldier who starved to death was just as much a war casualty as a soldier who was shot to death, most women quickly stepped up to the garden idea, seeing it as a vital component of winning the war. The effort held particularly poignant meaning for those women whose husbands, brothers, and other men they loved were thousands of miles away, serving in the trenches on the front lines of battle. These women knew that if they grew their own food at home, more food would be available to feed their loved ones fighting in places far, far from home.

The Japanese attack on Pearl Harbor, Hawaii, a few days before Christmas 1941, drew the United States in to World War II. Less than a month later President Franklin Roosevelt, who had, a few years earlier, inherited an America in economic collapse, embraced the view that "one man's hunger is every man's hunger." He advocated "freedom from want" as a critical aspect of what a victory over our enemies would mean for

America. Prompted by his feminist wife Eleanor, who had already plowed up a large section of the White House lawn to plant a victory garden of her own, Roosevelt had come to believe that a unified effort to overcome hunger and disease was the ultimate route to peace, and knew that women were the key to achieving this goal. He linked growing a home garden to middle class prosperity, setting the stage for growing food on a much smaller scale, and in urban rather than rural settings. The idea caught on and significantly eased the ongoing strain on the sparse, worldwide food supply.

The victory garden effort also emerged out of decades of economic depression and the resulting hunger that plagued all but the wealthy upper classes for most of the first half of the 20th century. The effort took firm hold when former ladies of leisure worldwide became contemporary women of action, and figured out that home gardens were the answer to producing significant quantities of food for the home front. Later, urban gardens became an integral part of the Marshall Plan, a large-scale Allied forces recovery effort to rebuild devastated European economies that had fallen apart with the end of World War II and defeat of the Axis powers.

When the war ended food moved beyond being a weapon of war to becoming a tool of diplomacy in the complicated adjustment to postwar life, both at home and abroad. Immediate fears of famine and starvation that had haunted war-torn Europe and threatened the United States lessened, eventually became a distant memory. It was not until post war prosperity gave way to socio-economic class divisions that widespread poverty began to raise its ugly head once again.

The Political Becomes Personal: Women's Land Armies, Victory Gardens and Public Memory

For many years on Remembrance Sunday we have not been asked to be represented. The question is, why not? Do we not deserve to be recognized ... why were we forgotten so easily after we were no longer needed? We were proud ... to serve our country. Those of us who are left are still proud to have belonged to the Women's Land Army, and we will never forget.

—Grace Wallace

The demobilization of the Women's Land Army at the end of both world wars forced women to surrender the personal freedom and sense of purpose they had enjoyed while doing wartime service. When the war ended hiring preferences abruptly shifted to favor returning soldiers, job prospects for women suddenly evaporated. It remains a dark commentary on American society that the ending of the wars women had helped to win propelled them backwards into their former lives. Instead of continuing to earn a regular paycheck the women who had helped win the war were sent back home to pick up where they had left off—changing diapers, mopping the floors and canning vegetables. It should have been that wartime service pushed women upward toward greater socio-economic status, workplace equality, and personal freedom, if they wanted this for themselves. Instead, most were demoted back into non-paying jobs as wives and mothers, whether or not they wanted to return to this life—and many did not.

Nevertheless, the experience of being an integral part of a widespread national war effort changed women forever, and in deeply personal ways that no misdirected social expectations or restrictive public policies can ever take away from them. Service in the WLA allowed women to discover their own valuable personal capabilities and develop a level of self-confidence they never knew they had. These attributes became an integral part of who they were as women and what kind of women they raised their daughters to become. WLA women would never forget how capable they were, even if their nations failed to recognize and remember their service and patriotism.

"Regardless of national intent or the programs participated in, women who cultivated the land during wartime not only cultivated victory, but also participated in spreading a new political and social culture of abundance focused on the production and distribution of food," writes historian Cecilia Gowdy-Wygant.[30] She goes on to observe that women who farmed brought about monumental changes in the way the western world viewed women's participation in the labor force, as well as impacting the availability of an abundant food supply.

In addition to taking jobs away from women, the end of World War II also marked the beginning of a new level of political activism among rural women. Midwestern farm women in particular took up the cause of the family farm, promoting their own vision of farm life and becoming staunch feminists long before the word ever entered the American vocabulary. They navigated the murky waters of a patriarchy built around land, agriculture, and family with a new sense of pride and self-confidence in their roles as wives, mothers, and strong, capable human beings. They renegotiated powerful shifts in gender relationships that allowed women everywhere to step up and make their voices heard, and the women of rural, Midwestern Iowa led the way.

In what she terms "the development of agrarian feminism" historian Jenny Barker Devine traces the path Iowa farm women took toward claiming public space and redefining their identities.[31] She writes that the stories of women who actively participated in the Iowa organizations "present examples of the ways in which women adapted their rhetoric and politicized aspects of their daily work, responded to female leadership at the state level, related to male leaders, coped with limited resources, and claimed a presence in male-dominated spaces in order to work toward favorable agricultural policies."[32] Relatively quickly, these actions within the Farm Bureau Federation, the Iowa Farmer's Union, the National Farmer's Organization, and the Iowa Porkettes (the auxiliary organization for the Iowa Pork Producers Association) created an opportunity for women to imagine new forms of rural community and redefine their own roles in it.

The means for achieving this new vision of rural life had been set in place during the earlier Progressive era, when social feminism took root around issues of public health, maternal and infant care, education, industrial safety, and homemaking as women's responsibilities. The progressive political framework elevated important public concerns from jobs women did to important responsibilities appealed to farm women, who were already gathering in one another's homes to talk about how to be more effective and efficient homemakers and how to apply their skills for the betterment of the wider community. "They practiced a 'politics of dependence' that allowed them to challenge male authority in state and federal policies, agribusiness and farm organizations by emphasizing their experiences as [wartime] farm laborers, in addition to their dependent roles as wives and mothers in heterosexual marriages," Divine explains. "Arriving at this point was part of an evolutionary process wherein women presented new interpretations of time-honored agrarian ideals that identified woman as public leaders."[33]

These sturdy farmwomen did not self-identify as feminists, because they believed their chosen work already set them apart from urban women who, they perceived, were at the center of the modern feminist movement. But to the outside observer, feminists are precisely who they were. More and more, hardworking farmwomen were claiming the right to make their own choices and define their lives on their own terms—they just weren't doing it the same way as the urban women leaders of the feminist movement they were watching unfold on television were doing it. And, unlike the urban feminist movement, rural women didn't declare war on men in the process.

Devine explains the urban-rural difference by noting that rural women rode the third wave of feminism by "abandoning essential definitions of feminism" in favor of promoting female empowerment rather than advocating for male oppression. This was because the women themselves were able to reconcile opposing ideas of caring and earning, dependence and independence, equality and mutuality, and understood that it takes both women and men, working together, for life at its best to unfold.

As the 20th century came to a close rural women activists found themselves at a crossroads. The rural population had shrunk to just two percent of the total population nationwide, local homemakers clubs that were the framework of rural women's activism were disappearing, and the National Farmers Organization shifted its emphasis toward marketing and services. Other farm organizations unraveled as paid consultants took the place of women's volunteer labor and leadership. Nevertheless, rural women continued doing what they'd always done—actively participating in the lives of their communities through their churches, schools, and other local organizations, and they saw these activities as the key to the survival of these important community partnerships.

Unfortunately, what Iowa farmwomen were not able to do was to successfully ensure passage of the Equal Rights Amendment to the state constitution in either 1980 or 1992. Still, they recognized that greater social, political and legal rights were the keys to their future prosperity, and pushed ahead anyhow, continuing to organize themselves around farm issues.

By early in the 21st century it was becoming obvious that total land use and ownership, especially in rural areas, was shifting rapidly and dramatically. The 2002 agricultural census revealed that women own half of the total amount of available farmland in the entire Midwest. A significant minority of these women are the principle operators of these farms.[34] These women also define sexism as a major obstacle to their success because they believe it affects their bottom line. Divine says some of the women report being exploited by tenant farmers they lease their land to, and they believe that farm service providers treated them differently from their male counterparts. They also believe they are perceived as emotional, confused, and lacking knowledge of good agricultural practices.[35] Some, but not all women also felt they had to earn the respect of male farmers, bankers and merchants, and then keep proving themselves again and again. Some women farmers also report feeling out of place in the traditional male meeting places such as the grain elevator, feed mill, local coffee shop, livestock auctions and sale barns.

As a result, women farmers began gravitating toward smaller operations, organic farm practices, and local sales outlets. These are easier for them to access and allow them to avoid the traditional male hangouts. "They favor sustainability over profitability and associate personal independence with community prosperity," Devine explains, adding that nevertheless, the issue of land ownership is what brings farm women together, because they realize that if they can take control of their own assets they can control the course of industrial agriculture. "Rather than demand equal rights and privileges within well-established farm groups, Iowa farm women, in the first decade of the 21st century want entirely new models for organizing that empower women to identify as farmers and producers using the time-honored strategies developed over the course of the 20th century," she writes.

Unquestionably the issue of gender discrimination is "dicey" and, in rural areas, more often than not, it seems to reside in the eye of the beholder. "If a man doesn't agree with me, I don't automatically think it's just because I'm a woman," says large operation crop farmer Kathy Nickel. "He might have a good point that I would be wise to listen to … and I don't want to work with a man who doesn't share his ideas, even if he isn't real smooth in his delivery."

Nevertheless, every woman farmer probably can recall a time when she felt discriminated against because of being a woman—if you ask her. However, most don't seem to spend much time either thinking or worrying about it. More importantly, gender discrimination does not appear to ever have been the reason even one woman farmer considered quitting farming.

THE WOMYN'S LAND MOVEMENT:
ANOTHER CHAPTER IN
WOMEN'S HISTORY ON THE LAND

It was the emphasis on gender politics that differentiates yesterday's separatist communes and collectives from today's female farmers.
—Joanne Stato

Critics of the 1960s feminist movement steadfastly blamed activist Betty Friedan for planting the notion that housework, cooking included, was drudgery and a form of female oppression, in the minds of American women.[36] They completely ignored the fact that Friedan made some good points. The social reality of most women's lives was that they had few options outside of the male-centered, male-focused, and male-defined, deeply entrenched social expectations that kept them in the kitchen, in the bedroom, and behind a vacuum cleaner. Only the bravest among women could think about challenging the notion that biology is destiny, and that having his babies, cooking his meals, and cleaning his house was the only way to keep a man—because another reality was that, for women, finding a way to adequately support themselves outside marriage was extremely difficult.

Friedan's timing was exquisite. Social unrest was smoldering just beneath the surface of social conformity. Mothers who had devoted their entire lives to home and family were taking to the streets to protest their sons being drafted to fight in a war in faraway southeast Asia that they believed was none of America's business and certainly not worth sacrificing American boys' lives. Support for granting voting rights to southern blacks was gaining a foothold, largely because northern women had already fought the voting rights battle once, and were predisposed toward lending their support to that cause again. Women saw these as causes worth risking everything for, and hitched their own concerns on to the broader issues already at play on the streets of nearly every city in the country. Sometimes it was hard to decide which protest to join, because there were so many worthwhile ones out there. But regardless of the cause, women everywhere were leaving the beds unmade and the dishes in the sink, and walking out the kitchen door into the sunlight of liberation.

Not surprisingly, most men weren't on board with Friedan's ideas. She was encouraging women to reclaim their lives, which men perceived as a threat to their power, and no one gives up power voluntarily. However, her detractors had foolishly overlooked an entire generation's attempt to re-contextualize domestic work as a feminist undertaking and entirely dismissed women's desire to claim the same rights men had always enjoyed, which included expressing their own opinions and desires, and living self-sufficient, independent lives. They failed to grasp both the feminist consciousness and the need all women have to live safe lives away from the social dangers any woman who desires to live her life on her own terms all too easily bumps up against. Men were afraid that if women became independent, they would, somehow, become less relevant, which would create a whole host of other problems most men really did not want to be forced to deal with. In other words, a woman living life apart from the socially prescribed roles her gender automatically imposes upon her, without her consent, faces inherent risks.

In 1960s America only the most courageous, or the richest, were in a position to pursue a path toward independent lives of their own. Most women did not fall into either of these categories, thus were imprisoned by widespread, deeply entrenched social expectations and left to suffer in silence. Women who did not want to be wives or mothers, and had no desire to follow other traditionally female career paths, needed to find some way to support themselves and fulfill their desire for an independent lifestyle. To make this even more difficult than it already was, they had to create a living environment that valued them for who they were, as they were.

This was the chief impetus behind the women's separatist movement of the 1970s that arose out of a much broader feminist movement that had begun splintering apart in various directions. Almost on cue, radical feminism suddenly collided with an emerging interest in organic farming, setting the stage for an unusual marriage of these two interests to occur. This coupling gave birth to a separatist movement among avowed feminists that focused on farming as a means for sustaining themselves.

The women who were following this path made a strong commitment to self-sustainability, and in the process created a rich opportunity for the re-emergence of women-led farming efforts. The concept of "womyn's land" became another answer to the liberation women everywhere. After all, women could now own land in their own names, and women were good at building support systems that drew in other women, so women joining together with other women to build farming enterprises seemed to be a match made in heaven.

Lesbian women in particular were drawn to this idea, thinking it would enable them to live the lifestyle they sought, and had great difficulty finding during an era when alternative lifestyles were generally unacceptable and fraught with political and personal challenges. These were women who had been socially rejected in urban settings and, as a result, were attracted to life in rural settings where they thought there would be fewer people to harass them. There was nothing not to like about the idea of gaining greater personal freedom and an opportunity to live among others of like mind in a supportive environment.

Various women-only, self-sustaining communes began to pop up, particularly in the rolling Green Mountains of rural Vermont and along the northern California coastline. Some groups bought existing farms and others bought acres of vacant land and built their communes from the ground up. Either way, the one thing they had in common was that they all aspired to live apart from urban interests, raise healthy, organic food, weave their own cloth, spin their own yarn, cut their own wood, and generally withdraw from the wider world into a much simpler, back-to-nature lifestyle.

Even though their muscle mass was useful, the women found they didn't want men helping them farm because, they discovered, when a man came into the farm's commune environment, the relationship dynamics changed. Inevitably, the men wanted to take charge and, sometimes to their detriment, these women were not interested in a man telling them what to do. Instead, they preferred figuring things out for themselves, on their own terms. As a result, sooner or later the man would be told to leave.[37]

In practice, women-only farming communes were driven, and sustained, by an enthusiastic amateurism, writes Rhian Sasseen, adding that, "oral histories of these farms are vague as to how much farming and sustainable living was actually accomplished."[38] She goes on to explain that the movement had lofty goals that included holding land for future generations, conserving and maintaining the earth's organic resources, and guarding against exploitation and depletion of land and natural resources. None of these desired outcomes shouted out solid, long-term economic viability.

Unquestionably, the idea of female empowerment through self-sufficiency is very seductive, but farming is dirty, backbreaking work and not every woman (or man) likes doing it. This was true even among those who sought the relative social safety of rural life. Infighting between those who held that sexual orientation is a choice and those who believed that heterosexuality was anti-feminist, erupted. Women who were seeking a place to live out their committed lesbian relationships often found that the white, middle-class women who frequently dominated the commune politics were not always welcoming to women of other races, lifestyles, or economic backgrounds. These deep divisions cracked the necessary resolve needed to hold the communes together and safeguard their long-term viability, despite the tremendous energy and profound commitment the women themselves were putting into them.

While the public face of the separatist communes' portrayed them as Mother Nature's ferociously loyal and forever faithful guardians, many were led by women who were woefully ignorant of good farming practices. They viewed farming merely as a means to the end goal of living off the land and entirely independent of men, and had no solid agricultural backgrounds or knowledge to support what they were trying to do. These women, while well-intentioned, did not come from farming backgrounds, know how to access the information they needed to farm successfully, often did not have the financial resources to purchase needed equipment and supplies, and had no idea how to successfully run a small business, which is what farming is. Furthermore, as lesbians in the 1970s, they were reluctant to reach very far in search of assistance with these issues, lest they be "found out."

Many argue that, as a social experiment, most women-only separatist communes were a failure. While it's true that most eventually died out, I don't believe they were failures at all. These communes were an important part of the larger women's movement that opened a wider door for 20th century women to walk through as they sought to make their own choices for themselves. And, what did not die with the commune movement, but rather has come alive in the 21st century, is the organic, healthy food movement that has created a flourishing economic marketplace for women-owned farms. The commune era fostered some women's keen interest in farming, and its lasting legacy is the opportunity to pursue this dream that women across all social classes and sexual orientations now enjoy.

One

Godspeed the Plow

Spirit Connects with Land, Food and Mother Nature

Though the wealthy and great
Live in splendor and state
I envy them not, I declare it
For I grow my own hams
My own ewes, my own lambs...
By plowing and sowing
By reaping and mowing
All nature provides me with plenty...
I have lawns, I have bowers
I have fruits, I have flowers
And the lark is my morning alarmer
So all farmers now
Here's Godspeed the plow...

—Agrarian Folk Song

Women have been farming for 14,000 years. They are the foremothers of today's agricultural enterprise, which began during the Old Stone Age hunter and gatherer era and continues today as clear proof that the biology is destiny notion is patently false. Since the beginning of time, women have been doing the work of farming commonly considered the sole purview of men.

The human farming story began around 12,000 BCE when practical concerns determined the male-female division of household labor. In simplest terms, since women needed to be available to nurse and care for the children, it fell to the men to search for meat as a needed protein source to feed their families. As a result, while men were stalking animals, women stayed closer to home, foraging for plants and seeds to supplement the family meals. Women began to notice that the seeds dropped from plants they picked for food eventually became new plants, which is one of the oldest natural processes in existence and remains basically unchanged 14,000 years later.

Figuring out that plants grow from seeds created by the other plants was a vitally important discovery for Stone Age women, who figured out that they could plant seeds and grow their food where they lived instead of having to carry their children on their backs and travel far distances in search of food. This discovery was as important to Stone Age women as the invention of the automatic washing machine 13,908 years later was to early 20th century women.

Soon Stone Age women wisely began using their natural nurturing ability to cultivate the seeds plants produced, enabling them to grow more food for themselves and their families. When they began using the plants they grew to feed animals they could raise for food, men didn't have to hunt as much anymore and found themselves out of a job. Soon they began moving in on the women's farming efforts and, before long, farming became a man's job.

Undeterred, women continued doing what they had always done— care for children, raise and cook food, and keep the household together and running smoothly.

In other words, women never really gave up farming when men began doing it, and the original women farmers undoubtedly passed their knowledge on to their daughters, who passed it along to their daughters and, perhaps, also on to their sons. Thousands of years passed and eventually women living off the land figured out that they were key players in a vital agricultural drama being played out in a much larger universe that someone other than themselves is in charge of running.

This mysterious universe possesses large quantities of energy expressed in various ways, with various levels of intensity, and is necessary to sustaining the natural world. Women intuitively knew they needed to learn to get along with whatever this mysterious life-giving force, which later became personified as "Mother Nature," was, because to do battle with this energy, they quickly realized, had proved futile.

Although it is not clear how giving this invisible, untouchable, yet clearly experienced energy that controls most things a female identity came about, it makes a lot of sense. Mothers are well-known for their ability to take charge and run things, and this is precisely what Mother Nature has proven herself quite capable of doing. Furthermore, time and again, she outsmarts anyone who tries to control or impose their will upon her, so eventually most people figure out it is best not to try.

"Women are very intuitively smart about nature," professor Corrie Norman, associate director of the Religious Studies Program at the University of Wisconsin–Madison, and keenly interested in women's connections with food and land, explains. "They know Mother Nature is running the show and that you might as well learn to work with her, because if you don't, you inevitably end up being sorry."

While not wanting to argue with Mother Nature seems like a wise decision, it's not always an easy one. "One of the biggest challenges I face is not being in control. During growing season, regardless of my plans the weather, or some other idea Mother Nature comes up with, decides what I do every single day. I almost never get to decide," crop farmer Kathy Nickel says. "If you like to plan ahead or are fond of thinking you're in charge of your life, even some of the time, then farming definitely isn't for you," she laughs.

Organic dairy farmer Sadie Zimmer agrees. "I'd love it if calves were born between 8 a.m. and 6 p.m., but their mothers absolutely don't care about what is convenient for me ... so during calving I'm up every two or three hours, all night long, regardless of whether it's snowing, raining, or a bottomless mud hole outside ... most of the time everything is fine, but I want to be there to support the mom, and in case something goes wrong ... sort of like being a midwife, I guess ... and women have been midwives since forever."

There's also the matter of a mother understanding her children better than their fathers do. A male dairy farmer who milked 95 cows twice a day once told me that cows are temperamental and having to deal with their mood swings is like having 95 wives telling him what to do every day. "Who needs that—really?" he asked me. "I can't keep one woman happy, how the hell can I please 95 touchy cows? I guarantee you it's a real pain in the ass trying," he said, scratching his head and kicking the dirt. Five years later, all his cows had been sold and he was crop farming.

Sadie also believes that cows have their own unique personalities, but doesn't find them particularly difficult to get along with. "I know them all pretty well, and can deal with their peculiarities—after all, I'm a mother too, and I know what it's like to have a baby, and be out working the next day ... sometimes I tell that to a heifer that's just calved, and she calms down pretty quick ... all she wants, and deserves, after all, is a little understanding of what she's going through ... just like we all do."

Even though women farmers and Mother Nature may share many similar traits, one does not have to be around farming for very long before beginning to wonder why anybody would want to make it their life's work.

This is not an easy question to answer, particularly as concerns women, who tend not to be solitary creatures or naturally inclined toward spending all day sitting atop a large machine pushing dirt around a big field, cleaning up after 2,000 pound animals or coaxing milk out of temperamental goats. Most women don't find talking to sheep as their chief source of daily conversation, living with an orphaned baby lamb who has taken up residence underneath their antique bathtub or spending all night in the bathroom babysitting a sick duck, a particularly attractive lifestyle choice. Yet this is exactly what women who feel, and seek, a deep connection with all of nature and the various non-human creatures included in this vast universe we are all part of, and deeply attached to.

"He'd hurt his foot and I couldn't leave him outside all night," Illinois farmer Andrea Hazzard explained to me when I asked to use her bathroom and came face to face with a very large duck. That the duck wasn't house-broken wasn't reason enough, in her mind, to not bring him into the house, and once that decision was made, the bathroom was the logical place to put him. "It ended up kind of a mess, but not the first mess I've ever cleaned up, and his foot is definitely much better this morning," she smiled.

It is an unusual woman who can be so nonchalant about the various possible consequences of a duck spending the night and, as it turned out, the better part of the next day, in her bathroom. Most women aren't interested in sleeping all night in a barn waiting for a heifer to calf either, which is what Sadie has been known to do. Regardless, even though the hours are long and the pay is low, neither woman is looking to switch careers. Instead, both have happily configured their unconventional lives according to the demands of their unique livelihoods.

Farming isn't a 40 hour per week job that includes paid benefits, access to human resources professionals, scheduled salary increases, or promotions. It is a 24/7–365 lifestyle that doesn't make room for vacations, weekends or holidays off—ever. "Your mother-in-law can get hit by a bus, your husband can blow out the tractor tire and you can go into labor with your first baby all in the same day—and the cows still have to get milked that evening," says farm wife Jeanie Lewis. She proudly adds that, "if you want to farm you have to accept that the farm is your life and you don't have another one, period, and anybody who thinks that'll ever change is wrong."

Kathy, whose farmer husband died suddenly in late summer, agrees. "I didn't have time to wallow in grief because we had to get ready to harvest. Some people might not understand this, but farmers do. Our neighbors knew that no matter how bad and how hard what had just happened to me and the kids was, or how deeply sad we were about it, there was still over 2000 acres of corn and soybeans that had to come in. We knew this was how life was going to go on for us after Vince was gone, and we had to deal with it. So we rolled up our sleeves and got it done ... and some farmers around here even took time out from their own harvesting to show up and help us out."

Living on the Land Is a Spiritual Endeavor

Forty acres and a goat can give you pretty much everything you need, and teach you just about everything you need to know.
—Will Campbell

By default, farming is a deep connection with the land. Good, healthy land produces abundant good, healthy food; conversely, land that isn't thriving fails to hold up its end of the life cycle-food cycle bargain. "Once you have lived on the land, been a partner with its moods, secrets, and seasons, you cannot leave. This living land remembers, touching you in unguarded moments, saying, "I am here. You are part of me," writes Ben Logan of life on his family farm.[1]

Women's natural connection to the land flows from the awareness that they are part of the land, and land is part of all human life, and the profound realization that they are the source of all life, makes them natural farmers. This is particularly true if one considers that the definition of farming is to cultivate, breed or raise animals and/or plants, within the context of a life cycle governed by the seasons of the land, and the process by which all living things shall eventually return to the dust from which they came sustains it. Farming honors this unchanging, and unchangeable cycle that has been going on since life first began.

Working with seemingly endless acres of dirt generously populated by various members of the animal and plant kingdoms, all of whom are living in a system of reciprocity with one another is at the heart of farming. All parts of this organic, interdependent system have inhabited the soil a lot longer than the farmer has been trying to grow things in it. And, because they were there first, native wildlife generally demand that the farmer learn to get along with them, and not the other way around. If a farmer balks at cooperating with the local animal kingdom, the animals always find some way to outsmart him, and are sure to get even. "I find it works best if I don't disturb the others things living around here," says permaculture farmer Suellen Tompson-Link.[2] "So I don't try to run the coyotes out of their den so I can plant that corner of the field. Instead, I just leave that space for them ... try to send them the message that there's room for us both. As a result, they can hunt where they want to, and unless they get very hungry, for the most part they leave my animals alone."

It takes solid faith, understanding, and courage to make a commitment to living as harmoniously with nature as Suellen tries to do, on land borrowed from its original inhabitants. Wisely, as it has turned out, she tries very hard to work with nature rather than to engage in a power struggle with her natural surroundings that, she believes she is bound to lose. She doesn't describe this relationship in spiritual terms, but she is very clear in saying that her connection to her land and the surrounding natural world sustains her.

As an outside observer of farming life, I'm very comfortable saying that the women farmers who participated in this book all seem to have a deeply spiritual view of both their work, and the land from which their livelihood emerges—but they don't necessarily articulate it. Some live actively and closely connected with God on a daily basis, while others are not necessarily comfortable talking about their life in spiritual terms, but they all see what they are doing as something much more meaningful, in the ethereal sense, than an ordinary nine to five job. Other than the farming community of nuns I spoke with, most don't refer to working on the land, and with various forms of nature, in words that reflect a concern with formal devotion, worship, contemplation, prayer, or sacred service, but will acknowledge that there is a mystical quality to what they are doing. It doesn't escape them that nature's miracles are occurring all around them every day.

"I can't say I'm either spiritual or religious, but I am a systems thinker," Suellen explains. "I don't think in terms of dominating anything, and I do feel very much a part of a much larger system that is the basis of who we are and everything we do, and I find this has a calming effect ... maybe grounding is a better word ... in the cycles of life and death that bring a natural sense of equilibrium to my life. Finding that balance is a huge challenge, and it works best when I remain very present to what I am doing."

Andrea describes her spiritual connection to the land in more esoteric terminology, referring to it as cosmic synesthesia—a neurological phenomenon whereby stimulation of one cognitive pathway leads to an involuntary stimulation of another pathway. Metaphorically, this is akin to an explosion in the brain resulting from one group of cells setting into motion a chain reaction that affects other cells. "I love land and I have a physical and emotional relationship to the land, all land. I can connect to land in a way that I can feel its pain or its exuberance," she explains. "I see and feel the earth as a larger version of myself. Trees and plants are lungs in reverse, water is like tears or blood or perspiration, a wetland is akin to a liver and bones are mountains and stones, soil is like skin. When I see mining or clear cuts in the forest it's an open wound on the earth or my own skin and if I allow myself I can feel emotional pain from it. We have a hard time accepting that we are made of the earth, everything comes from the earth, I am the earth, and you are the earth ... all life is of the earth ... a cosmos."

Roman Catholic theology, more than some Christian belief systems, teaches that all living things are created by God and, as such, must be respected and revered. Most of us don't give a lot of thought to, for example, a worm being one of God's precious creations, and have even a harder time mustering kind feelings toward nasty bugs, and other irritants lurking in the natural world. It takes an uncommon intellectual ability to engage in the higher order thinking that connects us to the animal and plant kingdoms in ways that become emotional reality. Sister Marilyn Rudy, who is a Roman Catholic nun is similar to Andrea in revering the land as place where reaching a state of cosmic oneness with something outside ourselves is possible. "I realize that we are all of one piece. I become at one with the soil. The plants, the animals, and the bugs find me irresistible. This experience is totally connected with the New Cosmology.[3] I am like a new person and I love it and am joyous." While Andrea's cosmic connection is with nature, and Sister Marilyn's is with God through nature, both are describing a similar experience.

Nan Bray, who made a dramatic shift by leaving a very successful career as an oceanographic research scientist in California to create a new life for herself as an ethically conscious sheep rancher in the Tasmanian Midlands, takes a less ethereal, more neutral view of nature. "Nature just is. We are not a particularly important or useful part of it, and long after human civilization has imploded, nature will still be there. It probably won't be in a form that would support us, as we seem hell-bent on destroying that. But it will be nature nonetheless. I find that quite comforting when I feel discouraged by the way we humans are abusing our life-support system. In the here and now, nature is a solace and delight for me, but I don't see it as having any particular spiritual attributes in and of itself."

Other women who have a conscious awareness of the spirituality associated with digging in the dirt and raising livestock see farming as a journey into an unfolding mystery that manifests itself in, for example, the transformation from a seed to a flower and then to a fruit or vegetable. "If you seriously meditate on it, there is an awful lot that can be learned from an ear of corn," professor Norman explains. "But you really, really have to be paying attention to capture this learning experience and all it offers."

While some women farmers tie their sense of spiritual fulfillment to land, others seek it in relation to the earth as a planet, and still others see it as part of the big picture that includes nature in all her forms. "Land is part of the natural world we hold sacred, and to which we all belong," explains Sister Myra Hill, who manages a large timber operation for her community of Strict Order Observance Cistercian nuns farming several hundred acres on the Iowa side of the Mississippi River. Although clois-tered, Sister Myra reflects the thinking of a much wider world of women religious of all faiths, and in various communities, who express a deep concern for the earth and all things living on it. These women believe that the earth is a shared domicile and everything that happens on it is inter-woven with the well-being of all living things. An awareness of this one, essential fact seems to be central to their spirituality, regardless of the finer details of the belief system any one of them subscribes to.

Nan explains her awareness of having a connection with the land as having begun as a child. "The time I spent in different wildernesses as a child and young adult gave me a feeling of belonging, in that 'greater than myself' sense, that has always been incredibly strong for me. I was happier, and more content, alone in the wilderness than surrounded by people in a city. Wild animals were always a part of that, but it wasn't until I started farming that the idea of domesticated animals contributing to that feeling of wholeness started to creep in."

Living on a remote South Pacific island among her Merino sheep has caused the evidence-based scientist Nan was trained to be to step aside in order to make space for a greater, more active acceptance of things that don't have an obvious explanation. "What I have done is to let in lots more trust in intuition, and to accept that there are many things I won't ever know," she says, noting that this has led to a new level of humility in the best sense of the term. "Maybe that's the key word: humility in the face of the amazing natural world we live in and its untold mysteries. There is a lovely cycle of things that must be done to care for the animals under my protection, and to ensure that the landscape is as healthy as I can help it to be, both for its own intrinsic sake and for the health of the animals (wild and tame) who inhabit it."

Over time Nan has developed a deep connection with her sheep, particularly since she has embraced the principles of shepherding. "The animals have taught me a lot—they have the nutritional wisdom to know what to eat, and my job really is to help them do that by working with the landscape and the weather.... I've also had to get to know the matriarchs of the flock—the non-breeding ewes who are the leaders the others rely upon. Without their cooperation, things don't go well at all, so I've had to figure out how to get them on board with the ethically sound program I was hoping to develop," she explains.

As she proceeded to create a collegial, mutually cooperative, rather than hierarchical, relationship with her sheep, Nan's life became one filled with events that have made her laugh, cry, bite her nails, and throw up her hands in exasperation. "Farming is one long journey of love and learning—sharing in the moments of joy and sorrow, frustration and hilarity, as I learn how to grow the finest wool in the world in the most sustainable way I can. It certainly isn't just a way to make a living—it's a way of life that I find deeply satisfying—it makes me feel like a whole human being."

Achieving wholeness and a sense of reciprocal relationship with the natural world requires a remarkable ability to surrender to nature and then to figure out how to work with, not against her. It also requires carefully observing and then studying the ways of the land, how it grows and sustains living things, how it self-nourishes and self sustains. Surrender also involves a commitment to seriously considering how human approaches to agriculture can mimic, or impede, the natural wisdom of the earth. This is important to conscientious farmers who must make what are, for them, many moral "what is best for the land?" and personal, "what is the right way to farm?" decisions, sometimes daily.

Women and men farmers alike have a profound awareness of land as a finite resource that can't be replaced or reproduced. As a result, few things about agriculture are more controversial than the use of farm chemicals, which are at the center of the best farming practices debate. The organic, biologic, mineral or chemical debate about the "right way" to nourish soil is ongoing and, at times heated. Farm chemical advocates argue that they are necessary to enrich the soil so it can produce the best possible crop. "If we stop using farm chemicals who is going to decide which 50 million of the world's people we won't be able to feed?" former Secretary of Agriculture Earl Butz famously noted. Many farmers agree with Butz and believe advocating for the halt to the use of farm chemicals is unreasonable.

Kathy Nickel crop farms several thousand acres, and believes chemicals get a bad rap. "It's not like we just throw them on," she says. "In reality, you almost need a chemistry degree to use them, and you have to pass a farm chemical safety course before you can even buy the chemicals ... the land has to be renourished somehow, and those of us with large crop operations can't farm totally organically, so I have to look to another way to replenish my soil." She uses organic material to enrich her soil when she can get it, but points out that there isn't enough fresh cow manure in the entire state of Wisconsin to adequately fertilize all her fields. Her point that even if there was enough manure available for her to go totally organic, trucking it in and spreading it would be prohibitively expensive and extremely time consuming is valid, and she would be unlikely recoup either the financial or time costs involved She also points out that farmers drink the same water everybody else does, so they try to be very careful not to overuse chemicals and risk polluting the ground-water.

Andrea believes organic farming, the chemical-free alternative to conventional farming, is the right way to grow food, but thus far has gone a different route, using her last name rather than the organic label to attract consumer interest. "It's not Organic, It's Hazzard Free" has been her farm's tagline slogan for several years. Her opinions on organic methods and certification are conflicted because, as she sees it, the labeling process takes the responsibility for how the food is produced away from the consumer and places it squarely in the hand of the government and third party certifiers, and this is unacceptable to her. "We have all heard the stories of organic free range chickens and dairy cattle being raised on corporate farms in a manner far from what most would consider organic. The laws of the national organic program are constantly under the pressure of large corporate entities pushing hard to loosen what used to be rather stringent standards. The label has been watered down and it is frustrating to watch because there are so many amazing farms that go far beyond the letter of the law to grow good food, and then you have this other very powerful contingent pushing in the opposite direction." She stresses her efforts not to stray from total transparency in her operation and believes those who know her and buy from her trust that she grows healthy food, and their trust is what matters most to her.

Sadie believes strongly in organic farming methods, and explains that, "the paperwork sucks." She feels the regulations around organic farming are very stringent, particularly once the federal government became the enforcer. "I have to keep meticulous records because the operation is reviewed every year and it only takes one slip up to jeopardize my certification." Her bottom line is that she feels that by adhering to organic farming practices she runs a much better operation. "The land is better off and the cows are happier, so they produce more milk," she explains while giving me a glimpse of the size of the paper files she has to maintain to keep her organic certification, which speak to the volume of paperwork involved.

As a permaculture, whole systems farmer, Suellen advocates integrating organic farming into the surrounding ecology to create mutually supportive, harmonious relationships among plants, animals and people that closely mirror those found in naturally evolved ecosystems. In the permaculture system she favors, insects are controlled by other insects rather than insecticides, and natural decay feeds the soil. "This idea originated in Australia, and as a native Australian, it makes perfect sense to me, so I do it here [Wisconsin] and it works just great ... it's very sustainable." she says of her small, diverse farm operation that includes raising meat animals, natural fiber production and food crops.

Mary Dunn, who raises Brown Swiss steers for meat, doesn't see a lot of value in the organic vs. conventional farming argument, nor does she consider the question a moral dilemma. "There isn't a farmer alive who doesn't want to raise a good product—and there's more than one good way to do that. I'm not sure it does agriculture or the food industry much good to have farmers arguing among themselves over which way is the best way to farm."

MY LAND IS MY HOME

The Mankiller family land defined who I am. During the period when Indian Territory was dissolved and Oklahoma became a state, the federal government attempted to destroy the Cherokee Nation by dividing up our commonly held land into individual allotments of 160 acres. The family land was allotted to my grandfather, John ('Yona) Mankiller, and passed down to my father, Charley Mankiller, and my Aunt Sally Leach. I am grateful that my father rejected offers to sell the land even in the very lean times our family faced after the Bureau of Indian Affairs relocated us to San Francisco. The land held deep memories of my family and the first ten years of my life. During my early childhood, my siblings and I gathered water from a cold spring where my grandparents had also stored melons, fresh milk, and butter. We shared that spring with bobcats, mountain lions, wild pigs, and an occasional deer. With a watchful eye for snakes, we turned over rocks looking for crawdads in the icy water. The banks of the spring were covered with a profusion of watercress and fragrant mint. God surely cre-

ated the spring with an abundance of love. It is protected on the
east and west sides by steep hills dotted with oak, hickory, locust,
and walnut trees. It is my favorite place to pray.

—Wilma Mankiller
Principal Chief of the Cherokee Nation

Wilma Mankiller's statement on the meaning of land as home and a sense of place reflects another meaning land has for those who feel a connection to it. bell hooks, writing on the need for a home and a sense of belonging, quotes from an essay by Scott Russell Sanders that identifies the importance of place as part of the larger picture connecting spirituality to the land.[4] "It is rare for any of us, by deliberate choice, to sit still and weave ourselves into a place, so that we know the wildflowers and rocks, and politicians, so that we recognize faces wherever we turn, so that we feel a bond with everything in sight," Sanders writes. "The challenge these days is to be somewhere as opposed to nowhere, actually to belong to some particular place, invest oneself in it, draw strength and courage from it, to dwell not simply in a career or bank account, but in a community … once you commit yourself to a place you begin to share responsibility for what happens there."

Neither Sanders nor hooks is likely aware of it, but they both are describing life lived solidly on the land in the same sense Wilma Mankiller describes the meaning of land as home and being in partnership with Mother Nature when you live there. It is the land itself—the dirt, the weeds, the gopher holes, coyote dens, sagebrush, rocks, hills and valleys, which provide farming women with their unique sense of place.

"She's has strong artistic sensibilities, and knew immediately, the very moment she drove in, that this was the place she was looking for, so she called me right away and we grabbed it," Gail Carpenter says, referring to her daughter Lindsey's discovery of the 44 acres they bought together nine years ago and now actively farm. "Something about the land itself spoke to Lindsey, and she's fallen so in love with it that she has taken steps to ensure it's never used for anything other than what we are doing with it right here, right now," Gail adds

Other women farmers are working land that has been in their family for several generations, and readily acknowledge the heavy responsibility that comes with this legacy. "This is our home farm—it's been in the family since 1847, and most of my ancestors, including my mom, who died last year, are buried right here, in the cemetery on a corner of these 240 acres … and I'm the first woman to farm it." Andrea explains, speaking of her farm in north-central Illinois. Over time Andrea has developed a very close, personal relationship with her land. "The land grows the food you put into your body, and you can't get much more intimate with or closer to something than that."

"There's definitely a whole spirituality women who farm and are connected with the land feel," explains professor Norman. She believes this spirituality begins when women engage in a soul-searching journey to find balance and center in their lives, and then try to make meaning out of what they discover. "The common theme seems to be an intense desire to become more of who they are, and reinterpret their lives accordingly," Norman says. "As far as we know, it's beyond rational, and mostly tied into wonder, gratitude and the desire for healing. What seems to happen for those who engage in this process is that they change their lifestyle, sometimes rather dramatically, in order to feel whole again—or maybe to feel it for the very first time."

Writer Margaret Roach, who abruptly abandoned her position as the editorial director of Martha Stewart Living Omnimedia and departed the perpetually noisy chaos in the City That Never Sleeps (New York) to live quietly on the land, has something to say about the journey toward wholeness.[5] "In 2008 I began a transition back to being just Margaret—writer and gardener. I traded the fast lane for my own dirt road," she explains, adding that it was neither an easy trip nor a smooth ride. "I am, in many ways, a solitary type. Work had been my village and my family." She left both to live in a rundown farmhouse situated on a few remote acres in upstate New York, and to, hopefully, find the "true home" that had eluded her in the city.

"On the way 'home' I had seen every manner of therapist and adviser (physical, psychiatric, financial, legal, and astrological), started buying weekly lottery tickets, and cleaned out every corner of my life to lighten the load I had to carry to the New World. I hired the professional matchmaker, writing a giant check despite my disappearing income, and wanting to head regret off at the pass by ensuring I didn't let happily ever after elude me if, in fact, money could buy you love. Bases covered," she says.[6] She even gave a treasured ex-boyfriend, who she was still hoping would see the light and mend his errant ways, the heave-ho.

While Margaret did not endeavor to farm per se, she did turn to something many women find great satisfaction in doing, which is to garden. She decided to engage in this activity on a much grander scale than one normally sees in a corner of the backyard. At the same time, she was looking for her essential self and learning how to make peace with her new lifestyle, which did not include a regular paycheck. She planted great expanses of flowers and large quantities of vegetables, with no particular plans for what she would do with the results. Eventually she figured it out.

Margaret believes it took her every bit of the two decades, spanning the time from when she found the land she eventually bought to finally arriving, or even beginning to arrive, in the sense of the total surrender, in the life she believes has always resided somewhere inside herself, albeit deeply hidden. She believes her journey really began when she took painter Andrew Wyeth's advice to heart. "I don't think there is anything that is really magical unless it has a terrifying quality," Wyeth says, thereby giving Margaret the courage to face her fears, and give up everything she had built her life around to transform the long distance relationship she had with her land into a committed marriage. It was a big change.

"Four months ago I was wearing designer clothes and living in fluorescent light. Today I was mucking out water gardens in the sun and refitting plumbing gaskets while my boy-friends [nine bullfrogs] looked on disinterestedly," she writes of her transformation.

This Land Is My Land

> The most common trait of all primitive peoples is a reverence for the life-giving earth, and the Native American shared this elemental ethic: The land was alive to his loving touch, and he, its son, was brother to all creatures.
>
> —Stewart Udall

Around the world, land, mostly the question of who owns it, is at the root of many intense personal and political conflicts, wars and deaths. Land ownership remains at the center of still volatile and unresolved issues in the Middle East arising from the 1948 United Nations decision to take land away from Palestine and give it to Jewish Holocaust survivors, enabling the formation of the state of Israel.

Closer to home, and more than 150 years ago, American settlers received permission from their government to claim land Native Americans had inhabited for centuries, and continue to firmly believe is theirs. Like the ongoing Middle East conflict, the Native American land-grab story will not end well until the U.S. government commits to restorative justice efforts toward the Native Indian population in the form of real amends for the harm done to them, and to their ancestors. In their eyes, the only way justice can prevail is to return the land they still believe is theirs to them.

One of the more infamous land feuds in American history arose between the Hatfield and McCoy families living on the Kentucky-West Virginia border—an argument that began in 1865 and lasted for the next 36 years. Between 1880 and 1891, this disagreement claimed more than a dozen members of the two families and caused the Governor of West Virginia to seriously consider mobilizing the state militia and invading Kentucky. Kentucky Governor Simon Bolivar Buckner, Sr., did not take kindly to this threat and ultimately it took an order directly from the United States Supreme Court to restore calm. In the meantime, more than 20 people had been killed or wounded.

Despite the court ruling, the two warring families continued to do battle at every opportunity, even after one of the Hatfield men was put on trial and found guilty of murdering one of the McCoy women. The judge ordered the offender executed by public hanging and the event, held in Pikeville, Kentucky, drew thousands to bear witness to what was, more than anything else, a statement of frontier justice.

The fact that the Hatfields and the McCoys fought each other so hard, for so long, testifies to the vital importance land holds in human life, and to the intense desire to own it. This is understandable when considering that, in addition to members of both the plant and animal kingdoms depending upon land for their survival; it is also a finite natural and economic resource that has both income potential and cash value.

Women Farmers' Concerns about the Food Supply

> *We should think long and hard before we turn control of our food supply over to foreign interests or big industry.*
> —Wisconsin State Senator Kathleen Vinehout

Although most people are not consciously aware of it, the food choices any individual makes are moral choices. The choice to never eat meat is a decision to avoid the violence associated with killing animals. The decision to keep a kosher kitchen is a commitment to uphold the dietary laws of Orthodox Judaism. The decision to avoid meat on Fridays and to fast during Lent reflects a willingness to adhere to the food restrictions imposed by the Roman Catholic Church. The decision to consume only organic food products signifies a refusal to participate in manipulation of the food system by any means, including antibiotic or other chemical use.

"Eating can be mundane or sublime, but either way it is an occasion for moral decision making within cultures that have a range of traditions and structures surrounding human nourishment," explains Rutgers philosophy professor Andy Egan.[7] He challenges his students to think about the social and environmental consequences of various eating habits, to reflect upon what ethical obligations, if any, humans have toward nonhuman animals, and to consider whether the answers to these questions generate moral obligations to adopt, or to abandon, particular eating habits.

Egan teaches a course titled "Eating Right: The Ethics of Food Choices and Food Policy" that explores how membership in certain cultural groups with specific culinary traditions relates to individual well-being. He suggests that the food choices individuals make lead to decisions about what actions society should take to influence how food is grown, processed, marketed, sold and consumed. "How are our individual and societal decisions about what to eat expressive of aesthetic, moral, cultural, and religious values?" he asks. Without question, women farmers have been struggling with this issue for a long time.

Past efforts women in agriculture have made to tackle complicated food supply questions have set the stage for the current concerns many women, and men, have for the current status of food production. In 2008 first lady Michelle Obama selected homegrown food as her major weapon when she declared war on childhood obesity and went on to choose healthy eating as her major domestic focus. Her efforts followed those of other first ladies with similar food interests, and she was not to first presidential spouse to plant a large vegetable garden on what was once part of the White House lawn.

However, the communal Womyn's Land Movement during the 1970s marks the modern beginnings of the current interest in organic farming methods and food products. Though the communal separatists' women farmers' ultimate goal of personal liberation never quite materialized to the extent they hoped for, their belief that women could successfully cultivate the land has endured. And though their approaches varied, these women were pioneers who helped to pave the way for greater interest in the food system that opened many doors for all of today's female growers. "As queers, as gays and lesbians, I think we've always been much closer to nature than other people. Our senses are keener, we nurture and we tend to have a larger view of things," explains Gael who, with her partner, Charoula, farms 250 acres in central Ohio. "There's lots we can do to help create a new world."[8]

The political locus for women farmers today has shifted from the liberation of women as the entire point of sustainable, organic farming efforts to a focus on the results of their efforts in the form of the quality of the food they produce. Many women farmers harbor real fears about a nationalized food system, which many believe is fraught with chemical misuse, synthetic additives, mislabeling, and antibiotic use. This deep discomfort with the food production system is what drives their efforts toward creating a better food supply.

"I have a huge concern about the health of the food system ... in 20 or 30 years there just won't be enough food to go around and what there will be won't be fit for humans to eat.... I'd like to do something about that," explains Iowa urban farmer Sonia Kendrick, who raises vegetables to supply the food pantries that feed Iowa's poor and homeless. She goes on to cite some staggering statistics about the food system in America's heartland.[9] "One in eight adults [12.5 percent] and one in five children [20 percent] go to bed hungry every night," she says, adding that 90 percent of Iowa food is imported, which ties food costs directly to oil prices. "Our food travels an average of 1700 miles from the ground where it grows to the plate where it's eaten," she goes on to explain. Most sobering of all, she projects that food production will need to increase 70 percent by 2050 to feed a projected world population of more than nine billion people.

Andrea echoes these concerns, taking them one step further. "The food system is in real peril, and I don't see men farmers worrying about it—so I guess it's up to the women to fix the problem ... and we can do it, because we've been growing food and feeding families for centuries." She has a good point, and is not the first woman farmer to make it.

Although, traditionally, farming has been regarded as men's work, women have been intimately connected to the land and the bounty it produces since the beginning of time, and as mothers, they are naturally concerned about what kind of food they feed their children. Further, supporters of women's greater involvement in agriculture speculate that if women farmers worldwide had access to the same resources male farmers enjoy, just in terms of land use and financial backing, there would be 150 million fewer hungry people in the world.

WE HUMANS MUST EAT

Let's face it—food is really important to people—and a bad donut
could destroy the world
                                                                    —Corrie Norman

Singling out donuts as the one weapon that could impart the potentially fatal blow to civilization as we know it is thought provoking. Professor Norman's point that food is at the center of human existence, and that consuming bad food has serious consequences, is valid. Food is at the center of almost everything people do, and it is rare for people to come together and not include food as part of the experience. To fully understand this, imagine Thanksgiving without sitting down to a meal.

Besides keeping us alive, food makes everything about life more bearable. It is impossible to imagine any celebration, religious or secular holiday, social gathering, grief ritual to mourn the dead or sentimental retreat into past memories that does not somehow involve food. Food is hospitality to guests, life-giving to the poor, and comfort for the afflicted. Thus, it is impossible to ignore or overestimate its importance, and it naturally follows that how food is produced matters to those who are paying attention to food as a significant part of their lives. People use food to make meaning for their lives, to bring themselves together with others, and to create important rituals that spiritually sustain them—a practice as old as civilization itself, and frequently centers on finding wholeness, meaning and connection.

The place where the search for oneness with the universe and the pursuit of good, nourishing food comes together is in the kitchen. For many, the search to make sense of the life that results from bearing witness to this alchemy is a spiritual experience. "Hunger, food, security, and love all come together in communion (becoming one) when bread is broken and wine is drunk," says bread baker Peter Reinhart, a former seminarian, and a member of the Eastern Orthodox, Christ the Saviour Brotherhood. Reinhart's communion analogy of joining bread and wine together brings to mind the Holy Communion ritual at the centerpiece of Roman Catholic liturgy. During the celebration of the Mass, the priest, by a process of transubstantiation, transforms bread and wine into what Catholics believe becomes the body and blood of Christ. The priest offers the changed substances to the faithful as a means of becoming one with Jesus and with the wider, worldwide body of Christ that is the Church itself. Notably, performing this ritual is restricted to male priests; women are never allowed to engage in this transformative act, even though every day, each time they cook something, they routinely transform food from one thing into another.

"There is an emotional reconnection with the self that occurs for women when they start paying attention to food, and an internal spirituality emerges that points women in the direction of a return to the land, of becoming more of who they really are, and allows them to reinterpret their lives and their relationships," explains professor Norman. She firmly believes much of this begins with the cooking rituals that occur in kitchens, which is where women, and everyone else, naturally gather. She explains that those who are concerned about food want to be involved in these rituals—as the farmer who grows the food, the person who cooks it, the person who serves it, the person who eats it, and as the person who cleans up afterward—and sometimes as a mother who passes her recipes on to her daughters.

Another aspect to this ritual is that, according to Norman, food movements often take on all the attributes of a dedicated belief system (i.e., a religion) for those who become deeply involved in them. Contemporary examples are the trend toward producing organic foods, adopting vegan or vegetarian eating habits, and the slow food (as opposed to fast food) movement. However, compared to many other food rituals, the concerns that have resulted in efforts to produce organic food are relatively recent. The notion arose from a realization that all farms are, in some sense, organic, and that injecting foreign chemicals in to the farming process can produce unwanted results that jeopardize the food supply. Organic producers avoid chemical fertilizer or pesticides, and the food that results is not processed using radiation, industrial solvents, artificial preservatives or other food additives commonly found in non-organic foods.

In order to market a food product as organic, the federal government must inspect and recertify the producer annually. Yet in spite of the regulations, the science backing up claims that organic foods are healthier than conventionally produced food is mixed. Nevertheless, those who are committed to organic farming methods, and the food it produces bear additional operating costs, keep copious records, and accept that, as a result of these efforts, their market is limited because the food they produce is more expensive. Sadie receives nearly twice as much for organic milk from her farm as does a conventional dairy farmer. "I get $33 per hundredweight, compared to $17 for a non-organic dairy," she says. The additional cost is passed along to those consumers who are willing to pay it.

Vegans and adherents to a vegetarian diet avoid eating meat, and sometimes also avoid dairy. Some vegans and vegetarians, sensing a certain cannibalistic quality to eating other sentient beings, avoid eating anything with a face, even viewing this as a spiritual practice. Others avoid meat, fish and/or dairy for health-related reasons, believing that plant-based diets are healthier overall, and result in less heart disease, cancer, and other inflammatory processes that can take hold in the body. Most people who adhere to specific dietary practices such as vegetarianism firmly believe what they are doing is good, and are not inclined to entertain challenges to this assumption. Speaking as a vegetarian myself, I've been on the receiving end of many comments about this commitment, which I made at age 13, after getting ptomaine poisoning from a lobster that had apparently died a natural death, and again when I ate a bad hamburger a few months later. What, for me, began as a desire to avoid foods I believed would make me sick, evolved into a discipline I'm very proud of, and I never hesitate to brag about my very low cholesterol numbers any chance I get.

The slow food movement, which began in Italy in the 1980s, in response to fast food rearing its ugly head, is another example of efforts to modify the way we all eat, as well as a heroic effort to preserve the social rituals around food. There is no other place on earth where food is as sacred or as packed with social meaning as it is in Italy, where eating is meant to be leisurely and enjoyed in the company of friends and family members. Any departure from that ritual violates the basic premise of the Italian cultural tradition to eat, drink, and enjoy each other's company. "I know I need to lose weight," a friend of mine told me recently, "but I grew up in an Italian household and I'd rather cut off my arms than not eat pasta." She also claims that it is unlikely there is an Italian alive, either male or female, who does not know how to cook a good Italian meal and take great pride in doing it.

The slow food concept gained traction when journalist Carlo Petrini became outraged upon learning of plans McDonald's had for a fast food restaurant in the center of ancient Rome, next to the historic 260-year-old Spanish Steps. A magnificent example of Italian Baroque architecture, the steps connect the upper piazza Trinita dei Monti, with its magnificent twin towers, to the Fontana della Baraccia in the lower Piazza di Spagna. The Spanish ambassador to the Holy See once lived on one side of the wide stairway, and poet John Keats lived, and eventually died in a home located on the other side.

Tradition holds that lovers from around the world who have been forced, for whatever reason, to part always agree to meet again at the Spanish Steps. Petrini believed that desecrating this storied romantic neighborhood by installing a fast food restaurant was, both for lovers and for most Italians, an unthinkable act. "What would fast food do to the food culture of Rome?" Petrini asked, strongly suggesting that it would, in fact, threaten the small local trattorias and osterias that are the local dining establishments where members of Rome's working class come together to enjoy each other's company. To change any of this was, in Petrini's mind, a travesty.

Petrini was passionate in his belief that fast food would ruin many beloved Italian traditions surrounding food, and because strikes are a fact of daily life in Italy, he took advantage of this commonplace occurrence to rally his friends around the fast food threat. He asked them to take a stand against "this global industrialization of food, and the social and culinary costs of homogenized eating," meaning fast food establishments everywhere. However, instead of picketing McDonald's, he armed the protestors with bowls of pasta, and directed that they sit down and eat it, thus declaring their allegiance to slow food.

Despite waging repeated, heroic, hard-fought pasta battles, Petrini lost the slow food war. McDonald's became a fast food occupation force that successfully encamped beside the Spanish Steps, where it has remained. However, unwilling to surrender, Petrini determined that in order to keep various possibilities for alternative food choices alive, it was crucial to create an "eco-gastronomic" movement that was concerned with environmental sustainability (eco), and the study of culture and food (gastronomy.) He knew that, somehow, the connection between the plate and the planet had to become part of the Italian mind-set regarding food, and that supporting and protecting small farmers and artisanal production was crucial to safeguarding the environment.

Eventually Petrini and Slow Food co-founder Folco Portinari drafted a Slow Food Manifesto that was endorsed by delegates from 15 countries and condemned the "fast food life" and its implications for culture and society: The rhetoric was passionate: "We are enslaved by speed and have all succumbed to the same insidious virus," the Manifesto proclaimed. "Fast Life, which disrupts our habits, pervades the privacy of our homes and forces us to eat Fast Foods.... A firm defense of quiet material pleasure is the only way to oppose the universal folly of Fast Life.... May suitable doses of guaranteed sensual pleasure and slow, long-lasting enjoyment preserve us from the contagion of the multitude who mistake frenzy for efficiency.... Our defense should begin at the table with Slow Food. Let us rediscover the flavors and savors of regional cooking and banish the degrading effects of Fast Food."[10]

Conviviality is the heartbeat of Petrini's Slow Food Movement, and taking pleasure in the processes of cooking, eating, and sharing meals with others is what the initiative has worked to restore. As a result, today the Slow Food movement's structure is decentralized. Each chapter (con-vivium) has a leader who is responsible for promoting local artisans, local farmers, and local flavors through regional events, social gatherings and farmers markets. Convivium members strongly support the efforts of organic food growers, and matches very well with the efforts of small-operation women farmers.

In the final analysis, however, spirituality is a nebulous concept and spiritual practices around food are eclectic, professor Norman emphasizes. "They can range from something as specific as the Jewish agricultural laws that dictate how you grow your food and what you do with it to thinking about how you eat in your house ... but food is nearly always somewhere in the mix."

Norman also agrees with popular notions that claim everybody is spiritual in some sense, but not everyone admits it. She views spirituality as separate from institutional religion and as a distinctly internal process. In that sense, working with the soil, growing things, and then eating what one personally grows, or using it to feed others, is one way to bring this internal spirituality into focus and connect it to something external. It's a transformative process that Norman believes allows women in particular to become more of who they already are. "Those who believe in God are keenly aware that it was God who created dirt, onions, turnips, and every-thing else found in the natural world, and want to honor that," she says

It Is Not about the Money

> Anybody who goes into farming thinking they're going to make a
> lot of money is in for a very, very big surprise!
> —Jeanie Lewis

Any woman brave enough to take on the daunting task of farming, particularly in today's world, where corporations overshadow everything, isn't merely a pioneer; she is a visionary. She is profoundly dissatisfied with the status quo and the state of the food system, and believes that something better, beyond current food ways, is attainable. Like all vision-aries, these women courageously exercise their independent judgment, often in opposition to conventional wisdom, and use their ingenuity to conceive new ideas, personify the "necessity is the mother of invention" mind-set, and discover innovative answers to recalcitrant problems. And, as pioneers, these women are risk takers willing to assume responsibility for their own lives and futures. They are brave enough to follow the road less traveled into perilous territory and, as a result, make life more fulfilling for themselves. And along the way, they make the world a better place for the rest of us, but they rarely get rich doing it.

"Farming is not a lucrative business venture," explains Sakina Bush, a member of the original group of Mendocino County, California, women who, as part of the wider-reaching Womyn's Land Movement, established an all-women intentional agricultural community in the 1970s that is still functioning nearly 50 years later.[11] Bush views the increased interest in locally grown food as an effort to take back control of the food system, and believes the only way to rescue a seriously imperiled food system is for women to turn toward farming, and to figure out how to sustain themselves while they are doing it.

Carmen Goodyear, another member of the Mendocino group, believes that no matter how technologically advanced society becomes, agriculture will always be at the foundation, and the reason is both obvious and amazingly simple. "You must be able to feed people," she says.[12] Goodyear also believes that a lifetime of farming has positioned her well to endure adversity and live frugally and independently well into old age.

Another remarkable quality women engaging in the hard work of farming possess is that the work itself draws women back into themselves and connects them to what they are doing day by day. This sense of doing what they were born to do provides a rare sense of satisfaction that can reach the spiritual plane. "Farming empowers women to move out of their traditional social roles," Womyn's Land Movement commune member Jess River explains.[13] "It resurrects a feminist view that has been lost and reminds women that there are plenty of interesting things to do that don't involve going to a shopping mall."

Nevertheless, as a small business enterprise, farming is unusually difficult. A farmer's most important partnership is with Mother Nature, and no other business relationship is quite like it. As the boss most farmers believe she is, Mother Nature is fickle, unpredictable, has a mind of her own, is not inclined toward compromise, adheres to a management style that can be very difficult for her employees to work with. And, no matter what kinds of problems she causes, she can't be fired for poor job performance. Not only that, Mother Nature doesn't email, text, Twitter, Instagram or carry a cell phone. She never answers her pager, doesn't keep regular office hours and only shows up for work when she feels like it, and then it's on her terms.

Furthermore, Mother Nature keeps her own counsel, and is not inclined toward taking advice from anyone. She, alone, is the decider about everything, including when to plant in the spring, when to harvest in the fall, and what to do in between. She decides when it rains, and when it doesn't. She can produce a tornado that wipes out a lifetime of farming in less than five minutes, a flood that moves rich topsoil miles away from where it belongs, or a lightning strike that ignites a prairie fire that can burn out of control for weeks. And when she feels like it, she also produces warm, sunny days perfect for growing crops and grazing cattle, gentle rains in just the right amount, at just the right time, slow spring thaws, and long, dry harvest seasons. In any given year, Mother Nature may forgive a hard winter, or make it one people talk about for generations to come. And, as mothers go, she can be exceptionally hard on her farming daughters—yet, to their everlasting credit, they love her anyway.

Bearing all this in mind, answering the question of why some women seek out farming as a way of life is no less difficult than trying to unravel the complexities of any mother-daughter relationship. Perhaps women instinctively understand the feminine traits ascribed to Mother Nature and can identify with them. Maybe biology is destiny in that all women are natural creators and nurturers, and some are drawn to farming as another form of creative expression. It could be that farming is a uniquely spiritual undertaking women farmers feel in a particularly satisfying way that they don't experience in any other profession.

What I do know about the answer to the "why farm?" question is that not one of the women farmers whose stories are told in this book ever mentioned earning money as the primary reason they farmed. In fact, other than to admit that staying afloat financially is an ongoing struggle, they only talked about money if I brought it up. Even then, most were not forthcoming about those details of their operations. "I try to make expenses, but I don't draw any salary for doing this," Sonia explains of her urban farming effort. "I'm obviously not doing this for the money—not at all. I'm doing it because it's the right thing to do, and that's one of the things I truly love about it."

Nan also questions the value of living a life in pursuit monetary wealth. "In my view, the only true 'wealth' comes from real things that are grown on the land. Everything else is smoke and mirrors (or rape and pillage in the case of mining/petroleum extraction.) To be part of a renewing cycle of growth is a great privilege, and carries with it a feeling of being part of something much greater than myself. I love being out on the land, and being a part of my flock … there is no greater reward."

All of the farming women live modestly and frugally, and while they are sharply aware of the need to survive financially, none seem to worry too much about how this will occur. They have confidence in themselves and faith in the effort they are putting forth—and whatever the outcome, it clearly gives their lives deeper meaning, even when they are barely making it. They understand, in their bones, that wealth is not found in bank accounts and that money isn't edible. It is very clear to me that none can envision doing anything other than farming and that all would agree with poet Wendell Berry's belief that "it is impossible to have health in mind, body and spirit without health in relationship to the land."

Two

Farming for the Love of God

*When you enter the land that I assign you, the land shall observe
a Sabbath of the Lord. Six years you may sow your field and six
years you may prune your vineyard and gather in the yield. But
in the seventh year the land shall have a Sabbath of complete rest,
a Sabbath of the Lord: you shall not sow your field or prune your
vineyard.*

—Leviticus 25:2–4

You can always find God in the nature you behold.

—Thomas Paine

Those who hold God close to their hearts usually agree that God and
nature are deeply intertwined. Land is part of this interconnected universe,
and those who place God at the center of their lives also view land as profoundly important to human existence. With this in mind, it is not surprising that the guiding scriptures of every religious faith make at least
passing reference to the moral, ethical, and sometimes practical issues
that govern proper treatment of the land. The common theme in all of
these scriptural mandates focuses in some way on directing the faithful
to take good care of the land entrusted to them.

The earliest written laws governing both secular and religious land
use arise out of ancient Hebrew traditions. These directives are found in
Leviticus, the third book of the Hebrew Bible and the third of the five
books comprising the Jewish Torah. While viewed as a religious text, what
Leviticus sets forth is, in reality, a structure for good farming practices
and a commitment to social justice that is as relevant today as it was in
700 BCE, when the words were recorded.

When, several centuries later, Christianity emerged out of existing
Jewish traditions to develop its own scriptural directives, it borrowed

heavily from the Hebrew agricultural laws to form its own rituals and regulations concerning land use and care. As a result, references to proper respect for the land and directions for appropriate farming practices appear throughout Christian scripture. Non-Christian belief systems also offer directives on the terms of land use. Islam addresses the care of land in reference to property rights and the wealth these rights include. Native American spirituality views the land as the source of all life—plant, human, and animal. Buddhists believe humans and the land are one, and if those who occupy the land do not care for and preserve it, they will not endure.

Perhaps because it is the oldest, Hebrew Scripture is the most thorough in directing how land should be cared for, as well as how the bounty the land produces shall be distributed. Rabbi Jill Jacobs, former director of Rabbis for Human Rights North America explains the scriptural focus on agricultural laws. "The Jewish agricultural laws, as expressed in the Mishnah and in other rabbinic sources, suggest a belief that one's land and produce is never entirely one's own, and six of the 11 *masekhtot* (tractates) that make up Seder Zeraim concern the obligation to dedicate a certain percentage of one's produce to sustaining the *kohanim* (priests), the Levites (who served in the ancient Temple), and the poor, who do not have land of their own," she explains.[1]

The Jewish laws also prohibit mixing two types of seeds in the same field and eating the fruit from trees that are younger than three years old, practices that are healthy for crops and fruit-producing trees. "In total, all but one of the tractates in Seder Zeraim are devoted to laws limiting production or limiting the grower's ownership of his/her produce, and although we do not observe the laws of *pe'ah* in the literal sense of leaving the corners of our field for the poor, Tractate Pe'ah remains a powerful statement about our responsibilities to the poor and our relationship to our property," Rabbi Jacobs stresses.

Leviticus, also obligates farmers to set aside part of the harvest produced from one's fields for those in need, places limitations on agricultural production, and instructs that a land sabbatical should occur every seventh year. Farming is expressly prohibited during the sabbatical year, allowing both the farmer and the land to rest, become renewed, and restored.

These agricultural directives were, in some ways, prophetic because they form the basis for what is known today as the Conservation Reserve Program. The CRP is an initiative of the U.S. Department of Agriculture that, among other environmental protections, pays farmers a yearly fee in exchange for removing environmentally sensitive land from agricultural production and planting species that will improve environmental quality.

Among both Christians and non–Christians alike, prayers and blessings continue to play a central role in the ritual observances centered on caring for the land. Fields are blessed each spring before planting, animals are brought to church annually to be blessed, the faithful pray for rain, for relief from floods, and for help rebuilding when other natural disasters occur. Rural church communities routinely pray for farmers, asking God to grant them a good growing season and an abundant harvest.

Some individuals and many organized religious communities, while not following the Old Testament laws to the letter, view all land as God's land, and take their responsibilities to it very seriously. They endeavor to live these out these mandates as an integral part of their commitment to doing God's work on earth. Equally important, the ancient directives about how to live on the land contained in Leviticus endure as rock solid advice any farmer, regardless of religious orientation, would be wise to follow. However, for those who farm for the love of God, these mandates underpin every decision they make. And, for Mother Nature's daughters, her land is their land.

Humble Laborers in the Fields of the Lord: The Sisters of Our Lady of the Mississippi Abbey

> I could have been very happy being a farm wife—except that I loved God more.
>   —Sister Gail Fitzpatrick, OCSO

"Farm with charm," Mother Angela, the abbess of Mount Saint Mary's Cistercian Abbey told 13 of the nuns under her guidance as she bid them good-bye in October 1964. This was not an ordinary goodbye, good-luck, see you soon farewell. The sisters were leaving Mount Saint Mary's because their abbess, who is believed to hold the place of Christ in their religious community, had accepted an invitation from Abbot Dom Phillip[2] of New Melleray Trappist Abbey near Dubuque, Iowa, to send the sisters west to establish a Cistercian Abbey as a companion community for the New Melleray Cistercian monks.[3] The sisters were going to Iowa with no thoughts of ever returning to live in their Mount St. Mary's home again.

Even though leaving the abbey to form a new community followed a centuries old tradition of their Order, saying good-bye to their rural

In 1964 Sister Columba Guare (left) stands with Mother Angela, the Abbess of Wrentham, Massachusetts, as the abbess says goodbye to the 13 sisters leaving the abbey to travel west to Iowa. Mother Angela, wearing the cross signifying that she takes the place of Christ in leading her community of Order of Cistercians of Strict Observance (OCSO) as their Mother Superior, appointed Sister Columba as the Mother Superior for the Iowa community that ultimately became Our Lady of the Mississippi Abbey. Both sisters are wearing the Cistercian religious habit of that time, which has since been modified (www.mississippiabbey. org).

Wrentham Massachusetts monastic home to travel to Iowa was not easy. It would mark the first time these sisters had ventured beyond the abbey walls since entering the Order of Cistercians of Strict Observance several years earlier. Most had come to Mount Saint Mary's in the late 1950s, as 16- and 17-year-old postulants aspiring to join the cloistered community and close the door on the outside world in order to devote their lives to God.

As members of a contemplative monastic order that lives apart from public life, the traveling sisters hadn't experienced the secular world outside the abbey since entering the convent. Most had never been in an airplane, did not know how to drive a car, and had never seen a television set. They didn't read a daily newspaper or listen to the nightly news either. While unaware of the details plummeting the wider, secular world outside the abbey walls into chaos, the sisters had, nevertheless, committed their lives to praying for this disordered world every day—and during the tumultuous decade the 1960s was becoming the world desperately needed these prayers.

They probably knew that the first Catholic had been elected president of the United States and then, 1000 days later, assassinated. But they did not, like most Americans who were glued to their television sets in the days after the assassination, see Jack Ruby shoot Lee Harvey Oswald, thought to be President Kennedy's assassin. Although, like all American Catholics of that time, they prayed daily for the conversion of Russia, the sisters probably did not know that the Soviet Union had planted long-range ballistic missiles in Cuba and then aimed them directly at the United States. They would have no way to grasp the depth of social tensions behind the escalating Vietnam War, were not likely to have heard The Beatles sing about Sergeant Pepper's Lonely Hearts Club Band or to know about the murder of three young civil rights activists in Mississippi.

In addition to the upheaval in the secular world, in 1964 the Roman Catholic Church, which is the foundational structure underpinning Cistercian life, was also in the midst of major upheaval. Pope John XXIII had convened the second Vatican Council in the over 2000 year history of the Church 1962, and it remained ongoing. Vatican II assembled Roman Catholic religious leaders to reconsider and settle doctrinal issues surrounding the church's relationship with the modern world. Lasting three years, the council was closely watched by both religious leaders and the Catholic faithful. Both groups were expecting major changes that could directly affect their lives, but in 1964 the final outcomes as concerned issues of faith, doctrine and morality, remained impossible to predict.

Like pioneer women a century earlier, the sisters had no certainty about what awaited them as they prepared to leave behind the protection of their abbey walls and travel to a place as unfamiliar to them as any foreign country would be. The 13 sisters chosen for the journey had entered St. Mary's expecting to remain there throughout their lives. They expected that, upon death, they would be buried in its peaceful cemetery alongside other members of their religious order, and some may not have been too enthusiastic about forsaking their abbey home for a place unknown.

However, the sisters had vowed obedience to their abbess. If she determined that she wanted them to travel more than 1100 miles west to the Iowa flatlands, establish a new monastery, and engage in farming to support themselves, then they were expected to gather their long black habits around their ankles, buck up and do as they were told.

Mother Angela selected Sister Columba Guare to be the Mother Superior of the new community, and Sister Columba, needing a mix of younger and more experienced sisters, had selected 12 sisters to accompany her. Eventually, three of the sisters found that going to Iowa as modern-day homesteaders proved to be too much for them, and they did not remain. Since then some of the original 13 sisters, including Mother Columba, have died, two are infirm, and four are still living in the abbey, which now numbers 15 sisters.

It is not unusual for nuns to be asked to take on a type of work quite different from that toward which they would normally gravitate, even going so far as being asked to do something for which they feel they have no skills at all. When this occurs, the sisters rely on God's grace to see them through, and believe they grow in reliance on God more easily when being stretched in new directions. With this in mind, the sisters set forth.

The sisters' response to a directive from their mother superior that they may not have felt fully equipped to handle is not difficult for me to imagine because I have yet to meet a Catholic nun who was hesitant to take on a challenge. Every one I've ever known has, one way or another, achieved whatever it was she set her mind to, or was asked to do. My guess is that none of the sisters blinked when they were told that they were going to a place they'd never been before and, once they arrived, figure out how to farm on land they'd never seen and, at the same time, set a plan in place to support themselves. Despite these formidable challenges, a wise person never would have bet against them—because one thing nuns everywhere have never been afraid of is hard work.

Within the abbey, work is always carried out in response to community needs. The sisters do not choose their own work and the abbess distributes community jobs among the sisters who are able. A committee of sisters assists the abbess by looking at community needs and fitting them with sisters' capabilities, but the abbess makes the final decisions. Jobs change frequently, to help the sisters remain detached from their work and continually focused on God. However, over time, all of the sisters perform all of the jobs required to keep the abbey functioning, whether it be cooking, washing dishes, doing laundry, weeding the garden or driving a tractor.

"Some monastic traditions depend on alms for much of their day-to-day needs. While this dependence on others has its own beauty, the Cistercian tradition instead gives a high place to work, especially manual work," Sister Gail Fitzpatrick, one of the original 13 sisters to make the trip west, explains. "We are a community of all women who must be responsible for ourselves, which is hard work, but we do it."

The sisters leaving Massachusetts for Iowa had learned farming the hard way—by digging in the dirt and operating farm equipment as part of their formation for religious life. They had spent several years preparing to make a permanent, lifetime commitment to the community at Mount Saint Mary's, and along the way had become good Massachusetts farmers. They had no reason to doubt that they could become good Midwestern farmers. However, Wrentham's climate is mitigated by its proximity to the Atlantic Ocean, and Massachusetts farming is very different from the challenges they would face in the Midwest.

The sisters would not have been familiar with blistering hot growing season marked by endless days of suffocating humidity and crashing thunderstorms that gain increasing intensity as they roll across the Great Plains of America's heartland during spring and summer. They had no prior experience with tornadoes or blizzards, and knew little about how frequently both could occur or how dangerous these storms could be. Ice storms that brought down power lines, raw, brutally cold winters, deep snow drifts and white-outs created by 50 mph winds were not familiar either. Weather-wise, Iowa had it all, but there was no Internet in 1964, and even if there had been, the sisters would not have used it, so they did not know what lay ahead of them on their journey.

"We were a little nervous," admits Sister Gail. "We really didn't know what to expect, in practical terms, when we got here, and we didn't know the New Melleray monks either. Shortly after we arrived, they invited us to dine with them, and when we arrived at the appointed time, we stood in a single-file line on one side of the dining room while they stood in a single-file line on the other side of the dining room, both sides just staring at each other. We stood there watching the food get cold, because no one knew what to do next!" she laughs. Today the two communities are much more comfortable with each other and often share religious holidays, feast days, and other celebrations together.

Gracefully ageless and amazingly articulate, Sister Gail has been an avowed Cistercian nun for more than 50 years. She is blessed with a quick smile, playful sense of humor and twinkling eyes that reveal a wellspring of serenity only found among those fortunate enough to be living a life that sustains them in mysterious ways that reach into infinite depths of their souls.

Sister Gail and I had met a few minutes earlier when I skidded to a stop just a few feet in front of her golf cart, which I unexpectedly encountered about half way down the abbey entrance road. The abbey turnoff isn't obvious from the main road and I'd missed it twice, making me late for my appointment and channeling my inner Catholic school girl anxiety over keeping a nun waiting. As a result, I was driving a little too fast. My embarrassment increased tenfold when I hit the brakes too hard and slid on the loose gravel right in front of her. She graciously did not comment on my rough arrival. Instead she focused on my car.

"Cute car," Sister Gail remarked, referring to my eight-year-old Mini Cooper, seriously in need of a visit to the car wash. "How is it for gas mileage?" she asks, eying the interior I suddenly wish I'd de-trashed before leaving home that morning. I assure her the gas mileage is satisfactory. She walks around the car a couple times, so thoroughly inspecting it I was expecting her to kick the tires. "Are you thinking of buying one?" I tease. She tells me she has no plans to buy a car, but at various times has had the opportunity to tinker with mechanical devices, particularly tractor engines, and finds cars generally interesting. I offer to let her drive it, if she can manage a manual transmission. She assures me that she's been driving farm equipment since before I was born, which we both know is an exaggeration, and has never stripped a clutch in her life. After one more tour around the car, she suggests we'd better get on with the interview, because in less than two hours the bells calling the sisters to prayer will ring, and that will end our interview mid-sentence, regardless of who is talking or what we are talking about.

I came to the abbey already aware that the monastic life cloistered religious communities of both women and men embrace is a straightforward, solitary existence. It is a wholly ordered world oriented toward contemplation of the divine mystery of a single, triune God who is father, Son and Holy Spirit. The sisters achieve this through a life devoted to ongoing communion with God and carried out within the monastery walls, hidden from public view. It is an environment where daily life is mostly silent and includes assiduous prayer, joyful penance, and work, all occurring in an atmosphere of supremely uncluttered simplicity. Women who enter into this particular form of religious life aspire foremost to develop an intense focus on their relationship with God, and this desire governs their every action. Outsiders are rarely invited into a cloistered community, and I am clearly aware of how fortunate I am that these sisters have allowed me to visit and are willing to take time away from their busy lives to tell me about their lives as farmers.

The abbey building itself, located about 100 yards further down the road toward the Mississippi River, is hidden by trees and is not open to casual visitors; however, there is a separate building where the sisters conduct their business with the outside world. "We don't decorate—we let God do that for us, using what comes in from the outside," Sister Gail tells me as we enter a small, unadorned meeting room having five large windows opening onto panoramic views of surrounding land that one could gaze upon for a lifetime and never completely take in.

"Ever since the Order was founded in France, in the 11th century, we have relied upon farming to sustain ourselves," Sister Gail begins, as we sit down to coffee and cookies she set out before my arrival. "And for centuries it has been customary that the founding members of any new abbey should number 13, reflecting the life and work of Jesus and his 12 apostles. So we 13 came to Iowa confident that there were enough of us to farm and do the work we needed to do—and we trusted that Mother Angela knew what she was doing. We felt sure God would show us the rest."

Venturing out into the unknown, to a place where none of the sisters had ever set foot before, was an act of faith and courage that immediately brings to mind the brave pioneer women who, a century earlier, left home and family to travel to the farthest reaches of the western frontier, intending to homestead on the Great Plains. I ask Sister Gail, whose religious name at that time was Sister Bernard, whether she felt like a pioneer when she came west. "I guess you could say we were pioneers of sorts," she agrees. "The difference was we arrived in an airplane rather than a covered wagon, and in those days we wore full length black habits and long black veils. Our clothes really were a lot bulkier than a cotton dress and a sunbonnet," she chuckles. She stresses that they believed they had been called by God to establish the new abbey, and this is precisely what they intended to do, which was a little different mind-set from most pioneer women. Bolstered by their unwavering faith that God would reveal to them what they needed to know, when they needed to know it, the sisters didn't worry too much about any devils who might be residing in details such as an unfamiliar climate or land that might not be particularly well suited to farming.

The sisters' temporary residence, for the next several years as it turned out, was a drafty old farmhouse bearing not the remotest resemblance to the serenely beautiful abbey they left behind. Their new landscape was 230 windswept acres stretching across hills and gullies along the main north-south highway between Dubuque and Clinton and east to the bluffs overlooking the Mississippi River. Their land had been donated by a benefactor who originally intended that they settle near Clinton, Iowa. "It's hard to imagine any place in Iowa unsuitable for farming," Sister Gail says, "but his first choice for us turned out not to be the best, so this land was purchased with proceeds from the sale of the original property. That actually turned out well because it also came with a house and a few outbuildings—so we had a roof over our heads right away."

The sisters named their new location Our Lady of the Mississippi Abbey, in honor of Mary, Jesus's mother, who is a patron of their religious life, and to whom the sisters express great devotion. It is a peaceful, prayerful setting located high above the longest river in the United States, and it's not hard to imagine that mighty waterway carrying the songs of praise to their God that the sisters sing every day many miles downriver.

The location is easy to fall in love with, but the lay of the land itself is obviously not easy to farm. "We were very grateful for the three large barns and the corn crib," Sister Gail explains. "But the land was in very bad shape and in no way ready for farming. We understood this immediately and began praying very hard for guidance on what to do next ... we had to find a way to support ourselves quickly, because we had no source of steady income. It is very, very important to us to be self-sustaining, and we were in a situation where we didn't have many options."

Although it was many years prior to the term "diversify" becoming a popular notion among farmers, a very forward thinking Mother Columba decided diversifying was the solution to their long-term economic survival. With this goal in mind, she sent Sister Rosemary on another airplane trip, this time back to Mt. Saint Mary's to learn how to make caramel candy, and bring that knowledge back to the sisters in Iowa. "That was a good decision in terms of bringing us income quickly, and it fit into our tradition of making candy to supplement our farm income. But our hearts still were in farming, and we really wanted to find some way to do it—and make it work," Sister Gail recalls. The small community kept praying, dialoguing about the problem, and waiting patiently until a clear picture of what they should do next presented itself.

Meanwhile, the sisters carried on with the monastic traditions they had committed their lives to following by speaking heart-to-heart with God daily, both directly, through personal prayer, and by sharing in the communal life occurring within the monastery walls. "Ours is a common life filled with unity of spirit in the charity of God, a bond of peace expressed as mutual and unbroken love of all sisters, and communion in sharing of all goods," explains Mother Rebecca Stramoski, the current abbess.[4] Sister Gail stresses that their common life is what sustained the sisters while they waited for clarity about their future.

Not long after the sisters' gave the "what should we do next?" question over to God, Dom Phillip, at whose invitation the sisters had come to Iowa, suggested sending one of his monks over to their abbey to work with the sisters' farmland and attempt to bring it to life. "Brother Placid became our farm manager, and he was—still is, actually—a genius at good farming practices," Sister Gail tells me. "When he came, we were so grateful we all rolled up our sleeves and got to work helping him out. He decided we should begin by withdrawing land from the soil bank and planting Christmas trees. The next year we put in row crops. Eventually we established a rotation of soy, corn, oats and alfalfa, and much sooner than we had dared hope, we had a working farm."

In the early days working in the fields meant that the sisters tied back their veils and secured their flowing sleeves with safety pins so neither would become tangled in the farm machinery, and then proceeded to dig holes to plant trees, drive a tractor, and pull a plow. "I really loved all of it," Sister Gail, who continued actively farming during the 25 years she later served as the abbess of her community, smiles broadly. "I was probably born to farm, and I'd still be doing it, except recently I've had to admit that I'm getting a little old to be driving a tractor around the hills ... but honestly—sometimes it's all I can do not to start it up and just take it out for a ride," she says almost wistfully. "That old tractor and I go back a long time and had a lot of fun together over the years, although sometimes Brother Placid wasn't amused," she reminisces, her face lighting up as she recalls what were obviously very happy days spent working hard to bring the farmland into production.

"One afternoon Brother Placid asked me to finish plowing the far eastern field, hopefully before the storms predicted for later that day rolled in. So, I hooked up the plow to the tractor and got busy. About half way through I saw Brother Placid waving madly at me from the edge of the field. I waved back and kept going. The next time around he was still waving, so I waved again and kept going. I finished up just as it began raining and, feeling pretty good about all I'd accomplished, I drove back to the barn. Brother Placid asked me how it went. I said fine—I'd finished it all up. Then he quietly pointed out that I'd dropped the plow off on the first turn and it went down into the steepest gully on the property, so if I'd managed to get the field plowed anyway, he'd have to call it a miracle, which is what it was going to take to get the plow out of the mud hole it would be in when the rain stopped. I said I'd help him get it out, and he said I'd already helped more than enough for one day and suggested I return to the house and pray for him.... I did as he asked," she says with a self-effacing laugh, "except mostly I prayed that he wouldn't fire me."

ORA ET LABORA: NOT YOUR AVERAGE WOMAN FARMER

The call to enter a monastery is Christ's invitation to seek Him in a particular community, place and manner of life. Entering a Cistercian monastery involves a long process of discernment, both on the part of the individual and of the community. This life continually calls us to conversion, charity, self-knowledge and mindfulness of God.

—Mother Rebecca Stramoski

The hard-working sisters are not ordinary women farmers. Instead of their lives being governed by the needs of the farm, it is governed by their religious vocation, and they fit farming into this life, rather than the other way around. "Our vocation is devoted to the mystery of Christ," explains Sister Kathleen O'Neill, a Cistercian nun for 32 years. "The Rule [of St. Benedict] is designed to safeguard the solitude and quiet needed to devote our lives to knowing Jesus and praying to know God's will ... we surrender our lives to live for God."

Everything about the sisters' daily life centers around prayer, and their orderly routine is clearly defined by the Rule of St. Benedict, an ancient, 73 chapter text on living a monastic life developed by St. Benedict of Nursia more than 1500 years ago. Benedict's purpose in creating and then recording these rules was to guide avowed religious men and women living communally, under the authority of an abbot, closer to God. The philosophic basis upon which The Rule rests, and which several religious orders of both men and women devote their lives to following, is "ora et labora"—to pray and to work. Both are equally important, and sometimes difficult to separate, because they are intended to occur in tandem, in an atmosphere of peacefulness of mind, spirit, and communal life that brings followers closer to ongoing worship of and connection with God.

Those who enter into the Order of Cistercians of Strict Observance are making a decision to become laborers working on God's land. They are embracing a form of working life provides an opportunity to participate in God's creation. In return, the community is able to provide itself with a means of financial support that is in keeping with God's will for them and for His land. So, while the order pays taxes on their agricultural land, they do not view it as belonging to them. "Our land belongs to God," Sister Gail explains. "Our job is simply to care for it in ways that we believe are in keeping with what God would want."

The sisters also believe that a life of fruitful aestheticism achieved through prayer and manual labor enables the mind and body to flourish as God intends. Doing farm labor also places the community in solidarity with all workers, especially the poor, with whom they share their bounty when opportunity arises.

Committing to life in a contemplative religious order requires a willingness to forgo the ways of the wider world and take up the strict discipline of monastic life—a decision that often involves considerable soul-searching. Sister Kathleen describes the early stage of the discernment process as a restlessness that, for her, led to "a Damascus experience." She suddenly realized she wanted to devote her life to God more than she wanted to marry the man she was engaged to, and more than she wanted to embrace living a traditional, upper middle class life as a wife and mother. Once she understood what she felt to be a calling to enter monastic life, she began a lengthy, purposeful, and carefully prescribed process of preparation.

For Sister Myra Hill, who runs the Abbey's 350-acre timber operation, embracing religious life was much more gradual. She became acquainted with the Rule of St. Benedict while in college and was drawn to the monastic ideals it sets forth. The stories of the desert fathers and mothers, who were the early monks and nuns who inhabited the deserts of Egypt and Syria in the 4th and 5th centuries, captivated her. "I began to wonder how I could give my whole self to God with as much dedication as the early desert dwellers had," she says. "I wanted to live simply and purposefully, focused on gospel values and not giving in to society's demands to produce, consume, and make money."

She says people sometimes ask whether she always knew she wanted to be a nun. "I have to answer 'no' she says, "and I am glad for the experience of having carried other dreams, hopes, and plans for my life. In hindsight I suppose I can see how God was planting seeds much earlier than I was aware, but I did not really begin considering religious life until I was in college." It took her several years of regular visits to the abbey, each followed by a period of reflecting on her experiences there, before deciding to make the Iowa Abbey home. "Community life offers encouragement and support on the path of discipleship, and provides many opportunities to serve my sisters with both my gifts and my weaknesses," she says.

The process for eventual admission into the community is rigorous and only those who seriously embrace the possibility of a religious vocation undertake it. "Generally a woman begins corresponding with the vocation director and comes to visit the abbey—ideally for several visits," explains Sister Gail, who currently serves as vocation director. "If this seems to be the direction God is leading her, then she returns as an observer, living and working with the community, inside the cloister, for several months. If both we and the applicant sense Mississippi Abbey may be the place God is calling her to, she applies to formally enter the community as a postulant, which is the first step toward eventually taking final vows."

When accepted as a postulant, the applicant gives up her job, distributes her material possessions, and enters the novitiate, where she comes under the guidance of the novice director, who instructs her in the nuances of living a committed religious life. This is her first exposure to the abbey's farming work, and lasts for five to ten months. When the postulant, novice director and abbess all believe she is ready, the postulant, in the presence of the entire community, takes her religious name, receives the Cistercian religious clothing, consisting of a white habit, white veil and scapular, and enters the novitiate. At this time, she also begins a two year process of intense spiritual and monastic formation, and all the while continuing to do farm work.

When the time feels right, the community again votes on the candidate to determine whether she will be admitted as a lifetime, permanent member of the worldwide Cistercian community. If the decision is to accept her, the postulant makes her solemn profession, legally renouncing all her property and her ability to inherit, and joins the abbey that originally admitted her into the Cistercian Order. She receives the full religious garments of the Order—the white habit; black scapular and veil; and a hooded cowl to be worn in church. Absent a change of heart, she will remain with the Cistercian community until her death.

The sisters all take vows of material poverty, chastity, and obedience to their abbess. "We do whatever is asked of us," Sister Louise explains, "and if we really struggle with it, or disagree, we can bring the concern to the superior. If she says 'I really want you to do this' then we do it to the best of our ability." The vow of obedience also includes nurturing the humility of spirit needed to discern God's will; keeping silent so God's voice can be heard and to enable constant communion with God; and humility—an openness to letting go of the self and allowing God to work within an individual, leading her toward greater love.

"We vow to obey God, the Rule, our abbess, and our community," the sisters explain. "All of us struggle with our own blindness and emotional attachments to our own wants and ways of doing things. The goal of obedience is not only a harmonious community, but primarily to assist each sister to grow in interior freedom from her own ego. We vow to remain all our life with our local community. We live together, pray together, work together, and relax together. We give up the temptation to move from place to place in search of a more ideal situation. Ultimately, there is no escape from oneself, and the idea that things would be better someplace else is usually an illusion. And when interpersonal conflicts arise, we have a great incentive to work things out and restore peace. This means learning the practices of love: acknowledging one's own offensive behavior, giving up one's preferences, forgiving. And we vow to live a simple, celibate life according to the customs of our monastery, and to be always open to change and grow. We are to accept with contentment the basic monastic regimen of our community and live out community decisions in a cooperative spirit. Above all, we must always be willing to ask forgiveness, to change our way of thinking and behaving, and to learn new and more loving ways of being toward other people and toward God."

However, on the deepest level, there is only one vow in monastic life—the vow to give oneself over to God completely. "I began monastic life with a heart filled with joy and awe, and a sense of coming home. And Jesus has never let me down in the 32 years since then!" Sister Kathleen explains, with quiet conviction and a broad smile.

Pope Francis strongly agrees with Sister Kathleen. "When a cloistered Sister consecrates her whole life to the Lord, a transformation occurs that one can never fully understand," the Pope told an assembly of cloistered sisters at an abbey in Assisi, Italy in 2013.[5] "Our normal thinking would be that this Sister becomes isolated, alone with the Absolute, alone with God; hers is an ascetic, penitent life. But this isn't the way of a Catholic cloistered Sister, it is not even Christian. The way goes through Christ

Jesus. Christ is always at the center of your life, of your penance, of your community life, of your prayer and also of the universality of prayer. And what happens on this way is contrary to what is thought is an ascetic cloistered Sister. When she goes on the path of contemplation of Jesus Christ, of prayer and of penance with Jesus Christ, she becomes greatly human. Cloistered Sisters are called to have great humanity, a humanity like that of Mother Church; human, understanding all things of life, being persons who are able to understand human problems, who are able to forgive, who are able to pray to the Lord for people. Your humanity comes on this way, the Incarnation of the Word, the way of Jesus Christ. And what is the sign of such a human Sister? Joy!" Unquestionably, Sister Kathleen agrees with the Holy Father.

However, in reality, monastic life is rigorous and disciplined, and not all avowed sisters remain with the community throughout their lives. Three of the original 13 sisters who came to Iowa left the order before professing their final vows. And, three years ago Sister Sherry, a fully professed sister, and the most recent abbey farm manager, left the community. "Sherry was still young enough that she could do something else with her life," Sister Gail explains, adding that her departure was "a very difficult loss for us."

Sister Gail Fitzpatrick, OCSO, leads vowed members of her community, including Sister Nettie, Sister Joanna, and Mother Rebecca in singing the Psalms of the day together in choir, after the farming chores are finished. The sisters follow the Psalms with Compline, the final prayers before the Great Silence begins, marking the close of the day (David Peterson Photography).

The Rule sets forth the manner by which the sisters' daily life of prayer and work will occur. "It balances life—

keeps it from getting too screwy," explains Sister Louise. "And when the bell rings, we stop whatever it is we are doing and go to church to pray." There are no exceptions to this practice, regardless of the activity the sister is engaged in, whether it is plowing a field, preparing a meal, or sorting the laundry.

The bell rings seven times each day, which begins at 3:30 each morning with Vigils, which calls the sisters to rise from sleep, followed by four hours of grand silence during which Lexio, a daily reading of the Divine Office,[6] occurs, and ends with Compline at 7:15 p.m. In between are Lauds (morning prayer), Terce (mid-morning prayer), Sext (midday prayer), Non (midafternoon prayer), Vespers (evening prayer) after which grand silence is again observed. The sisters retire to their cells at 8 p.m. Between these times the sisters eat, carry out their assigned work on the farm or in the candy factory, and converse as necessary, without engaging in idle chit-chat. "Silence is so very important to being able to hear God speak," Sister Kathleen explains.

Unlike committed religious women and men who live more public, secular lives, monastic contemplatives focus on praying for the world, similar to what those of Jewish faith describe as tikkun olam, a prayer for healing and repairing the world recited three times each day. The sisters endeavor to live in a partnership with God, and at all times are praying for knowledge of the right steps to take that will help the world, thus bringing greater honor and glory to God.

Contemplative monastic orders like the Cistercians leave the apostolic work of the church—teaching, nursing, engaging in social welfare work, offering spiritual direction, doing missionary work, or engaging in political action—to other orders of religious women. Theirs is a quiet life devoted to God and actively farming is one of the ways they are able to both express this devotion in daily life and, at the same time, sustain themselves.[7]

"Sadly, today very few monasteries can support themselves just by farming," Sister Gail explains. "The sisters in religious communities everywhere are all older, and fewer young women are entering the monastic orders, so we've all had challenges finding ways to keep supporting ourselves." Currently there are 1800 contemplative nuns worldwide and five cloistered abbeys for religious women in the United States. All have had to figure out how to enter into the 21st century in ways that allow them to remain true to their traditions. Often this has involved making some very difficult business decisions, particularly in terms of selling land and buildings. However, most have tried very hard to keep some form of agricultural endeavor as part of their efforts to survive going forward.

"We were lucky—this abbey was established just as Vatican II was occurring and all religious were being called upon to reflect on religious life. We had an opportunity to modify some things—it was very exciting time," Sister Gail says. Among the adjustments the order made was to replace their long, medieval-appearing black habit and veil with a cream-colored, leather-belted, ankle-length garment, black cowl and shorter black veil. They added a prayer robe that symbolically removes the sisters from the world of work and guides them into the world of prayer when they enter the chapel.

Another change Vatican II brought about is that the sisters no longer surrender their entire identity upon entering the community. They no longer forsake their given name for a religious one, as had been the tradition for centuries. "I entered the order as Gail Fitzpatrick, took the religious name Sister Bernard when I made first vows, and after Vatican II returned to my baptismal name," notes Sister Gail, who has seen a lot of change during her more than half century in the order.

Unlike previous times, when nuns wore only their religious clothing, today the sisters who work on the farm wear tennis shoes, Levis, muck boots and sweat shirts in the fields, and their religious habit the rest of the time. "It was a practical decision—it's dangerous trying to run a chain saw in a habit, even with the sleeves rolled up," a strong, robust Sister Myra explains, adding that the decision does require them to have a few more clothes than they would normally need.

However, for Sister Carol, who entered the community as a life-long University of Iowa football fan, this change is a special blessing. As a show of support for the team, every Saturday during the playing season she wears a U of I sweatshirt while she works. Because there is neither a radio nor a television set in the monastery, she has no idea how her favorite team performs each week until one of the abbey employees brings her up to date on Monday morning, but she prays for them every game day anyway. Her prayers payed off during the 2015 season because the Iowa Hawkeyes, who have not been a winning team in recent years, were undefeated going into the Big Ten Conference playoffs.

Another modern change in abbey life is that rather than being assigned to particular work tasks, sisters are guided to find work within the cloister that both meets the needs of the community and suits their own interests. Sisters Myra and Kathleen are both musicians, so are able to lead the sisters when they sing their prayers. Sister Gail actively farmed until, in her words, she "just got too old to be doing such things," a claim I personally find very hard to believe. Currently she helps with administrative tasks and fills in when needed on the caramel candy production line. All this is in keeping with St. Benedict's directive that every sister "be given some work to do so that she will not be idle. Weak or sickly sisters should be assigned a task or craft of such a nature as to keep them from idleness and at the same time not to overburden them or drive them away with excessive toil."[8] For the sisters at Our Lady of The Mississippi Abbey, this has been challenging because the community has grown older and the younger sisters able to do farm work are few. "We've had an increase in interest among younger women who believe they may have a calling to monastic life," Sister Gail says, "but overall our average age is on the higher side."

Farming Is Doing God's Work on Earth

Be still and know that I am God
—Psalm 46:10

Other than addressing the need for meaningful work, St. Benedict's Rule does not directly address how farming is to be conducted, land acquired, or economic sustainability achieved. Monastics seriously apply themselves to the humble task of earning their living, with the intention of not having to beg or become a burden to anyone. What sets the monastic approach to work apart from that of the wider world is the attitude the monk brings to it. For monastics, work is a functional activity that is not motivated by a desire for career advancement, success, accumulating wealth or acquiring goods. Instead, its function models the principles of subsistence farming to make ends meet in ways that support and sustain the monastery and bring balance to the daily rhythm of the monastic life, while at the same time avoiding greed in any form. In other words, in the monastic tradition, enough truly is enough.

The stewardship of monastic land arises from the daily inspiration the sisters receive from the celebration of the Mass, which is the ritual liturgy for worship, and the associated scriptural readings they study for four hours each morning. Monastics strive to live in harmony with the seasons and remain attuned to the natural world as manifest by the influence of the local weather on farming efforts. They study proper nurturing of the soil, calculate the proper moment for planting, understand what is needed for proper growth, and make precise decisions about when to harvest. As a side benefit, the community plans their meals according to the farm calendars, allowing them to balance their diet by eating seasonally.

One of the principles monastics try to implement is synchrony between their farming schedule and the rhythms of the church year. They endeavor to blend the seasons of Mother Nature and Holy Mother Church together in their daily experience, particularly during Lent, which is the period leading up to Easter and a time of sacrifice and denial in preparation for celebrating Christ's resurrection. Lent and Easter are times for both spiritual rebirth and rebirth in nature. In the northern hemisphere, it is also the time to prepare for planting and new life from the land.

Every monastic farm, including Our Lady of the Mississippi, begins the planting season by blessing their fields on May 15, the feast of St. Isadore the Farm Labourer, who is the patron saint of farmers. St. Isadore is an example of a lay saint of humble origin who attained a life of sanctity through doing ordinary work extraordinarily well and is believed to

Sister Gail, joined by Sisters Genevieve, Grace and Kathleen, all members of the community of Cistercian nuns at Our Lady of the Mississippi Abbey, sprinkles holy water across their farm land as part of the annual Blessing of the Fields. This spring celebration occurs on May 15, the feast of St. Isadore the Farmer (David Peterson Photography).

understand how hard farm labor is and through prayer and heavenly intercession, assists the farmer in making it easier.

Sometime during the early fall of each year livestock farmers look to St. Francis of Assisi, the patron saint of animals, to bless their livestock. Over the years, this practice has extended to include pets, which are brought into church for the ceremony, when the priest is willing. More often, priests in rural areas go out to the farm to invoke the blessing of St. Francis upon the livestock.

Monastic farmers also express devotion to Saint Fiacre, the patron saint of gardeners, especially those who grow vegetables. Fiacre is called upon to aid those charged with clearing weeds and brush and stones from the garden, and if he does not help directly with the digging and the heavy lifting, he can at least grant patience and persistence in performing hard labor that is never finished. He is the saint for lowly things and for increase, and his blessings are sought by those who love springtime and planting, summer, and harvest, the smell of turned earth, and the joy of a flowering land. The vegetables St. Fiacre grew around his monastery were said to be superb, so those asking for his intercession believe he possesses special powers to ensure successful vegetable crops.

"Although we have a large farm we love dearly, we have never been able to bring it to the point that it has become the major source of income for us," Sister Gail tells me. She explains that the present goal is to sustain their land and keep it healthy and beautiful, keep the farm operating in the black, and rely on their candy sales as their primary financial base. Clearly this is a wise economic decision in today's agricultural economy, where most farm families cannot support themselves on their farm income, and expecting a farm to support an abbey and 22 sisters is unrealistic. Nevertheless, in order to increase their bottom line and stretch the farm income as far as possible, until very recently the sisters did most of the hands-on farm work themselves.

"We did it all ourselves for a long time, but we are getting older and have had to pass on much of the heavy work to hired employees because there just aren't enough of us to get the work done. We also decided to rent out some of our land, and right now this adjustment is allowing us to attain our goal," explains Sister Gail, who thinks like the career farmer she was. "Many of our sisters are older now and work mostly in our gardens and orchards, providing food for our table. Cattle graze on our land and corn, soybeans grow ... one sister is a beekeeper, and we sell whatever honey from those hives that we don't use ourselves. These efforts, plus the timber operation are about all we can reasonably manage ... and

Brother Placid's decision to diversify, and to do it the right way, has helped keep the farm solvent and out of debt."

The farm management issue has presented challenges for the sisters, particularly after Brother Placid retired. "We managed the farm ourselves, but relied heavily on a hired hand to help us run it," Sister Myra explains. "He was good at what he did, but he didn't understand monastic life, and it wasn't a normal working situation—the sisters were making all the decisions, but asking him to oversee the daily operations. He had an entire community of nuns telling him what to do, and that's a very difficult situation for anybody," she acknowledges with a chuckle. "We were his bosses and his primary workers, and were supposed to start work at 8 in the morning, but sometimes we wouldn't show up until 10:30 or 11 because the community needed to dialogue about something, and that took priority. The, after an hour, we had to stop to pray, so he had no control over the work schedule. We struggled along together for a while, making do as best we could, but we completely understood when he decided to leave—after all, on any given day he had at least 10 women he perceived as having a direct connection to God telling him what to do, and that's an awful lot to expect anybody to deal with!" she laughs.

The sisters went back to taking turns managing the farm themselves, one after another, which was not the ideal arrangement either. Not everyone in the community was interested in, nor naturally inclined toward, agricultural management, and everything was complicated by having increased the farm size to 620 acres. "This certainly wasn't the best time for us to add acreage, or try new management models," Sister Gail, who was serving as Abbess at the time, explains. "But the farm next door was being sold for development, and this was going to very negatively impact us, so we felt we had no choice except to purchase the land. Ultimately we made the decision for the sake of the land itself ... and because we feel so strongly that nature is a gift from God and we want to do all that we can to preserve the beauty of the land and care for it in ways that God's entire kingdom, the plants, the animals, and we humans, can reside upon it in harmony.... I guess you could say we wanted to be sure we were providing hospitality for all of God's creatures."

Sister Gail, known as Mother Gail during the 25 years she was abbess of the community, decided the farm worked best with just one manager, and appointed individual sisters to assume responsibility for the farm as their primary task. Before she became the current abbess, Mother Rebecca acted as farm manager, and later Sister Sherry took over for three years, until she left the order. "We were in a real quandary when Sherry left, and

While waiting for the official Blessing of the Fields ceremony to begin, Sister Grace sits on the tailgate of the farm pickup, reading prayers to St. Isadore the Farmer. The sisters pray to St. Isadore, the patron saint of farmers, to bring them an abundant growing season (David Peterson Photography).

then someone who understands monastic life and thought he could work with us arrived. He has good hands-on skills and knows how to fix things, which helps a lot! I honestly don't know what we would possibly do without him," Sister Gail says, adding that it's really up to him, and the younger sisters, to keep things going now. He manages the farm leases for the crop and pasture land, with the requirement that it all be farmed organically. The sisters also maintain a large enough garden to feed themselves year round. "Our garden requires a fair amount of work of its own, apart from the farm—and we'd never give that up, no matter what," Sister Gail smiles.

As a result of Brother Placid's 1965 decision to take some land out of crop farming and plant trees instead, the abbey, under Sister Myra's guidance, is now engaged in a diverse timber operation. "We have hardwoods, pine and very high-quality walnut," she explains, adding that she relies heavily on the advice of a forester to determine best management practices. Working with the timber operation is also where the sisters who like operating chain saws get their chance. "Several of us don't mind pruning the trees and thinning things out, so we took a couple quick lessons in chain saw safety, put on our goggles, and got to work," Sister Myra beams proudly, adding that "it's kind of fun."

Late last winter the forester told Sister Myra the community could probably sell off 200 walnut trees in late spring. She presented the idea to the sisters, and the decision was to go ahead with a sale. "The forester and I marked 200 high-quality walnut trees for sale and he helped me put the trees up for bid, she explains. "I actually went to the bid opening, and there were three bidders. The highest one came from two loggers in Belle-vue, Iowa. They harvested the trees, and I think they sent the wood to Germany and China."

The sisters do not sell their wood to New Melleray Abbey, which maintains a worldwide casket manufacturing business just down the road. "New Melleray buys wood in much larger quantities than we have available, and the volume allows them to purchase at a lower price than we can get by putting the wood up for bid on the open market," Sister Myra explains.

This year the timber yield helped keep the entire farm operation in the black, and afforded the abbey the opportunity to pave a road the sisters had wanted paved for several years. "Being good stewards of our land is paramount," Sister Gail stresses. "Obviously we can't afford to go into the red, , but beyond that, we're not trying to make money off our land, and every decision we make reflects our intention that the land remains well cared for, just as God would want it to be."

"Work cannot be the major aspect of our life," Sister Myra adds, but it feeds our prayer life, allows us to express our spiritual self through action, and it's definitely possible to pray while working with our hands, outside in nature ... in that way our life itself becomes a prayer. And in farming we are brought so very much closer to God."

Five minutes before noon the abbey bell rings once, signaling the approaching time for noon prayers, and the end of our conversation. Walking out I thank Sister Gail for her time and tell her how much I've enjoyed talking with her. Before getting into her golf cart, she eyes my car again. "Want to race me to the gate?" she winks.

At that moment the abbey bells ring again, and without another word Sister Gail pulls a sharp U-turn and takes off back down the hill toward the chapel at a pretty good clip, waving back at me as she goes.

Driving away from the abbey, I found myself reflecting on what a unique group of women the sisters of Our Lady of the Mississippi Abbey are. Each has surrendered her life to a very structured regime focused on prayer and work, day in and day out. They faithfully adhere to centuries-old rituals that begin each day in the darkness before sunrise and end in early evening. Yet, in order to support themselves, they must work with Mother Nature, who is unpredictable, often difficult, and doesn't care about the sisters' need to fit the farm chores into their prayer schedule. While most farmers say key to successful farming is flexibility and putting the farm first, the sisters take a different approach. They resolve the tension between needing to pray and being flexible enough to meet Mother Nature's demands by always putting prayer and their relationship with God first. The result is a community of the most profoundly content women I have ever met, and I couldn't help wondering where this well-spring of happiness arises from.

Although theirs is a cloistered existence, perhaps the sisters sense of deep peace arises from having the good fortune to be living the life they feel called upon to live, in a place where they know they will long be at home upon God's land. Or, maybe their peacefulness is simply because they don't have to worry about bad hair days and never waste time wondering what to wear, which is enough to make a lot of women very happy. Regardless of the explanation, all of these women are deeply in love with, and devoted to God, and seem to experience this state of being in a way that falls far beyond ordinary understanding. For me personally, knowing that I had just spent time in the presence of a truly remarkable group of women unlike any I had ever met before became a deep awareness that has remained with me for a very long time.

Feeding the Hungry Is Precisely What Jesus Would Do

> Truly I tell you, whatever you did for one of the least of my brothers and sisters, you did for me.
>
> —Matthew: 25

"I spend a lot of time wondering what God wants me to do with my life," Sonia Kendrick sighs. She pauses for a deep breath, looking into the distance for several minutes before continuing. Her statement does not surprise me. Since meeting her a few months previously, it's been obvious that figuring out what God wants her to do with her life is not only very important to Sonia, it is a continuous question that is never far from her thoughts. There is no doubt in my mind that each day she works very hard at finding the answer to this pressing issue in her life. "I'm truly not sure I'm on the right path, but so far God has been opening doors for me, so I just keep walking through them," she finally says.

We are having this conversation in late September, in an abandoned warehouse on the outskirts of Cedar Rapids, Iowa. Sonia is currently elbow-deep in water, cleaning the dirt off freshly harvested carrots. The bright orange one she hands me is shaped more like a baseball than the slender root it is supposed to be. "This is what happens when I don't thin them out well enough ... but they're just as nutritious as the perfect ones, and God doesn't mind the imperfections, because we all have them—even vegetables," she laughs, sweeping her long, honey-colored hair back from her face.

It takes Sonia about 90 minutes bending over a sink to hand scrub 50 pounds of root vegetables. "I could wash those 600 pounds of radishes over there in about an hour if I had an automatic vegetable scrubber, but I don't," she tells me. She apologizes again for having to work while we talk, rather than sitting down and giving my questions her full attention. I doubt Sonia ever sits down anywhere for very long.

Sonia Kendrick proudly shows off carrots harvested from her first crop as an urban farmer in Cedar Rapids, Iowa. The farming effort is part of the Feed Iowa First initiative Sonia founded (Anthony-Masterson/Terra Firma Films).

Sonia rents this drafty old warehouse from Cargill Corporation, a multinational production agriculture conglomerate with several food processing plants in the Cedar Rapids area, for one dollar per year. This gesture of corporate generosity has been a big boost to her efforts to provide the poor, hungry residents of the Cedar Rapids area with fresh produce, and is one of several lucky breaks that have come her way since she first conceived the idea of feeding fellow Iowans. Each boost has enabled her to further pursue her urban farming dream with missionary zeal, in hopes of rescuing the nearly 27,000 residents Cedar Rapids and adjacent communities of Marion and Hiawatha who don't have enough to eat. Together, the three communities have a population of about 211,000 and comprise most of Linn County, which boasts some of the richest farmland in central Iowa. The area poverty rate is 15 percent, and an estimated 21 percent of the entire county population suffers some form of food insecurity[9]—a problem that has profoundly disturbed Sonia ever since she returned from a yearlong National Guard deployment in Afghanistan in 2004.

"Food security is a matter of national security," Sonia tells me. "I saw first-hand what hunger does to people, and can testify to the awful things it drives them to do. In Afghanistan starving people are digging through rancid garbage, running across dangerous roadways to get to the supply truck when it arrives, and risk their lives in hundreds of ways just for food every day." she says, her eyes welling up. "I came back realizing what lack of food does to people, but I had no idea what to do about it—I just knew I had to do something—because people will go to war to get food … and I know God doesn't want it this way." Although she is sure mass starvation isn't God's plan for the world, determining what she could do about the threat has taken her a long time.

Finding the "right path" is a difficult personal undertaking for anyone seeking their place in the universe. For Sonia, it has been an especially long, circuitous journey that began while growing up in rural Iowa, in a family of fundamentalist Christian hippies she refers to as "Crippies." Sometimes called "Jesus freaks," Crippies called for Christianity to return to its most primitive beginnings. Most believed their life's work was to develop and nurture a heart filled with peace and love that flows out of a personal encounter with the living Christ. They also believed that this encounter was the first step in fostering a personal relationship with the Creator of the universe.

As Sonia explains it, being a Crippie isn't how you dress, or even what you say, so much as it is a total lifestyle governed by the principles Jesus preached in his Sermon on the Mount. "Jesus loved the outcasts, and he reached out to the rejects, which is what I'm trying to do," Sonia explains, adding that the Sermon on the Mount is where Jesus also set forth the Beatitudes, the Lord's Prayer, and other principles of Christian life. Crippies were the major Christian element within the 1960s hippie counterculture movement, and became the forerunners of what has since evolved into the Conservative Christian influence that is evident in today's political culture.

To the greatest extent possible, Sonia's family lived off the grid among other, like-minded Christians, and interacted with the wider world outside their immediate environment only when necessary. Eventually Sonia was able to attend public high school and "within minutes" of graduating she committed a dramatic act of teenaged rebellion against both her religious background and pacifist upbringing by enlisting in the Army. Not surprisingly, this threw a bomb squarely into the middle of her family relationships.

After completing four years on active duty with the Army, Sonia enlisted for a five-year tour of duty in the Iowa National Guard. Not long after, she was suddenly, and unexpectedly, deployed to Afghanistan. It wasn't until she returned from 12 months in a war zone that she found her way back home to Iowa, and back to God. "This hasn't been a smooth ride," she says with a nervous laugh and intense gaze. Then she stops laughing and stares down at her dirt-encrusted hands. "The truth is, it has been a terrible, very difficult struggle ... and I've paid a huge price ... but I still feel like what I'm doing is what I'm supposed to be doing, right here in Cedar Rapids, at least for right now ... and that has helped me to keep going"

Cedar Rapids is Iowa's second largest city, just behind Des Moines, the state capital located 100 miles straight west. Neither city is a place anyone would be quick to describe as easy on the eyes. Primarily an industrial center, Cedar Rapids sits on the tip of a traffic artery connecting it to Interstate 80, a major east-west highway that is a major corridor for Midwest interstate commerce. Typical of most towns scattered throughout the Iowa flatlands, this densely populated community of 1784 people per overcrowded square mile lacks many distinguishing features. A quick, non-scenic windshield tour reveals a lot of old, frequently abandoned buildings randomly scattered among typical urban neighborhoods consisting of small, dingy white rundown houses. Most have unkempt dirt yards, little to no green grass, with front-yard chain link fences separating neighbors from each other.

Outward signs of prosperity are rare and powerful evidence of ongoing economic struggle is everywhere. The town's visual suggests that an urban, non-profit fresh food initiative, which is what Sonia is trying to develop, would be quick to catch on, but as she explains to me later, it has proved surprisingly difficult for the program to gain traction.

Sonia's urban farming efforts flow from an idea that began as an intense "I need to do something meaningful with my life" feeling that surfaced after leaving the military. She underwent a dark, lengthy period of soul searching, mostly focused on trying to answer the unanswerable question of why a loving God lets things like the starvation she saw in Afghanistan happen. "I felt angry at everybody, abandoned by God, and disillusioned with my country … and because of all this I was in no shape to try to get, much less hold onto, a regular job," she says. "I had gotten married just before I got my orders for overseas deployment, had two children soon after I returned, and then realized that my husband wasn't saved [had not accepted Jesus Christ as his personal savior] and couldn't understand what I was talking about in terms of wanting to do what God wanted me to do. But he was supportive of my decision to go back to school for a degree in agronomy, figuring this would give me time to figure things out—and hopefully settle down and get a paying job."

For six semesters, sometimes in good, but mostly in bad weather, Sonia drove back and forth from Cedar Rapids to Ames, home of Iowa State University. The trip put 2400 miles per month on her car during a time when gas prices were moving toward record highs. By the time Sonia completed her degree requirements she estimates she had driven around the world about one and one half times, at an average cost of $3.96 per gallon of gasoline. The lengthy journey gave her the solitude she needed to think about her future.

"No matter how I thought about the hunger issue, I just couldn't get past the fact that Iowa is a farm state and we grow a lot of food here, but 340,000 Iowans have limited or no access to nutritious food on a daily basis. Then I found out that 90 percent of Iowa's food is imported, and that most of the foods Iowans eat travels an average of 1700 miles before finally arriving on our plates. That we're feeding everybody else in the world, but not ourselves really, seriously bothered me," she explains, acknowledging that importing this much food to a state whose entire economy is based upon growing food is crazy. It is also a significant fuel cost and energy issue passed on to Iowa consumers in the grocery store checkout line.

In spring, 2011 Sonia decided that a good way to bring attention to the hunger issue would be to walk the entire 100 miles between Cedar

Rapids and Ames to attend Iowa State University graduation ceremonies and receive her diploma—cum laude. Her graduation walk for hunger was a clever idea that brought her considerable local publicity as well as a Damascus moment, when she suddenly realized that what she really wanted to do about solving the hunger problem was to become a farmer. "I had a degree in agronomy I wasn't sure what to do with, and finally it all made sense.... I could grow food," she exclaims.

However, finally finding the answer she was looking for and then figuring out what to do with this information are two, very different things. While Sonia was trying to determine what to do next, she was also discovering that graduation itself brought forth a new set of issues she had to face. "My husband figured that now that I'd finished school I'd finally get a paying job and be home to help with the kids—and all I could think about were hungry people," she explains. "Nearly a third of the people in my own county live in a food desert, without access to fresh, healthy food, and I discovered this to be true myself, first hand, because, without a job, I was depending on a food pantry too. All I knew for sure was that I wanted to farm, but I had no idea where to begin. I'd given up on trying to figure it all out for myself and finally admitted that I really needed God's help, so I started praying very hard and asking for it."

One of the darkest clouds hanging over Sonia's farming dream was the fact that she didn't own land. "I didn't have the benefit of access to a family farm, or the money to rent tillable farmland, so the practical reality was that I couldn't pursue farming, no matter how much I wanted to ... my husband was still pressuring me to get a job and I didn't care, because all I could think about was farming land I didn't have. We both knew this didn't make any sense, and things between us were getting worse ... but I still couldn't let go of this intense feeling that God wanted me to do something about the food problem." At this point Sonia was forced to admit to her husband what he had already begun to realize, which that was getting a job that provided a steady paycheck just wasn't a priority for her.

By now Sonia had been home from Afghanistan for eight years, and although she accepted that "God's time doesn't necessarily mesh with mine," she was getting impatient to fix the food problem she saw all around her. One day while driving to the food pantry she realized that urban Cedar Rapids has a lot of vacant lots scattered throughout the city. "These are plots of unused land just sitting empty, and I kept thinking that Jesus would say 'don't mow—grow' and this became my mantra."

The two big, unanswered questions facing Sonia now were what to grow and how to actually do it, particularly in unenriched urban dirt that, by any measure, isn't the best growing medium for producing healthy, nutritious vegetables. "Some of my first ideas didn't work, but Iowa has a rich farming heritage, and I believed that sooner or later I could figure this out," she says. "A few days later, when I was at the Alliance Church food pantry, I noticed they didn't have any fresh produce, and yet outside they had more than an acre of unused land just sitting there. Three churches had already turned me down when I proposed using their vacant land to grow food, but I decided to screw up my courage one more time and have a little talk with Alliance," Sonia chuckles. This conversation finally produced results, quickly giving birth to Feed Iowa First, an organization she brought to life by acquiring just one acre of land.[10]

Actual food production began the next spring. Sonia began growing the vegetables she promised Alliance she would donate to their food pantry in exchange for the use of their vacant land. The first year that acre produced more than 2,000 pounds of carrots, tomatoes and other vegetables that went to the church's Abundance of Love Food Pantry. "Finally, I was a farmer," she smiles broadly.

It turns out Sonia has a lot more than a green thumb—she also has ten green fingers extending in several directions, and can grow money as well as vegetables. Her boundless enthusiasm for her idea of feeding Iowa first and boundless faith that God is with her, showing her the way nurtures her efforts to expand the organization.

As Feed Iowa First gained traction, Sonia developed the deep conviction that the church, not the state, bears the chief responsibility for feeding the hungry. This belief enabled her to forge a successful long-term, food producing partnership with Alliance Church. Using this success as her model to propel her cause forward, she began approaching other churches in the greater Cedar Rapids area, asking them for permission to use some of their spare land to grow food. "Cedar Rapids is a pretty religious community, and there are a lot of churches, so I didn't expect this to be too difficult—but it turned out that it was, and I'm still not exactly sure why," she puzzles. "The ministers get it about the hunger issue, but the church members not so much, apparently because they're not motivated by fear [of not having enough to eat or of encountering God's wrath by not feeding the hungry]" she says.

Nevertheless, a few churches did agree to allow her to grow food on their spare land. But what the church members didn't seem to understand, Sonia found out the hard way, was the need for them to become directly involved in the planting, caring for, and harvesting the food. "They'll give money to the food pantry, but they don't want to get any dirt under their fingernails ... we're supposed to be a Christian nation but, for some reason I can't seem to get all these supposedly Christian people to actually make the effort to show up and help me out with this," she says, frowning. "They'll give me money, which I do appreciate very much, but they won't give me their time, and both are important."

This isn't to say that everyone in the participating churches ignored what was happening in their churchyards. Joe Clark, a volunteer at the Hillside Wesleyan Church farm site tries to spend three or four hours each week helping with chores. "I asked myself what Jesus would do, and the answer was that if I really want to serve Jesus I need to help feed the poor," he says, adding that he's grateful for the opportunity to fulfill this scriptural mandate.

Dave Martin of St. Wenceslaus Catholic Church and Chris Formanek of St. Andrew's Lutheran Church are both active in their church communities and praise Sonia's effort as an opportunity for parishioners to become involved in an important ministry. "It's simple, low maintenance, and any church can do it," Martin points out.

Urban minister Martin Dwyer, executive director of the Mission of Hope, a 24/7 Christ-centered ministry offering physical, emotional, and spiritual help to former offenders and others in need says the food produced through Feed Iowa First helps the organization serve 20,000 meals per year. "We feed an average of 50 people a day, just from right here in our own immediate neighborhood, and the magnitude of blessing this fresh food brings to us is hard to imagine ... there's just no way we could ever afford to buy it."[11]

At the same time, Sonia was using her remarkable energy and enthusiasm to recruit more churches to commit land to grow food she was also using her smart business head to bring corporate sponsors from within the larger Cedar Rapids business community into the Feed Iowa First organization. She was also developing a two-dimensional model for solving the hunger issue. "By 2050 food production has to increase by 70 percent if we are going to feed the earth's population, which is projected to be 9 billion people by then," she tells anyone who will listen, "so we have to grow food to feed ourselves, and to do that we also have to grow new farmers."

The food part of this multi-solution approach to the hunger problem has been easy and has expanded quickly. By 2014 Sonia was actively farming 25 acres of land in various locations around urban Cedar Rapids. Her partners now include seven local churches and four industries. The result is over 30,000 pounds of fresh produce she now distributes to five food pantries and delivers to between eight and ten food sites, including veteran organizations and Meals on Wheels. She also drives a "vegetable bus" into low-income neighborhoods. However, as an agronomist, she is not satisfied with her per acre production and does not view a 30,000 pound harvest as a huge success. "This is only 1200 pounds per acre on average, which isn't a great crop," she stresses. "If I had some equipment and more volunteers helping me, we could enrich and work the soil properly, and do much, much better," she says.

From the beginning, mechanical and human assistance have been hard to come by. As the result, Sonia's labor-intensive urban farming effort struggles along without enough workers to meet the need. "I get a few volunteers from the church community, but this still hasn't caught on strong with churches, and just as many volunteers come from places like Cargill and Rockwell-Collins," Sonia says. And the struggle to find the money to obtain needed tools and labor-saving machinery is never-ending. "God's played some jokes on me with the tractor issue," she laughs, adding that she's learned that "God gives us what we ask for, even when we're not prepared to receive it ... so you have to be careful what you ask for, and when you ask for it." To prove her point, she explains that, soon after getting Feed Iowa First started, she began praying for a tractor, and one morning in early spring she received a phone call from someone offering to give her one. "I had absolutely no place to put it, so I had to turn it down ... it was sad."

After Cargill offered her their old warehouse, Sonia decided to try raising money for another tractor, and in six months had enough to purchase a small one new, just in time for the spring planting season. The tractor was the single piece of equipment that helped her most in her quest to farm more land and grow more food. Then, a few weeks into the growing season, someone stole it.

"I know people are in need out there, and they steal things because they need them. I just hope the person who stole the tractor really needed it ... but I need it too," Sonia says, still visibly upset by this piece of bad luck with her only piece of farm equipment. The tractor, which was not insured against theft, was never recovered.

Nevertheless, Sonia still holds onto deep faith that it'll all work out somehow. "We make do with what we have. What else can we do? People are still hungry," she shrugs, adding that she is confident God will send her another tractor when she's ready to receive it, so she has stopped fretting over it. "I also need a green bean picker ... actually any kind of harvesting or vegetable processing equipment would really help."

Sonia Kendrick drives her green vegetable bus through poor urban neighborhoods in Cedar Rapids, Iowa. The bus delivers fresh vegetables grown in the urban fields around the city to residents living in designated food desert areas where fresh fruit and vegetables are not readily available (courtesy Sonia Kendrick).

Meanwhile, the Feed Iowa First farming project remains entirely dependent upon hands-on human labor. This is backbreaking work, carried out in the hot sun during the hottest days of the humid, airless Iowa summer. "I need a lot of people to help pick and wash tomatoes, carrots, beets, kale, peppers, potatoes, and lettuce … 15 tons of fresh vegetables is a lot, much more than just one person can manage," Sonia says, pointing out the obvious.

Just when she began to think she couldn't continue with her farming by hand business plan any longer Feed Iowa First secured partnerships with local businesses, including Rockwell Collins, Cargill, and the Hy-Vee grocery store chain, and a few more churches, schools and individuals stepped up. Volunteers, from among employees working for the sponsor companies began to come forward to offer their time, and bringing their children along to help. Sonia believes this is another important piece of the permanent solution to eradicating local hunger. "These kids are learning a valuable lesson about where food comes from and how to grow it," she says.

Teaching people to grow their own food is another dimension of Sonia's hunger solution vision—and fits perfectly into the proverbial notion that giving someone a fish enables them to eat a meal, while teaching them to fish allows them to eat for a lifetime. She remains acutely concerned about "a very real energy crisis" in the food system that is partly responsible for the acute hunger problem in this country. "People need to learn to grow more of their own vegetables and feed themselves, and we need to figure out how to farm without being dependent upon fossil fuels and figure out how to move away from a transportation-based food system to a locally based food system," she says.

Sonia also believes that far too many people are nutrient deficient, that we all are too dependent on fast food, and packaged, processed food. "We need more farmers, and there are fewer and fewer of them It's really hard for young or beginning farmers to get started ... the entire burden of feeding people in the future will be on our young farmers and there just aren't that many of them," she explains.

The United States Department of Agriculture estimates that, simply to maintain the current food system 10,000 new farmers will have to take up farming each year. Sonia believes most of these new farmers will come from urban backgrounds and will farm small plots of land. She has a good point. If an aspiring start-up farmer hasn't inherited land, he or she will need substantial assets, farm management training, access to operating capital at reasonable interest rates, and land—and none of these is easy to come by.

John Whitaker, Iowa Farm Services Agency executive director, shares Sonia's concern about the importance of encouraging new farmers and the challenges this presents. In addition to making himself available to offer advice and resources, he believes getting people to participate in the process of learning how to farm is a huge challenge. Sonia answered this concern by inviting fellow veterans with an interest in learning how to farm to participate in the new farmer program she envisions.

Although certainly not the first obstacle she's faced, getting people interested in farming is proving much more difficult than she originally envisioned. "Beginning farmers face multiple obstacles in Iowa. The cost of land is at record highs, and to qualify for a low-interest Farm Service Agency loan the applicant must show proof of farm management experience that includes three years of profit," she explains. Her solution was to convince Whitaker that donation records kept by Feed Iowa First would count toward these requirements for people who are interested in beginning to farm and willing to volunteer with the organization. "Each year we could train a new farmer and those farmers, in turn, would train volunteers to tend gardens at other churches," she said, describing an ever-widening circle drawing in potential farmers. She estimates that there are about 800 unused acres surrounding Cedar Rapids churches, and another 500 acres in the greater Marion and Hiawatha areas that are potential growing sites.

"If we got a new farmer started in each region of the metro area, we could rotate crops and manage the output more effectively," Sonia explains while drawing detailed diagrams of how this would work. According to her plan, the donated Cargill warehouse would become the central distribution center for the produce, and interns from the city's Blue Zones project, which runs several farmers' markets in metro Cedar Rapids, would deliver the fresh vegetables to the food sites. This would be a win-win: feeding the hungry and developing new vegetable farmers. Sonia has also made efforts to get the word out to potential new farmers to apply for the Farm to Food Donation Tax Credit. This program allows Iowa farmers who donate self-produced items to food banks and food pantries to receive an Iowa state tax credit amounting to about 15 percent of the value of the donated items, up to $5,000.

There are many benefits associated with participating in Feed Iowa First's beginning farmer program. The opportunity to gain three years of hands-on farm management experience and build a record of production through the inventory of fresh vegetables donated to food banks are two big ones. Evaluation of farming and farm management skills by Feed Iowa First staff, access to ongoing educational opportunities; and support for establishing a positive relationship with the Farm Service Agency going forward are additional bonuses. Elizabeth Blood, one of the first to participate in the new farmers project, expanded what began as a back yard garden into more than a half-acre of green beans that will be donated to Feed Iowa First for food pantry distribution. "Sonia and I developed a wonderful mentor-mentee relationship and it's been nothing but a good thing. She's given me the confidence to bite off something way bigger than I ever would've tried just on my own," Elizabeth says.

Sonia has also forged a relationship with an inner-city Cedar Rapids high school, and managed to twist some arms into donating enough money to build a walipini, which is an approximately 12' × 12' underground greenhouse heated by solar energy, on the high school grounds. Students will maintain the greenhouse themselves, and the resulting produce will enable the school to have its first-ever fresh salad bar. "This is one way to get teenagers to eat their vegetables," Sonia laughs.

Sonia spends the dormant winter months fund-raising for Feed Iowa First. So far, she says, God has sent money her way when she's needed it, but this doesn't mean she hasn't had to do her part. "I spend a lot of time beating the bushes for money, and manage to raise about $40,000 each year, which isn't enough, but it keeps us afloat, as long as I don't draw a salary," she explains. At the top of her wish list, if she had more money, are buying better seed, obtaining equipment, finding some way to do a better job of watering during the dry spells, and enriching the soil, which badly needs it.

Sonia has brought her vision a very long way since the idea began germinating in the spring of 2011, when she didn't know anybody who could help her get started, and had no idea how to begin figuring that out. "I'd talk to two or three people every week. One man, who was well known, and well connected in the community, asked me about my credentials, and about who I knew that could vouch for me, and I didn't have an answer for him, so I shrugged my shoulders and walked out—and then cried a lot. A while later I ran into him at a local food event, and he asked me what I was doing there? I told him I was getting to know people who would be able to vouch for me some day. He laughed and said he thought my idea was a good one, and that it would work OK. His endorsement meant a lot."

Meanwhile, Sonia's credentials have grown at least as much as her stature in the community. In addition to earning a degree in agronomy, being appointed to Linn County's food systems council, and named a Sister of the Planet for the international poverty fighting organization Oxfam, she helped found Iowa's Women's Veteran Farmer Coalition. In 2014 she was named a White House Champion of Change. And, she is working on a graduate degree in sustainable food systems.

Sonia believes that to be truly human and at home, in the deepest sense, is to live in synchrony with nature, which is God's creation, and that any circumstance that alienates people from their truest home takes them away from God. Using her faith to guide her in every decision she makes, she has done some amazing things. "I lost my faith at one time, and then prayed really hard for it to come back ... making Feed Iowa First work for good is how God has returned it to me," Sonia smiles. "I couldn't do any of this without His help, or His love."

Three

Farming to Heal a
Troubled Soul

*I came to this farm because I thought it needed me, and found
out I needed it a lot more.*
—Suellen Thomson-Link

Anguished people often seek out rural life when circumstances beyond their control have badly beaten them up. Emotionally battered and bruised by hurts they never saw coming, and circumstances they never knowingly signed on for, these are folks who find themselves with nowhere else to turn. In some sense, they are running away from whatever it is that life has, sometimes cruelly, and always without their permission, visited upon them. They retreat to rural settings because they are emotionally lost and do not know where else to go, and they intuitively know that the land doesn't care who they are or what has befallen them. The land will always welcome them for as long as they want to stay.

This is particularly true than for recent combat veterans, particularly those involved in the Iraq and Afghanistan wars. Many returned home suffering from psychologically damaging post-traumatic stress disorders[1] that took them to dark emotional places, they were not equipped to handle. Desperate to save themselves, many came to believe their only way forward was toward a life where there are not so many people around to bother them. They may have been seeking communion with a God unknown, comfort in the predictability and beauty of nature, solace in the predictable routines of daily life among animals whose demands are few, or simple solitude, so they can regain control of a life that feels lost to them. No matter their reasons, they are seeking, and counting on, nature to heal them.

Looking to rural life, nature and land for healing is something others who have suffered overwhelming emotional trauma brought on by more ordinary life events also do. No matter the loss or hurt, people who have had profoundly emotional reordering experiences often seek out a simpler life. Often they find that nature is their true soulmate and once coming to terms with this realization, few ever return to the life from whence they came. Many of these seekers turn to farming as a means to support themselves while they await emotional and sometimes physical wholeness once again.

Whether those seeking nature to bring themselves back to life knowingly sold their souls to the devil and then experienced an acute attack of seller's remorse, or the devil stole their soul away from them when they were not looking, does not really matter. When trouble comes, yearning for the comfort nature, land, and wide-open spaces provide, is a life-saving response to an unmanageable life.

Nature points the way to something vastly larger, more encompassing, and so very much more important than every-day life affords. It moves with a unique rhythm and energy that comforts the afflicted, and afflicts the comfortable in ways that demand they start paying attention to their life and surroundings. Nature allows us to stand still, on solid ground, while being nurtured, sustained, and welcomed back to ourselves—and one sure thing about farming is that it always involves the solid ground beneath our feet.

Kinkoona Farm: Land That Laughs

> After my divorce, I knew I needed nature and land to heal, and I
> looked hard for a place that could do that for us.
>   —Suellen Thomson-Link

In terms of loss, divorce is no different from death. A once deeply loved and valued relationship has been lost, and the loss hurts. The grief that follows such a profound loss creates a deep well of emptiness in a once happy life, profoundly rearranging the emotional and often structural bearings of those who experience it in ways from which it is often difficult to recover. This is particularly true when the changes wrought by loss include finding oneself alone as single mother with three young children to care for and raise.

For Suellen Thomson-Link, grief following the divorce that signaled the end of her marriage took the form of a decision to leave her suburban lifestyle and purchase a 35 acre abandoned farm in southern Wisconsin.

"The kids and I—we'd been through a lot and were hurting ... life felt very much out of balance. I intuitively knew nature could heal us, and wanted to create that opportunity," she explains. She spent a lot of time looking for "the right farm" because the one thing she was certain of was that she wanted a place that needed her at least as much as she needed it.

A native Australian, Suellen is a tiny, pixie-like woman who, during her nine-year marriage, discovered that chasing the typical American dream was, for her, deeply unsatisfying. "Wealth takes a lot of forms that don't involve money," she says. "Pursuing economic success and living a suburban lifestyle had drawn me so far out of balance I found myself in a state of profound disequilibrium, and I knew that if I was going to survive and move forward I had to find some way to reconnect with nature and allow it to rebalance me...." I also knew that if I went under, we [her children and herself] would all go under, so I simply had to do this. Plain and simple, it was a matter of personal survival."

Suellen's lengthy quest to restore her own, and her children's, emo-

Suellen Thomson-Link (second from left) stands under the large bur oak tree that first welcomed her and her children, Syon (left), Sundara (third from left) and Acaya (right) to the new home they named Kinkoona Farm (courtesy Suellen Thomson-Link).

tional balance finally took a positive turn one early spring afternoon. Out for a Sunday drive, she came upon a For Sale by Owner sign pointing down a gravel road several miles off the main north-south highway through a rural Wisconsin county. She turned into a narrow, overgrown opening between two large oak trees, drove across fifty yards of unmowed grass, and eventually discovered an abandoned farmhouse. Built in 1856 and nearly hidden by bushes left to grow wild, the structure looked solid, but had not seen a paintbrush in over a century. It also lacked indoor plumbing, and all the windows had been shot out. It appeared that, in recent years, the structure had become a cozy home for raccoons, possums, and various other native wildlife common to the surrounding area.

Nevertheless, Suellen felt the old house emitted the positive energy she was seeking. Its setting, in the shade of a spreading 200-year-old bur oak tree that she says she actually felt reaching out to her, convinced her that she had finally found the place she has been looking for. "I bought it immediately, exactly as it was, which was just barely standing," she says, adding that she used cash from her divorce settlement to pay for it. "I got quite a good deal because the overall condition of the place didn't provide the seller with lot of negotiating power," she smiles.

The day Suellen closed on the real estate deal and took official ownership of the property she strapped on a tool belt and got to work. "I don't have any interest in fancy decorating and wanted to preserve as much of the original farmhouse structure as possible, so the repairs weren't as extensive as someone else might've done," she explains. She was anxious to move her young sons Syon, 7, and Acaya, 5, and her toddler daughter Sundara, age 3 at the time, away from the suburban life she felt was crushing them, so her immediate goal was merely to create an inhabitable home as quickly as possible. "I hired out most of the work on the house because that involved plumbing and electrical, as well as carpentry, all things I couldn't do. While that was going on I focused on the outbuildings, which were in much better shape and a little easier to work on," she explains.

The result, after a few short months, was a comfortable, welcoming house, a tall, sturdy, albeit old red barn sitting on a stone foundation, and several newly roofed sheds. The chicken coop became a utilitarian home-schooling classroom for Syon and Acaya, and a playroom for Sundara. "I wasn't afraid of the work, and from the beginning I knew that restoring this farm to good health would restore us to good health too, so I was all in." Because they knew the farm was going to be a healing environment for them, and because laughter heals, eventually Suellen and the children decided to name the farm Kinkoona, the Aborigine term for laughter.

"From the beginning the kids were a very, very big part of this," Suellen, emphasizes. Because she has always homeschooled them, using a self-generated curriculum, she cleverly began using the farm, and their restoration projects, as a learning laboratory. The daily farm chores, out of which Suellen created assignments, became an integral part of the children's various learning experiences. "They never complained about doing chores," she laughs. "They were able to learn very effectively, on their own schedule, according to their interest areas at the time, and it has worked out wonderfully well."

Almost immediately, the kids began acquiring various pets, including geese, pot-bellied pigs, a puppy, and a few chickens. Suellen, on the other hand, took a year to settle in before giving serious thought to the operational side of farming. She played out various scenarios in her head, and determined that, since she had no practical knowledge of, or experience with, successfully running a farm, she had a lot to figure out before she could actively farm, and was facing a steep learning curve. "I was 43 years old and went into this feet first," she admits. "But I love a challenge, particularly learning new things, and most of it turned out not to be that hard to figure out," she says of her eventual decision to enter into the world of permaculture farming—a technique that requires the farmer to work for rather than against nature.

"I felt drawn to the ecology and sustainability of permaculture methods, which approach farming as a sustainable ecology involving interrelated systems among, and between, plants, animals and humans," Suellen eagerly explains. "A fully functioning permaculture farm meets all the needs of its inhabitants by providing food, shelter, fuel, and entertainment, while being entirely self-sustaining." In some respects, permaculture farming is very much aligned with the goals of many early, and present-day, homesteaders seeking true self-sufficiency by living off the land, and it's not hard to understand how this would be a very attractive notion for someone like Suellen. Like many who divorce and never want to be dependent on anyone again, she makes personal, freedom, independence, and self-sufficiency a high priority. She says the fact that permaculture farming originated in Australia in the 1970s was mere coincidence. "It just made sense to me, in all the ways that nature itself makes sense to me," she stresses. "I didn't discover that the idea came from Australia until much later."

Permaculture emphasizes utilizing naturally growing, native plants that have practical benefit either as food, insect control or for medicinal purposes. Wasting valuable time and important resources to cultivate ornamentals and plants prone to disease is not favored.

The natural strengths and abilities of the land, and the needs of the humans and animals it supports, drive the decisions about how a successful permaculture farm operation is designed. Creating this kind of farm requires very thoughtful planning combined with a concerted effort to copy nature's blueprint. For example, the amount of sun an area receives, the potential for wind damage, and drainage issues all come into play when making planting decisions, and in order to thrive, and the growing needs of the plants must closely match naturally existing land and soil conditions.

Native animals, birds, and insects are also part of a sustainable permaculture ecosystem. If domestic animals are part of the farm design, the farmer must consider how they will fit into the bigger picture. For example, chickens can be fenced into a crop area or garden at the end of a season to clean it up, and pigs, who are good routers, can till an area before planting. At Kinkoona Farm Suellen does both. "The key to permaculture farming, and to economic success, is diversification—and this includes finding many uses for one thing. For example, I raise 170 sheep for wool, and butcher the males for meat, but not before they've been sheared. So they are useful for not one, but two purposes, wool and meat." She sells the wool as batting, converts some into felt for heavy blankets, and produces hand-made mattress toppers, chemical-free comforters, woolen pillows, and zabutons stuffed with organic wool.

"Everything is individually made from wool from our own sheep. I hand wash the fleece in a citrus chemical free wash/scourer using an old hand-crank wringer washing machine I picked up cheap at a farm auction. The fleece is then sent off to the mill where is made into batts without the use of oils on the rollers or any anti-static sprays/chemicals. When it arrives back here, my very skilled and kind Amish neighbor makes a cover from a delightful, 230 thread count organic cotton sateen and then quilts it with organic cotton yarn. The fabulous result is an organic, chemical-free comforter or mattress topper," Suellen explains, expressing great delight in her decidedly low-tech operation that marries exquisite craftsmanship with a production method that results in an economically sustainable business plan that produces an environmentally friendly product.

Suellen acknowledges that she would love to sell her wool as yarn, but wool is expensive to process and the lag time between sending it to the mill and receiving it back dyed, spun into yarn and wound into balls is too great. "I would have to carry a lot of expense on the books until the yarn is sold, and besides, I prefer raising different kinds of sheep, which produce particular kinds of wool suitable for specific uses ... and to produce and sell enough yarn to make it profitable requires a larger flock than I can maintain," she explains. Almost as an afterthought, she says she has often though that knitting a sweater from yarn spun from the wool of a sheep she has raised and cared for would be deeply satisfying. As a knitter myself, I happily tell her that raising my own sheep and processing the wool into knittable yarn is something I have always wanted to do. She laughs at this notion, and then explains that the process from sheep to sweater would no doubt make me appreciate the result of the knitting project a lot more.

True to the small, organic farm tradition, this includes an intentional, focused effort to raise happy animals. Suellen takes great pride in knowing each of her sheep personally, and has named nearly all of them, many of whom she helped bring into the world while spending many cold March nights in the barn during lambing season. She now routinely expects more than 80 live births each spring.

The current population of the farm's animal kingdom includes horses, a donkey, two pot-bellied pigs so friendly they can occasionally be found

Suellen Thomson-Link gives a friendly pat to one of several large (1300- to 1800-pound) pigs roaming freely on her farm. The pigs' natural rooting behavior helps cultivate the garden soil in the spring ahead of planting (photograph by the author).

inside the house, five dogs, ducks, geese, quails, chickens, a turtle, a chameleon, a parakeet or two, and too many cats to count. Nearly all of them have names. "We're really just one big happy family!" Suellen laughs.

This happy family also includes an estimated 50,000 worms that also have an important place in the farm operation. "To assist in management of winter animal bedding, we created a vermiculture project by building four 5½' × 3' bins out of recycled boards and adding red worms. It is inspiring to watch the ongoing work of these wonderful creatures whose efforts create terrific composting material for the plants," she explains, adding that they have not come up with names for them all, yet. "We're still working on that," she chuckles.

The health of farm's watershed is crucial because humans, animals and plants all depend upon clean, running water. Consequently, water resource management is another important part of the self-sustaining farm operation. The water system at Kinkoona Farm is intricate and carefully designed to reverse the effects of pollution, control erosion, effectively purify, and utilize rainwater. "I believe strongly in closed water systems to reduce water waste," Suellen explains. "Initially we focused on erosion control and began by rebuilding the slopes, which had been worn entirely away by cattle prior to our arrival. We laid down old hay over the eroded soil and let nature rapidly compost it into the dirt needed to repair the gullies that had formed from years of bad flow. Then we built a stairway for the sheep, redirecting their path from one pasture to another, away from the slope. The stairway has a slight curve and we made each riser step from salvaged barn beams and backfilled mostly with sand. The result is that instead of the run-off water washing down the slope and creating erosion gullies, each step redirects it back into the hillside."

The second aspect of effective water management has been to put gutters on all the outbuildings and the barn, allowing rainwater to be collected and stored in two 1,500-gallon tanks, thereby reducing the need to pump water out of ground wells. "The water passes through three screens and the initial roof run off is flushed out of the system before the clean water is collected in the tank," Suellen, now a certified permaculturalist, explains. "This supplies our stock troughs and gardens. We also have a variety of rain barrel systems for water collection to supply our smaller, more distant gardens." Recently she and the boys, now in their late teens, constructed an aquaponics system to provide a closed water environment for growing both plants and fish in a confined space. The waste fish produce is rich in nitrogen, which enables plants, both those grown for market and those other fish feed off of, to flourish "We have also added a pond stream system utilizing an upturned satellite dish and the natural downhill slope on our property ... eventually I hope to install a rain garden," she says.

Completing her diversity design, Suellen added vegetable products and today supplies fresh sunflower sprouts, grown year-round, to several restaurants, sells her meat to three local area markets, and is a vendor at some of the Chicago-area farmers' markets. "Syon and Sundara initially started the organic sunflower sprout business. They grow year-round and are marketed to restaurants in Milwaukee and Madison," she explains. "When the demand grew, Acaya wrote an agricultural sustainability grant, and Sundara carried on with it," she explains. As a result of the grant, Sundara was able to purchase seeds for planting colorful and unusual vegetables for two restaurants owned by a chef who Suellen describes as a "virtual Monet with food." Southern red and green okra, chocolate and orange bell peppers, spiral broccoli, multi-colored beans, and carrots are now grown year-round in the farm's 96-foot greenhouse, which Acaya salvaged from a junkyard, for free, and repaired. "The restaurant clients will buy any vegetables we grow, and I like growing unusual ones. It's definitely a shifting, but constant, market," Suellen smiles.

For Kinkoona Farm the entertainment aspect of life on a fully functional permaculture farm involves hosting groups of friends for potluck meals, music and, sometimes, dancing. Syon and Acaya remodeled a section of the big barn to make space for these activities, and repurposed some of the wood into an elevated dance floor that is also used as an improvisational dance stage. "We enjoy some wonderful evenings out here in summer," Suellen, a trained dancer, says.

Prior to entering the world of farming, Suellen, a licensed occupational and dance therapist, worked in pediatric mental health, focusing on traumatized children and youngsters who have gone afoul of the law. She brought these skills to the farm by opening a day camp for juvenile first offenders the court had placed into a criminal diversion program. The initiative was a natural outgrowth of the three-day summer camps for local elementary school children she runs from April through August most years. Both activities are aspects of the diversity plan Suellen implements to keep farm income flowing, and are among several wise decisions she made that helped her to survive the deep recession that settled over the economy in 2008.

Besides being an additional revenue stream, the children's camps have provided an opportunity to share a lifestyle Suellen and her children deeply appreciate and are grateful to be part of. "I looked around me and wondered: 'Are our kids just walking by without noticing what we played amongst as children? Do they even know what a carrot looks like in the ground? Do they know how to identify the trees and plants that grow wild around them? Too many kids visit Kinkoona and don't know how to shell peas, how to take responsibility to see a project to completion, how to repair things and make something from the odds and ends lying around … things don't have to come out of a kit, nor do they need to beep, nor do they change channels. This really is a wonderful place for children … sort of like Old MacDonald's farm, only it should probably be called Old Kinkoona farm," she laughs.

Syon, Acaya, and Sundara all help with the camps, which begin by bringing the campers along while they do their morning chores, including feeding the animals. The camp experiences are carefully designed to encourage total immersion into farm life, with the goals of heightening the children's awareness of the natural world that surrounds them and fostering both responsibility for each other and for tapping into their own creativity. A mixture of ages is encouraged so that sharing occurs at a variety of levels, with no more than six children at a time participating. "We expect the children to go home dirty," Suellen explains. "I believe a lot of our children are becoming nature deficient. Keeping our children in touch with nature is so important, and will not only help them become more aware and conscious people, but will also keep our future generations caring for the environment that surrounds them and thus help to preserve its beauty … so if someone wants their city kid to get a taste of farm life, this is definitely the place!"

Suellen strongly believes women are natural farmers and should be proud of that ability. She hires out only the jobs she absolutely cannot do for herself, using a fulcrum system, a red flyer wagon, the kids' ability to help out, and nature, as her main tools. "My experience is that men want to take charge of nature rather than working with it, and when the focus becomes only on the economic value of the land and the economics of the farming operation, nature is nearly always disrupted … and that is never, ever a good thing, so when I'm doing the work I'm sure that's not going to happen." she says.

The farm operates in the black, "but just barely," Suellen explains. Most of the profits are folded back into expanding the operation, which has included adding another 13 acres of pasture and no-till cropland. Living expenses come through court-ordered child support and Suellen's off-farm employment, which has recently increased from three to five days per week. "I've just started my own business, providing therapy services through a regional health care provider, and getting that established is taking up more of my time right now. Nevertheless, I do not expect that to go on forever—and I hope it won't, because the quickest way for me to get out of emotional balance is to start focusing too much on money ... the farm is paid for and I can cover the bills, which is enough. I don't need new clothes or a new car every year."

If this seems like a busy life and a lot of work, it is. Collaborating with nature is a serious commitment that requires focus and concentration, and does not leave a lot of time to wallow in sadness over all that was lost when the divorced occurred. For Suellen, keeping busy doing the hard work of maintaining the farm has been a great healer, as well as a labor of love for a multi-talented, high-energy woman who is both tenderhearted and tough-as-nails. "My biggest challenge is that there aren't 36 hours in a day," this single mother head of household sighs.

Admitting that she could not do any of this without her kids, who are as invested in the farm as she is, Suellen explains that she went into the farming enterprise knowing she had to make it work. "With three children to raise by herself, failure was never an option," she admits. What she does not talk about is the courage it took to make this giant leap into the unknown, or where the self-confidence it takes to succeed comes from. "I'm a non-linear thinker, so if something doesn't work, I'm quick to try something else, until I get it right.... I'm also a systems thinker, so I look at every problem as one part of the system we're all part of, and know that the answer is somewhere in that system," is all she'll say about how man ages so effectively.

On any given day, Suellen makes the tough decisions farming requires while, as a single mother, she runs an efficient household that includes raising three thriving teenagers and holding down a full time off-farm job. She expects her children to be responsible for helping to care for the animals and sharing in the farm work, keeping everything clean and orderly, and excelling in their studies. "We work hard together, and get along together—and we're all so much better for it," she says, with well-deserved pride in what she has created. "We all relate very, very well to each other and to everything else ... the dogs don't chase the cats, the kids all get along, and I focus on building up individual skills and abilities, not on differences or creating competition. I expect a positive outcome from everyone ... and I dream big dreams."

Australians are not generally religious, Suellen says, but she admits that she finds her farm and its natural surroundings provide her with a spiritual home. "The cruelest thing that could ever happen to me would be to get on the financial/building wealth treadmill and end up in a shopping mall because I don't have anywhere else to go or anything else to do," she proclaims. There is little chance that will ever happen, because Kinkoona Farm is, as the name implies, a happy, healing place. "Thirteen years of living here has taught us that this is the right place to be—and it has also given me a legacy to pass along to my children."

Suellen's self-designed healing program and home-schooling educational system have both been very successful. Today Syon is studying veterinary medicine back in Australia and Acaya is pursuing an interest in electrical engineering. Sundara, who has not yet completed her high school-level studies, is gaining valuable business experience by helping run the farm's sprout and vegetable business, which has grown dramatically since the farm first began.

The remaining unanswered question is where Suellen finds the energy to do all the things she does, and do them so well? Her answer is simple: "I'm part of the farm and the farm is part of me. We nurture and sustain each other, and this well-integrated system gives me all the energy I need."

Suellen's enduring legacy to her children will be much more than just a farm. She is creating an inheritance that joins the courage of an incredible pioneering spirit with an abundance of practical skills, coupled with the remarkable survival instincts that can only be found in the experience of bringing an expired farm, and a family of grieving souls, back to life once again.

Answering the Call to War and Ending Up on a Farm

> When the difference between war and peace is blurred, female soldiers seem more approachable to other [civilian] women and children, and that they may ultimately be more effective than an all-male or mixed gendered combat units.
>
> —Iraqi War veteran

Before engaging in urban farming to feed the poor[2] Sonia Kendrick spent eight years in the military. Within days of graduating from high school, and wanting to rebel against her conservative Christian upbringing, she joined the Army, thus taking on an obligation she knew virtually nothing about. It was peacetime, and she saw this decision as a chance to serve her country and, at the same time, earn valuable job skills. She found she liked military life, and when her Army enlistment ended, she signed on for an additional, five-year tour of duty with the Iowa National Guard. As her military commitment was drawing down, she felt ready to leave that life and was eagerly looking forward to her imminent discharge from an uneventful eight years serving her country. Now 27 years old, she had married a fellow Iowan and was eagerly looking forward to building a new life with her husband, beginning in a few short weeks.

When she decided to sign up for the Army, Anna Mann[3] was 19 years old and had just completed what had turned out to be a much more expensive first year of college than she had anticipated. She saw military service as a quick way to earn some much-needed money, and as an added benefit, upon completing her tour of duty she would become eligible for the educational benefits afforded to former military personnel through the GI Bill.[4] When the military recruiter handed her a list of job possibilities, Anna chose civil affairs specialist because the job description sounded no different from serving in the Peace Corps, except she might, under certain circumstances, be required to carry a gun. She quickly settled into army life and, with no military conflicts on the horizon, the possibility of serving in a war zone never entered her mind.

After several episodes of urban homelessness that began when she was 15 and included periodically living in her car, rural Georgia native Althea Raiford enlisted in the military as a way to focus her life. Her first choice was the Air Force, because she believed it was the safest branch of the armed services, but the Air Force had a two-year waiting list, which, since she was homeless when she walked into the recruiting office, would not work for her. She settled for the Navy because they would accept her right away, not because she wanted to be a sailor. She went on to become a member of the Naval Construction Force (Seabees) whose primary job is to build military facilities such as bridges, dams, airstrips, and other infrastructure. Althea found Navy life satisfactory, and like both Sonia and Anna, she had given no thought to the possibility of going into combat.

Sonia, Anna, and Althea each signed up for military service for different reasons—financial need, expressing a teenage rebellious streak, and the desire to focus an unfocused life. What all three young women had in common was their youthful enthusiasm, dreams for a bright future, and the sense of invincibility that comes from being inexperienced in all the ways life can whip a person into becoming someone they don't want to be, yet are helpless to prevent. All three women had grown up in peacetime, and when each volunteered to serve their country in the military, war was not anywhere on their own or their nation's radar screen.

Although these women found that having to follow orders was not always fun, in peacetime the stakes for doing what their commanding officer told them to do were relatively low. As a result, none of these women found the military life they had signed on for particularly disagreeable and they all decided to remain in the military beyond their initial four-year tour of duty. "The comradery is huge—and anybody who says blowing stuff up during maneuvers isn't fun is lying," Anna, who served eight years, reminisces, wryly adding that one thing she likes about being a farmer now is that every so often she gets to shoot something.

While completing her military obligation Sonia learned electrical wiring and she knew this ability would be a valuable employment skill after she returned to civilian life. She also found that she enjoyed serving her country. As a Seabee, Althea had the opportunity to travel to many parts of the world, functioning as a master at arms,[5] and she intended to make the Navy a career. "It kept me focused, and I needed that," she says.

Then, on September 11, 2001, foreign terrorists successfully attacked the American homeland. While most civilians did not immediately interpret this event as an act of war, the military wasted no time in viewing the attack as the deliberate actions of forces hostile to American interests, and knew what the response would have to be. No one, not even President George W. Bush, had anticipated the attack, and no one, including those currently on active military duty, knew what to expect as a result of it. Their only choice was to sit back and watch the political events play out.

The president's decision to wage a war on terrorism by attacking Iraq and Afghanistan baffled many Americans. Since nineteen of the twenty-one terrorists were Saudi Arabians, many saw this action as a senseless and confusing response to the catastrophic events of September 11. Most Americans began to realize that terrorism is a blurry, supremely illusive concept, and trying to mount a successful military campaign against a concept is fraught with strategic difficulties that, realistically, are impossible to overcome. However, from the military's perspective, the president is their commander-in-chief, and if he says the nation is going to war, then the nation is going to war—and the military is responsible for carrying out these orders.

When, less than two years later, President Bush landed on an aircraft carrier and declared "Mission accomplished," thus signaling the end of major combat operations in Iraq, America, and those serving on active duty in the United States military, believed him. However, despite proclaiming the successful end to a war in Iraq, guerrilla warfare in the region increased dramatically, widening the Iraqi insurgency. American military casualties continued to mount and the realization that currently serving soldiers likely would see active combat grew. The war that the president had declared over was not even close to ending; instead, it was intensifying. At the same time, that same war became much more controversial among politicians, the American public, and those serving in the military.

Many saw the situation as one whereby America was attacking a country that had not attacked us and, similar to the opposition surrounding the Vietnam War a generation earlier, the nation was not of one mind about whether this was the direction the country should be going. "It's different when we're attacked and have to defend ourselves, but to just go start a war against an elusive enemy and kill a lot of people, including innocent civilians, is stupid," was a common theme among those who disagreed with the president's decision to invade Iraq. Some current and former service men and women, particularly those with prior combat experience, agreed. These were the circumstances Sonia, Anna, and Althea suddenly found themselves facing.

Like most others serving in the volunteer military in 2001 these three women did not knowingly sign on for military action on the front lines of a foreign war. They were being drawn into a collision with a fractured, deeply foreign culture they had no knowledge of and didn't understand and, similar to other currently serving, active duty military personnel, they had no choice about whether or not they wanted to be sent into a war zone in a place they had never heard of and had no interest in finding out about. They were flying blind into the sunrise of war and had no way of knowing how the experience was going to draw them in and reshape them, regardless of whether or not they wanted it to. Yet, all three women were proud to serve their country, and had voluntarily joined the military to do that. "I wanted to be a hero for my country," Sonia says.

Nevertheless, being sent into a foreign combat situation blindsided Sonia, who never saw it coming. The National Guard mission is to protect and rebuild the homeland after natural disasters and, when needed, to keep the domestic peace. Guard personnel are reservists who usually report for active duty one weekend per month, with two additional weeks set aside for military maneuvers in summer; the rest of the time they hold down regular jobs and lead ordinary civilian lives. Normally they are not called to fight in foreign wars, unless they are desperately needed, and at no time in recent memory have National Guard personnel been sent into foreign combat situations.

However, in 2001, the United States did not have a large enough active military force to engage in a foreign war, and needed to call upon all available personnel to swell the combat-capable ranks to an acceptable level. When the telephone call came telling her she was going to Afghanistan, into a war zone, regardless of how shocked she was, Sonia had no choice other than to report for active duty.

Other issues were also at play in the Iraqi and Afghan wars. One was that, in prior wars, women who enlisted in the military had been assigned to non-combat, support roles, primarily office work and nursing care, and were not placed in direct combat situations.[6] Another was that while young men have to register for the draft at age 18, women do not, and because actual conscription into military service has not been in effect for more than 30 years, the U.S. is entirely dependent upon a volunteer military force. As a result, in 2001 the United States did not have a large enough active duty military force to fight a war anywhere unless women serving in the military were placed in active combat situations. When the U.S. commenced combat missions in Iraq, Kuwait, and Afghanistan, women soldiers were, out of necessity rather than military policy, front and center in this preemptive strike war effort.

Although combat fatigue and post-traumatic stress reactions are known to occur among men who fight in active combat situations, no one really knew exactly how being in active combat situations would affect women, whose emotional and psychological make-up differs dramatically from that of men. However, because Iraq and Afghanistan were not ordinary combat situations, in reality it was impossible to speculate how fighting a war there would affect either male or female soldiers.

Most of the Iraqi and Afghan war efforts involved targeted airstrikes rather than ground attacks. They evolved from intelligence data claiming to identify areas of greatest military threat. As adjunct combat activity, ground troops went into small, remote villages and rural mountain areas to flush out civilian insurgents. American soldiers encountered women and children who strapped bombs around their waists and threw themselves at them while they were walking through the villages, creating unspeakable carnage. While local women and children threw grenades under military convoys, their husbands, brothers and sons acted as snipers, sitting on top of buildings waiting to shoot at U.S. ground troops. This was not conventional warfare and Sonia, Anna, and Althea, as women soldiers, were about to discover a suddenly reordered world they never knew existed, never expected to encounter, and were not emotionally well-prepared to cope with.

None of the three women ever thought their war experience would propel them into the dirty life of farm work. Ultimately this is exactly what happened, but not before war had stolen away their previous life, leaving them with a heavy emotional burden to bear.

THIS IS WHAT WAR
REALLY FEELS LIKE

There are perhaps many causes worth dying for, but to me, certainly, there are none worth killing for.
— Albert Dietrich, U.S. Army

No tinsel of trumpets and flags will ultimately seduce women into the insanity of recklessly destroying life, or gild the willful taking of life with any other name than that of murder, whether it be the slaughter of the million or of one by one.
— Olive Schreiner, South African
feminist writer, 1911

"When I got that phone call saying we were being deployed to Afghanistan, I really couldn't believe it," Sonia says. "A couple days later they sent us from Iowa up to Camp McCoy, about 200 miles north into Wisconsin, where we sat waiting for further orders. This went on for a long time and our families kept coming to say goodbye. Pretty soon I just couldn't take it any longer—there's only so many goodbyes a person can say." Finally, one cool, sunny day, not very different from many other days during the spring of 2003, she marched out of her barracks in full battle gear directly onto a military transport plane to make a 16-hour trip to a place she had barely heard of. She was leaving behind the rolling green hills and bucolic countryside surrounding Camp McCoy strapped inside the fuselage of a troop transport plane. "We were packed in tight—three soldiers deep on each side, with Humvees chained together, front to back, in the middle aisles ... and the chains rattled for 16 hours straight," she says, holding her hands over her ears. Eventually the plane landed in the hot, barren Afghanistan desert, and the deplaning soldiers walked through the looking glass.

Sonia was among the first boots on the ground ordered to carry out aggressive combat missions in Afghanistan. She was neither emotionally nor psychologically prepared for combat, and found being greeted every morning by the Muslim call to prayer deeply unsettling. This repeat experience, day in and day out, instilled a sense of ongoing, imminent danger that immediately placed her on emotional high alert and kept her that way for the entire next year. "It was like knowing a bomb was going to drop somewhere—you just didn't know when or where, or how close to you it might fall," she explains.

Eventually Sonia was assigned to combat aircraft refueling duty at Bagram Air Field. "These big fuel transports would come in riddled with bullets and leaking fuel everywhere, all over the place, and we had to deal with it," she explains, adding that aircraft fuel is very explosive and they had to be extremely careful not to ignite it. Soldiers had to act fast both to keep the acutely flammable liquid from spreading and to save what fuel they could from the bullet-riddled planes before sending them for repairs. At the same time, as quickly as possible, they had to go back onto the airfield and refuel the planes waiting to take off on the next combat mission.

It was extremely high stress, very dangerous work because as a supply depot, Bagram Field was particularly vulnerable to enemy attack. Every soldier assigned there knew they were just one hand grenade or one spark away from the entire operation blowing up, taking them along with it. All the ground crews knew exactly what the planes they were refueling were going to do after they left the field, and that both civilians and military personnel would die as a result. Sonia began feeling like an accomplice to murder.

After several weeks at Bagram, Sonia was sent to forward operating bases near Gardez and Kabul, where the fighting was even more intense. She remained there, continuing to perform the same aircraft refueling job she had done at Bagram Field, until she returned to Iowa several months later. By then she felt like a murderer herself.

In 2003, Anna was sent to Kuwait. "When we got there [Kuwait] we didn't even really know where we were, and we spent a lot of time just waiting around for something to happen. There were two women and 3000 guys, all waiting for orders," she explains. Eventually she was sent to Bagdad, as part of the Shock and Awe offensive, whose sole purpose was, through the use of overwhelming power, to crush the enemy into extinction. Merely by following orders, Anna suddenly found herself an active participant in an effort, using whatever means possible, to create spectacular displays of force designed to rapidly paralyze the enemy and destroy its will to fight. In this case, the enemy included local civilians deemed a threat to U.S. military operations.

Although, in theory, minimizing civilian casualties and collateral damage was part of the Shock and Awe initiative, in reality sparing civilian lives is nearly impossible in a guerrilla war. Often it is impossible to tell the difference between an innocent civilian, an enemy soldier, or an insurgent, who could be a man, a woman or a child, and a soldier has no time to stop and consider all the possibilities. Further complicating this kind of warfare is that the goal of rapid dominance over the enemy drives Shock and Awe tactics, thus requires quickly disrupting communication, transportation, food production, food supply lines, and infrastructure, with the intent of rendering the adversary impotent in its ability to fight back.

Using Iraq as an example, Harlan Ullman, one of the architects of the Shock and Awe military strategy explains it this way: "Shutting the country down would entail both the physical destruction of appropriate infrastructure and the shutdown and control of the flow of all vital information and associated commerce so rapidly as to achieve a level of national shock akin to the effect that dropping *nuclear weapons* on *Hiroshima* and *Nagasaki* had on the Japanese. You're sitting in Baghdad and all of a sudden you're the general and 30 of your division headquarters have been wiped out. You also take the city down. By that I mean you get rid of their power, water ... in two, three, four, maybe five days they are physically, emotionally, and psychologically exhausted."[7]

Anna's role in Shock and Awe was to go out into the streets of Baghdad ahead of military attacks to warn Iraqi civilians of impending danger. She, along with five other soldiers would drive into the communities, draw their weapons, enter the houses, and, through an interpreter, tell the people to take cover. They never knew who was waiting for them on the other side of the door, or whether the civilians they were trying to warn were part of the insurgency. "It was pretty dangerous ... several guys were shot up pretty bad, and my interpreter was killed," she explained.

Anna's mission was not the sort of activity that it was a good idea to think too much about, either before or afterwards. "Yes women can go to war, but their positions are supposed to be limited to non-combative situations. While the idea is noble, it is also not working ... especially in the Army. In the Army, some women soldiers are used to body check other women but it is at these checkpoints that some of the fighting occurs. The military is a good old boys club and women soldiers are not always trained for these situations ... leaving them very vulnerable for attack," Anna says.

In 2003, Althea was deployed to Camp Morrell in Kuwait where she maintained security for base camps. She also worked as a convoy commander, a job not many women soldiers step up to do. Nevertheless, she volunteered for the most dangerous runs, which included bringing supplies, weapons, and personnel to the frontlines. "I was single, and if something happened to me I wouldn't be missed as much as the soldiers who had husbands, wives, and children waiting for them back home, so I did it," she explains. She does not reveal the wellspring of loneliness that must have accompanied this courageous decision—or the level of bravery or commitment to her fellow soldiers that her actions displayed. Women convoy commanders were few, and Althea found that she was good at the ducking and dodging maneuvers the assignment required, particularly when she was taking in supplies and bringing out the causalities the Blackhawk helicopters had rescued. She believed this was better than sitting out the war in an office. "Sometimes it seemed like women had to do more than the men, but it also felt like we've come a long way but are still in the same place."

None of these three women were familiar with the nations of Iraq or Afghanistan before being deployed there, and when their orders sending them there came through, they had no idea where they were going and no time to understand what they would be doing after they arrived. In an instant, they were transformed from smiling, relatively carefree young women into combat soldiers fighting an unconventional war bringing them face to face with death every hour of every day. Nothing ages a soldier faster or changes her more.

From Battlefields to Farm Fields: Coming Home

> Nobody survives a war—everybody dies somehow, and I was really
> angry about all of it.
>
> —Sonia Kendrick

Returning home from combat duty half a world away was not anything like Sonia had imagined, or was expecting. The military had failed to let families know when the transport plane bringing their loved ones back to them would arrive at Camp McCoy, and there was no one waiting to greet the battle-weary soldiers when they deplaned. Without fanfare, they walked into an empty aircraft hangar. Not having husbands, wives, children, parents, grandparents, siblings or friends standing there, crying and happy to see them back safely, was a crushing disappointment for these emotionally exhausted soldiers.

Eventually they were loaded onto a bus and driven back to central Iowa where, emotionally and physically exhausted, they were dropped off at the Cedar Rapids National Guard station and told to call someone to pick them up. "I went to war proud to serve my country, and came home feeling something I didn't even understand. As I was looking out the bus window at people going in and out of a Walmart, all I could think was, 'These people have no idea what this country is doing to other people—and they don't even care.' I was so angry.... I felt like a murderer ... and I didn't know where I fit in anymore," she says, still choking up at the memory of her unceremonious bus ride home from war eleven years earlier.

While trying to figure herself out, Sonia enrolled in the agronomy program at Iowa State University. She also gave birth to a daughter, and then another one. "My husband was patient about my finishing my degree, but he was counting on me to get a job when I graduated ... and I had no clue what I was going to do.... All I knew was that I couldn't work in a regular job, even if that's what my husband wanted me to do ... it wasn't an unreasonable expectation—it was just one I couldn't meet." She was not aware of the rage building inside her—all she knew was that she did not feel safe anymore, always had to sit facing outward, with her back against a wall, and did not trust anyone. The only time she felt safe was digging in the dirt.

This feeling of deep unrest went on for several years. Then, one day while she was weeding an acre of vegetables on one of her urban farms located near a veterans' assistance center in central Cedar Rapids, one of the veterans, who had been observing her gardening activities for some time, walked over and suggested she pay them a visit. She had no idea what prompted the invitation, but eventually she accepted it. "I learned that post-traumatic stress disorder (PTSD) can be quite a long time coming to the surface, and clearly PTSD was exactly what my problem was," she grimaces.

While not all returning combat veterans suffer PTSD, many do. It differs by degree for everyone who develops the disorder, and some who treat the problem think it also varies by the type of war and even by gender. In other words, fighting in a pre-emptive strike war is very different from going to war to defend one's country; standing up to guerrilla warfare is very different from military to military engagement; and fighting a discernible, clearly identified enemy is very different from going up against an ill-defined concept labeled terrorism, hoping to defeat it. Male and female soldiers will internalize and interpret the same wartime experience differently; and officers have different experiences from enlisted personnel.

Nevertheless, all PTSD sufferers share a similar set of physical symptoms and emotional reactions that Althea, Sonia, and Anna each describe experiencing in some way. They were living in a ticking time-bomb world comprised of sudden flashbacks triggered by something as insignificant as a backfiring car, endless nightmares only exhausting, sleepless nights can prevent, angry displays of temper erupting out of nowhere, ever-present depression and an unrelenting sense of imminent danger. "I'd had an entire year of life and death experiences, and saw a hell on earth most people can't even imagine ... and I didn't think anybody cared—or understood—or even wanted to try to understand," Sonia sighs. "It was unimaginably lonely."

The anger of having answered a call to war they never expected to hear, only to return to country they feel is either indifferent to the war they fought or too cavalier in its attitude toward what returning soldiers have been through is something many Iraq and Afghan war veterans express. Some say they do not want to be thanked for their service by civilians who have no clue about what it was like to pull the trigger on a gun that killed another human being someone other than themselves had declared the enemy. Many feel the skills they learned in the military failed to, as promised, seamlessly transfer to civilian jobs. Others express a psychological inability to leave the battlefield behind and return to a life filled with expectations others have for them to be happy, raise a family, pay a mortgage, and hold down a "regular job." They want post-military life to open the door to something they can do well, that holds some meaning for them, and gives them a sense of satisfaction, and they find out that nothing does. "I'll never be happy again—at least not the way I was before I went to war," Sonia says.

When they leave the military, many soldiers find themselves unprepared for the confusing, unexpected sadness, and grief that accompanies the loss of the day-by-day, life and death intensity of war, and are profoundly lonely for the camaraderie only found among fellow soldiers. They don't understand why they miss the unrelenting pressure and stress that they experienced in combat, but they do miss it. They loved trying for the perfection the military demands of soldiers, and don't know how to handle not being able to pursue that goal anymore.

While combat soldiers derive no meaning from the death and destruction they were intimate participants in during wartime, deep down many soldiers want, more than anything, to go back and fight again. They found that fighting a war was the greatest excitement they have ever known, far surpassing any previous life experiences they had. Being a combat soldier made them part of a team, and that team was focused on something much larger than, and so far outside of themselves that it brought greater meaning to their lives than anything before, or since, has been able to do.

These painful, yet brutally honest truths are difficult to acknowledge and, for some ex-soldiers, induce a crippling guilt. They find themselves so ashamed that they are unable to admit their deepest secrets to anyone. Meanwhile their anger and frustration mounts, often evident in its ugliest forms only to those closest to them, or to other soldiers like themselves. Added to their burden is that returning home from a war some of their buddies didn't come back from is a heavy burden to bear, and for some induces profound survivors' guilt.

When they come back home and return to civilian life these enlisted soldiers aren't soldiers any longer, and they don't know where, or how, to fit into a world they no longer like very much. A once familiar life, in the community they called home, no longer feels like their life, or their home. Nowhere feels like a place where they belong and they find themselves adrift in a world they once knew intimately, loved dearly and went to war to preserve. They never anticipated that serving the nation in wartime would have the net effect of isolating them from their fellow citizens whose freedoms they fought to protect.

Another unanticipated truth many soldiers, including Althea, Anna and Sonia, encountered upon their return from the war zone was that public sympathy for soldiers returning from combat bearing the invisible wounds of war is lacking. This was particularly noticeable among those who felt that because both men and women soldiers had joined the military voluntarily, they knew what they were getting into and should just "man up and deal with it," no matter what "it" turned out to be.

This is the world, and the life, Sonia, Anna and Althea returned to after their tour of combat duty ended and they left the military to return to civilian life. They all felt like strangers in a strange land, and they did not know what to do with these feelings.

Sonia's husband waited patiently while she tried to sort herself out after returning from combat duty. However, his expectation that she earn a paycheck never wavered and he did not share her enthusiasm for the urban farm project she began after completing her degree at Iowa State. "I was spending 40 or 50 hours a week on this idea and wasn't drawing any salary—I still don't—and he was very frustrated with all of it. He's a good man and he'd stood by me through a lot, and I really could understand his point, but I still couldn't do what he wanted me to do. Eventually we decided to stop fighting and get a divorce. I told him he could have everything—all I wanted was the girls half of every week, which he agreed to. The irony is that in the middle of all that was going on with us he found Jesus and got saved," she says quietly. And, she wonders whether, if this had occurred sooner, the redemption might have helped them work through their problems before divorce became the only solution.

Sonia went so far as to sign an affidavit attesting that she would forgo child or spousal support because it would be a significant financial hardship on her husband. The decision propelled her directly into a life that includes the everyday struggles of living in urban poverty. She draws no salary for her farming work and supports herself by working one 24-hour and one 16-hour shift per weekend at a group home for the disabled, where she earns $10.30 per hour, which is less than $1500 per month after taxes. She also receives disability payments. She says she does not mind her work routine, because her two daughters, now ages 10 and 8, are with their dad on the weekends, and she needs to "keep busy doing something … and I really do love the farming during the week."

Through talking with other veterans Sonia eventually found her way back to the God she was rebelling against when she signed up for the Army so many years before, and figured out a way to channel her concern for hunger into the urban farming initiative Feed Iowa First.[8] The work gives her life meaning. "Farming is a peaceful way to live, and gives me a sense of mission and focus. I can still be useful and be of service to others, even with my PTSD. I can't fight in wars and be a hero to my country anymore, but maybe I can be a hero in my own community," she smiles, expressing a newfound hope she never wants to lose.

Anna's anger erupted randomly, often at inconvenient times, and it took her a while to figure out that it was aimed at both war itself and at the military. "War movies aren't even close to the reality of war," she says, adding that portraying the horror of war "can't be faked on a screen." She came home feeling like she had attention deficit hyperactivity disorder, and found that every little stress was a big deal far out of proportion to the reality of the situation. "I had survivors' guilt, and had lost all my self-confidence, but the VA[9] kept telling me there was nothing wrong with me." By now she was married and had tried several job options, including returning to school, but nothing seemed to work out. "What I should've done was go on a retreat someplace for a couple years, but no one was telling me what was wrong with me, and I couldn't figure it out, so I didn't know what to do."

Eventually Anna was able to force the VA to pay her the five years of benefits she was due, and she was then able to turn to farming as a means to reground herself. "I got into farming through eating…. I'm a good cook and I know how to grow things, so it's almost a perfect job for me now ... and once in a while I get to shoot something," she chuckles. "Plants and animals don't judge me. If I don't feel like working I don't ... it's a quiet life and there aren't a lot of people around." She enjoys being her own boss and takes great pride in being the creative and successful small business owner that farming has allowed her to be. "Trying to fit into the civilian work paradigm made me look stupid, and farming has given me my confidence back ... gradually healed me from the demons of war."

Little by little Anna has expanded her business by using her cooking skills to make homemade jams and jellies from the fruit on her 16 acre farm. She carefully and humanely raises animals for organic meat, which she sells at the local farmers' market in Mount Airy, North Carolina, during the summer months. "People care about where their food comes from, and I give them a high quality product that I try to price fairly, and keep the money local," she says. Eventually she hopes to grow her operation enough to hire another veteran to work with her.

After Iraq, Althea became a guard at Guantanamo Naval Base in Cuba, which was her last active duty assignment. She acknowledges that, "a lot happened" during her wartime service, but doesn't talk much about it because one thing the military taught her was to "suck it up and drive on." Her brother, Matthew, also a combat veteran, admits that while he knows Althea "went through a lot," he doesn't know many of the details about all that occurred.

Needing to earn money, Althea took a job with a civilian security firm, but her heart was set on returning to the farm that had been in her family for six generations, even though it could not support her. "This [owning a six generation working farm] is unusual for a black family," she explains, adding that she and her brother were both very surprised when her grandmother deeded the Brunswick, Georgia, farm over to them a few years ago. For Althea the timing was perfect. "I was ready to leave war behind me and bring back something that was lost ... and I had a lot of unseen scars that needed healing."

Gilliard Farm encompasses 25 acres Althea's great-great-great-grandfather originally acquired after the Civil War. It has been pesticide and chemical free since 1876, making it an organic farm before the term ever came into existence. "I protected our country and its rights, now I can protect the land by being a good steward of it, and helping people eat," she explains, adding that she intends to push hard for more organic farming methods, particularly among black farmers, because Gilliard Farm is the only organic farm operation within 100 miles of Brunswick.

Althea's brother has a green thumb, and she has a heavy equipment operator's license, which she feels makes them perfect partners in keeping the family's land healthy and its farming legacy alive. "Women are natural farmers, and I actually find it odd more women aren't doing it," she says. "Women can see the glory in nature in ways other people don't.... I'll plant a little tree and some people just see a stick—I see a young tree getting ready to grow."

Althea tears up talking about becoming the heir to the historic farming traditions her family has passed on to her and stresses that she feels called upon to preserve it all. "This place is healing my soul.... It's where I first learned to deal with my fears, and I sleep better, and feel better here ... it's brought me inner peace."

WOMEN DO NOT VOLUNTARILY GO TO WAR—SOMETIMES WAR COMES TO THEM, AND AFTERWARDS THEY FARM

There's no shortage of victims in a war, and soldiers aren't the only ones.

—Sonia Kendrick

Bosnian native Nada Marcovic's[10] war experience was one that American civilians have never encountered. Until 1980, she had lived her entire life under the reign of Yugoslavian leader Marshall Tito, who was widely regarded, both inside and outside of Yugoslavia, as a benevolent dictator. Tito had allowed Yugoslavians to enjoy as comfortable a life as was possible under a Communist regime, and as a result, Nada had a car, a house with central heat, an income, a thriving young family and a relatively comfortable life in this coastal Balkan country of 3.87 million people, bordering the calm, blue waters of the Adriatic Sea.

In 1980, Tito died, resulting in a period of political unrest. By the early 1990s the Socialist Federation of the Republic of Yugoslavia he had created was coming unraveled. The country had infrastructure and economic problems, and belligerent opposition between the Republic of Bosnia and Herzegovina and the self-proclaimed Bosnian Serb and Bosnian Croat entities within Bosnia and Herzegovina erupted. Republika Srpska and Herzeg-Bosnia forces, being led and supplied by Serbia and Croatia respectively, began a program of massive ethnic cleansing carried out by military and paramilitary personnel. This action, which can only be described as a bloodbath, caused Yugoslavia, a mostly rural country almost entirely dependent upon an agricultural economy, to fall into bloody civil war. Suddenly no one was safe any longer.

In less than five years more than 100,000 Yugoslavs were buried in mass graves, 20,000 mostly Bosnian women were raped, and 2.2 million people were displaced from their homes and communities. The bucolic former Yugoslavia was in shambles. "Four or five people in a family were killed, leaving only women to care for the children," Nada explained.

When the shooting finally stopped, just before Christmas 1995, Nada, who by now was the single mother of two daughters, with one having a significant handicap, and caring for an elderly mother, felt the need to try to bring the opposing sides together because, in her mind, this was the only means of survival. Entirely lacking in economic resources, she had nothing to work with other than the remarkable personal resolve to start rebuilding her war-torn country, an abundance of wild raspberries growing in the region, and hundreds of displaced women who needed work and desperately wanted to find their way home again.

Nearly everyone in the former Yugoslavia lost their land and the livelihood it had provided them. Fertile farm fields were now mass graves, filled with nameless dead, and many thousands more, mostly men, were declared missing. Their homes and villages had been bombed out, the economic infrastructure was shredded, and women without husbands, brothers, or fathers to help them, and often with several children to provide for, had nowhere to turn. Bosnia's new social reality was that there were very few able-bodied men left. With nearly 100 percent unemployment, the entire economy and infrastructure of what had once been a functional eastern European nation was in ruins. With few men available to form a viable labor force, rebuilding the necessary social and cultural infrastructure that allows society to function fell to the surviving, mostly displaced women.

These were the circumstances Nada found herself up against when she founded the Maja Kravica Women's Association to help women organize and begin learning how to deal with their circumstances. Like civilian war victims everywhere, these women had not signed on for the devastating personal and political destruction that befell them, setting them adrift with nowhere to turn and no social or personal supports to fall back upon. Nada knew the surviving women had to learn to take care of themselves in ways they had never had to do before. Utilizing the knowledge and skills she knew these women already possessed, she sought economic opportunities for them through agriculture and cottage industries. Most Bosnian women already knew how to can jams and jellies, make candy, knit, crochet and sew, and do crafts, and these talents could easily be turned into income-producing activities, if a market could be found, or created.

Nada's office was in an abandoned elementary school within walking distance of her "new home" in one of the few buildings still standing in her village. "We had to accept the path we were on and move forward," she explains, entirely lacking in self-pity.

Nada began by making it possible for women who had lost land to access land again, so they could obtain government loans to grow food. Building upon the widespread availability of naturally growing fruits in the area, she founded a women's agricultural cooperative to represent women's agricultural interests, obtained a bank loan for start-up funds, and then reached out to survivors on both sides of the conflict. Out of this effort came the Insieme Raspberry Cooperative where 400 Serb and Bosnian women farmers work side by side to process and sell their fruit, which grows wild in the region. In the beginning the co-op employed 20 to 30, mostly single-mother headed families who benefited financially, as well as emotionally, by having meaningful work that allowed them to begin rebuilding their integrity and self-respect. As they began to heal from the ravages of war that had taken everything from them, these women became the centerpiece of post-war economic recovery efforts.

A woman of incredible energy and optimism, Nada intends to expand the co-op to include education on planting and cultivating vegetables and other plant crops, as well as raising chicken and turkeys. When he toured Insieme, the Bosnian Minister of Agriculture and Commerce was so impressed by what he saw he proclaimed, "Women are the best part of society!" Nada's response was a simple one: "We have to rebuild our families."

Nada also believes that women have a very difficult time returning to communities affected by war. She explains that those who do find their way home need to know how to do everything, fix everything, and find some way to become whole again despite, the unspeakable horrors that have befallen them. "It's hard to believe anything good can ever happen unless the country can heal, and it is women who can bring the warring factions together," she says, with strong, roll up your sleeves and get to work, determination.

Nada's story is one of experiencing the ravages of war from the other side. She was victimized in a different way from Anna, Sonia and Althea. Nevertheless, all four women suffered the consequences of events they never saw coming and, more poignantly, they all were innocent victims of a conflict they never signed on for, and quickly found they wanted no part of. However, none were inclined to wallow in their misfortune for very long, and all four found that the pathway to healing and going forward with lives that war had changed forever led them to farming. They found their way back home to their communities, and to themselves, by returning to the land.

None of the women in these stories began life as farmers. Each of them sought out, in their own way, a connection with the land and the wider universe to hold them up during a time when they felt lost and their hearts were broken. No matter the circumstances that emotionally leveled them, instinctively each seemed to know that farming would reconnect them with what is truly life sustaining and went forward seeking solace in nature to enable this healing to occur. Their stories testify to the power of Mother Nature, and only the foolish would dare question her ability to comfort and heal—or doubt that she is a supremely good mother who can always be counted on to wrap her arms around a battered soul and restore it to life once again.

Four

Don't Let Your Daughters Grow Up to Be Farmers

Making a Living Off the Land

That the much-celebrated small-scale farmer isn't making a living is the dirty secret of the current movement.

—Bren Smith

Farming is a hardscrabble life. Yet, there is a certain amount of satisfaction in continually pushing up against economic uncertainty and managing to remain financially afloat. But the ugly reality in this scenario is that while farmers work very hard, most manage to squeeze out a profit margin that routinely falls somewhere between slim and none.

"If you don't believe that farming is intrinsically unprofitable, try it," writes Gene Logsdon, who spent more than 70 years in farming, doing everything from hand-milking cows to editing a farm journal.[1] "Rent or buy some farmland, rent or buy some equipment, rent or buy someone at a living wage to do the work then put out a crop of corn, soybeans, cotton or any other major market commodity—except, maybe, marijuana. I defy you at year's end to show me one penny of real profit. There's more profit in making bread wrappers than in growing wheat to put in them. If you decide to do the farming work yourself, you may make a slight return on your labor, but that is not what a good capitalist calls profit ... farming is not a moneymaking proposition in an industrial economy. Never was, never will be," he writes, adding that this intrinsic non-profitability is the chief reason nearly all industrialized nations subsidize farming.

Logsdon firmly believes that the relationship between farming as a profit-motive endeavor and the actual profit farming generates is not complicated. "The way money grows is not the way plants, animals and humans grow. Corn or sheep grow at their own sweet rate, whether interest rates are 3 percent or 15 percent ... the demands of exponential money growth are lethal to a pastoral economy. The way manufacturing produces goods is not the way nature produces goods. A farmer can't 'gear up' or 'gear down' a corn field, or change it to a wheat field half way through the production year to meet new shifts in the market economy," he points out. He is correct. Extreme weather conditions do not have the same direct, make or break effect on factory production that occurs with farming, when one hail storm, or one tornado, can wipe out an entire year's worth of food crops, livestock feed, or a poultry or dairy operation.

"A factory can heedlessly extract product out of raw material knowing it will be years, even centuries, before the raw material runs out. In farming what you extract from the soil you better replace, and quickly, or yields decline. Because you must return to the soil what you take from it, where, in a capitalistic sense, is the profit going to come from?" Logsdon asks. Since most people need to make a living somehow, and are reluctant to work for nothing, he raises a reasonable, and pressing, question that those who grow our food are continually asking.

Logsdon also believes the only profit in farming is in land values, and not in production, noting that farmers, who never work overtime, because they work all the time, have extreme difficulty calculating their labor costs. "For reasons that not even psychiatry can figure out, some of us will often farm for free just for the pleasure of working ourselves to death. We all really should be seeing shrinks, but we can't afford to," he says. He has a point. However, there is also a certain amount of deep, personal satisfaction in doing a job one truly loves, regardless of the demands or the financial return, and the real difficulty comes in having to give up such a job.

Ocean farmer Bren Smith would agree with Logsdon that even with a small-scale farming operation profit is very hard to come by. "At a farm-to-table dinner recently, I sat huddled in a corner with some other farmers, out of earshot of the foodies happily eating kale and freshly shucked oysters. We were comparing business models and profit margins, and it quickly became clear that all of us were operating in the red. After the tools are put away, we head out to second and third jobs to keep our farms afloat. Ninety-one percent of all farm households rely on multiple sources of income. Health care, paying for our kids' college, preparing for retirement? Not happening. With the overwhelming majority of American farmers operating at a loss—the median farm income was negative $1453 in 2012—farmers can barely keep the chickens fed and the lights on," he writes.[2]

Smith, who dropped out of school at age 14 to become a commercial deep-sea fisherman relies on USDA subsidies and foundation grants, rather than retail sales, to make ends meet. Over the last decade he has hustled wooden crafts to tourists on the streets of New York, driven lumber trucks, and worked part time for any nonprofit that would hire him. He says day-dreaming about having kids some day is the far cheaper alternative to actually having them.

Today, Smith, who owns Thimble Island Oysters, doesn't have kind words for high-priced community supported agriculture shares and local farmers' markets as a retail income mainstay for small farmers. "These new venues were promising when they proliferated over a decade ago, but now, with so many programs to choose from, there is increasing pressure for farmers to reduce prices.... And while weekend farmers' markets remain precious community spaces, sales volumes are often too low to translate into living wages for your much-loved small-scale farmer. Especially in urban areas, supporting your local farmer may actually mean buying produce from former hedge fund managers or tax lawyers who have quit the rat race to get some dirt under their fingernails," he says. "We call it hobby farming, where recreational 'farms' are allowed to sell their products at the same farmers' markets as commercial farms. It's all about property taxes, not food production. As Forbes magazine suggested to readers in its 2012 Investment Guide, now is the time to 'farm like a billionaire,' because even a small amount of retail sales—as low as $500 a year in New Jersey—allows landowners to harvest more tax breaks than tomatoes."

Smith also finds the competition from non-profit farming initiatives such as Growing Power, an urban farming enterprise in Milwaukee, Wisconsin, very discouraging. Released from the yoke of having to show a profit, he believes the non-profits are doing some of the most innovative work in farming and, at the same time, escaping the iron heel of the free market. "Growing Power received over $6.8 million in grants over the last five years, and its produce is now available in Walgreens stores. How's a young farmer to compete with that?" he asks. Smith also points out that when nonprofit farmers want a new tractor, they ask their board of directors, but every other farmer who needs new equipment has to go begging to the bank.

Restaurants that buy local, Smith believes, are the perfect example of good intentions arising in idealism-heavy social movements that lead to bad outcomes. They are also part of the problem. A general rule of thumb is that a chef has to keep actual food costs at or below one third of the menu price, and when the restaurant's other operating expenses are added in, the profit-loss margin narrows considerably. Going organic, which is attractive marketing as well as a higher cost, therefore higher risk, business venture, can mean the farmers' contribution to the total meal is even smaller. "Capping the farmer's take to a small sliver of the plate ensures that working the land remains a beggar's game," he explains. "The food movement—led by celebrity chefs, advocacy journalists, students and NGOs [non-government organizations]—is missing, ironically, the perspective of the people doing the actual work of growing food. Their platform has been largely based on how to provide good, healthy food, while it has ignored the core economic inequities and contradictions embedded in our food system."

Smith's argument fails to recognize that increases in food costs are passed on to consumers, so the proportional profit margin for the small business, organic food restaurant remains steady. In other words, if farmer costs increase, wholesale prices increase, and the consumer pays for all of it. However, his point that the farmer is not receiving a fair price for the food he or she produces is valid.

Food writer Michael Pollan's take on small farm operations is intimately connected to the notion that growing food is participating in an entire food system enterprise.[3] "When I began writing about agriculture in the late '80s and '90s, I quickly figured out that no editor in Manhattan thought the subject timely or worthy of his or her attention, and that I would be better off avoiding the word entirely and talking instead about food, something people then still had some use for and cared about, yet oddly never thought to connect to the soil or the work of farmers," he says.

Pollan also believes that, as consumers, we are all implicated in the broader farming enterprise behind our massive food system, and are responsible for making food production profitable enough for small-scale farmers to earn a living by growing the food others eat. This is unquestionably true; however, not all independent farmers manage small-scale operations, and not all farmers fail to stay financially afloat. To the contrary, some do make a living from farming.

Farming 6000 Acres Is Farming Nine Square Miles

> Sure farming is hard work, but so are a lot of other things.
> —Kathy Nickel

In 2011, Kathy Nickel was the wife of a farmer and the nurse manager of the Waupaca County Hospital emergency room. Kathy's hospital job enabled her family to have health insurance and provided additional, off-farm income that supplemented her husband's grain operation and side businesses, helping to ensure that both remained solvent. Besides her paying job, Kathy also kept the farm books, tended to the house, and helped Vince, her husband, with chores on weekends.

Located just slightly east of the dead center of Wisconsin, Waupaca County, with a population of 52,000 is somewhat denser than many rural areas peppering the state; otherwise, it is typical of thousands of rural counties across the Midwest, where glaciers from the last Ice Age flattened the region into miles and miles of farmland. Scenic is not the first word that comes to mind when describing this landscape, where the ratio of hard-driven pickup trucks to not very new cars traversing beat up roads is about five to one.

Waupaca's consolidated school district is the county's largest employer and, in terms of usable space, the new high school is the county's largest building. The hospital is the county's second largest employer. Both provide vital, steady incomes to their employees, most of who come from farm families who are still struggling to recover from the 2008 economic recession

Kathy and Vince were both born and raised in Waupaca County. They dated for 11 years before finally getting married when she was 31 and Vince was 37. They built a strong partnership together, and had been a good team for more than 25 years, until one mid-summer day in 2011, when everything suddenly changed.

"It was an exceptionally hot Sunday morning in mid–July, and for some reason I decided to leave the breakfast dishes and ride down the road with Vince to have a look at our new grain dryer and storage facility. He was in the process of putting in a computerized 120,000 dry bushel capacity air transport storage system and wanted to show me how it worked … we weren't there more than 10 minutes when he sat down, complaining of feeling dizzy. I'd done emergency nursing long enough to know right away that he was having a stroke … and less than 24 hours later his brain was completely gone," Kathy explains wistfully. "I thought taking Vince off the ventilator would be the hardest decision I would ever have to make, and in a lot of ways it was, but it also turned out to be just the beginning of having to make a lot more hard decisions."

Kathy recalls this story on a sunny winter afternoon while we are sitting at her kitchen table, strategically placed in front of a large window.

Kathy Nickel stands next to her computerized 120,000-bushel grain storage facility on her crop farm in Waupaca, Wisconsin. Being able to store grain to sell when the market price is up is important for the financial viability of an operation as large as Kathy's (photograph by Sara Bresden).

We are drinking some of the best coffee I've ever tasted while watching two cardinals argue over who owns the birdfeeder. She slides a plate of homemade cookies toward me, and wonders aloud why I am interested in her farm story? I'm too taken by what I see out her kitchen window to offer a fast answer.[4]

Kathy's snow-covered farmland stretches out flat in all directions from this window, for as far as the eye can see. A few large trees provide summer shade and a winter windbreak for the neat one-story house that appears slightly smaller than the attached, several vehicle garage; otherwise, very little interrupts the landscape between the front porch and all sides of the surrounding horizon, for as far as the eye can see.

A remarkably cheerful woman with a ready smile, Kathy seems reticent to shift the conversation over to telling me about a farm operation she is rightly very proud of—and yet truly amazed that people find both interesting and remarkably unusual. "We build this house in 2001, just ahead of the old farmhouse falling down," she tells me. "It was a purely practical decision—we had two kids and needed something to live in that was at least as reliable as Vince's pickup truck," she chuckles.

Kathy's demeanor bespeaks strength, confidence, and a no-nonsense approach to life. Clearly, she is not prone to self-pity, or inclined toward spending endless hours wallowing in grief, and is not given to worrying about things she can't do anything about. "I've always been of the attitude that no matter what happens, you keep going," she says simply, volunteering little else about the emotional train wreck that had befallen her just over three years ago.

"This land is the home farm. Vince's parents bought it when Vince was 6 months old, and from that time forward, until he died, he'd never lived anywhere else. He grew up on this land and made it his own … and we never lived anywhere else either." Taking a deep breath, Kathy acknowledges that Vince's dream was to build up the farm operation and eventually pass it on to their son Ben, just as his dad had done for him. "Farming was in his blood … and it seems to be in Ben's blood too … so we'd always planned on Ben taking over some day. Unfortunately, that day came much sooner than we ever anticipated…. Ben was just 16 years old when his dad died, and suddenly that distant someday had arrived, and with it a lot of uncertainty."

Kathy explained to her son that with his dad gone nothing about their future was certain. "At that time we were farming 3000 acres, which is 4.7 square miles of land, and by any measure, that is a large crop farm operation," Kathy admits. In a county having a population density just over 70 persons per square mile, the Nickel farm already comprised a significant portion of the local farmland.

"Ben helped out, and knew a lot about the nuts and bolts of running the farm but he was still in high school when Vince died, and was a starter on the high school football team. He was far too young to step into his father's boots just yet…. I knew that, and even though he wanted to do it, deep down Ben knew it too."

Kathy knew Ben loved farming just as much as his dad and grandfather had loved it, and she didn't want to let Vince's dream for Ben die. But, she had no idea how to keep it alive either. "I didn't know what to do, and didn't have a lot of time to think about it because it had been a very hot summer and we had 100 acres of wheat needing to be harvested in the next few weeks," she sighs. "I was raised in the Christian faith, and believe that the Lord helps those who help themselves, so when trouble comes, you pick yourself up and deal with it. There was never any question in my mind about doing that—I just had to figure out how."

That answer began to appear just a few days later, while sitting at the kitchen table talking with Ben and trying to figure out how to bring in the wheat crop. "Ben knew a lot more than I realized, and right away he showed me how to do some things, including turning on the irrigation system so the other crops didn't dry out while we harvested wheat. Then, I called the folks who'd installed the new corn dryer and storage bins and told them I needed someone to come out and show me how to run the computers…. I understood the old auger system for moving corn, but had no clue about running this new one, and we had a crop coming in pretty soon, so I had to learn how to do this right now. It didn't take me long to catch on because, honestly, I was absolutely floored at how easy this new system is to operate—it is amazingly easy," she smiles, "you could do it— no problem." I'm not sure I believe her, but she reassures me this is true.

Meanwhile Vince's brother made sure Ben could safely run the combine and be able to help Kathy harvest the wheat—and he got that job done mostly on his own, with some help from his two uncles and a cousin. "In the middle of all this I suddenly realized that I really could manage this operation myself. I wanted to do it for the kids, but it had also been

Kathy Nickel talks with her son Ben as he prepares to take the tractor out into the fields to begin spring planting (photograph by Sara Bresden).

Vince's and my life together, and the farm meant everything in the world to me too…. The bottom line was that I just didn't want to give it up. By the time we had the wheat crop in I had built up enough confidence to think seriously about keeping the farm and running it myself…. A few days later I made up my mind that was what we were going to do and gave notice at the hospital."

Kathy found that her decision received mixed reviews, both from her kids and the wider community. "My daughter Bailey was 13 at the time, and she kept reminding me that I was a nurse, not a farmer," Kathy laughs. "I knew everybody else in town was thinking pretty much the same thing." She also suspected many of their friends would think she was probably out of her mind to make such a sudden and dramatic career change within weeks of losing her husband. "I know you're not supposed to make any major decisions for a year after a death," she says, "but a farm doesn't just stand still waiting patiently until you're ready to decide what to do next, so I didn't have the luxury of taking all the time I needed—I had to start making decisions right away, and some of them would be big ones." Nevertheless, she kept quiet about her plans for the future for as long as possible but, in a small town, news travels fast, and there's never any shortage of opinions about what folks are, or are not, doing. From that perspective, the less than enthusiastic reaction to her plans for the future forthcoming from some people did not surprise her.

Kathy made the decision to leave a 28-year nursing career behind and take over managing a 3000-acre crop farm because it was what she wanted to do, and what she strongly believed was best for her family. She never had any illusions about the limitations her hands-on farm experience imposed upon her, but she had a good grasp of the business side of the operation, and knew this "counted for a lot" going forward. As a result, having people think she was a little crazy to be doing what she had determined she wanted to do didn't bother her as much as it might bother some people.

Kathy viewed the possibility of keeping the farm and running it herself a little differently from many others, taking more of a "why not?" approach to her decision. "Admittedly I didn't grow up on a farm, but I did grow up in a family-owned small business I'd helped out with since I was a teenager. And, I'd kept the farm books for Vince from the beginning, which was, counting the years before we were married, 36 years ago, so I knew the ups and downs, who we did business with, and where the money went…. I had management experience from running the ER [emergency room] so I know how to work with people. Somehow, I just felt sure I could figure out the rest. Besides, deep in my heart it just seemed like the right thing to do."

Kathy stresses that she wasn't naïve about what she was getting into. "I knew I had a lot to learn, but the fact was, I really wanted to keep the farm that Vince and I built together. So, I set about figuring out how to do it. From the beginning I knew I'd have to quit my job, roll up my sleeves, and get to work, so that's what I did," she says matter-of-factly. She doesn't seem to grasp how remarkable, and courageous, her decision to quit a well-paying position with a guaranteed future and jump into farming on this scale, under these circumstances, actually was.

Kathy readily acknowledges that it might have been an entirely different story if they were livestock farmers. "I'm not sure I could've done it if we had dairy cattle … jumping into crop farming with both feet is very different from milking a dairy herd twice a day, and if that was the situation I'd had to deal with, I probably would not have been able to make the same decision," she says.

The farm operation Kathy took over included a fieldwork side business involving contracts with seven other farmers in the township. "We have 3 semis and one straight truck, so in the fall we combine and haul their crops to the co-op, and then do their fall tilling. In the spring we till and plant, and in between we'll spray for them if they want it," Kathy says, adding that she's just now getting back into this. "The summer Vince died I told our contract farmers I wasn't sure we could get their harvest work done, but I would help them find someone else. As it turned out, we did manage to get most of it done, and some other farmers in the area, including Vince's brothers, stepped forward to help us. Everyone was very understanding and wanted to come back to us as soon as we could take them, so I worked hard to be sure we could make that happen. Fortunately, we've been able to keep those contracts, which are both another income source for us, as well as a lucky break."

Kathy has high praise and deep affection for Vince's remaining family, particularly his brothers, DuWayne and Ellwyn, who live nearby, and are her closest family. Both Kathy's and Vince's parents, Vince's sister and one of her two brothers died before Vince did, and her only remaining brother lives in Georgia, so she has almost no extended family of her own and none nearby that she can call on in a pinch. Realizing this, Vince's family enfolded her into the family as one of their own. "Vince was the youngest of the brothers, and losing him was really hard on the others, but they stepped up right away to help mentor Ben, and be there as a sounding board for me.... Even though Vince is gone, they've kept me, and the kids, deep inside the family circle, and that means the whole world to us, and especially to me," Kathy emphasizes with rare emotion. "I've been through a lot, and am still standing partly because of all the support from Vince's family ... not all families would've held us so close or done what they have."

While she admits that she realized, from having lost other family members, that unexpected things could happen, Kathy says she had never given any thought to the possibility of becoming a young widow and single parent to two active, involved teenagers. When life unexpectedly propelled her into that situation, she accepted it just as she had accepted previous upsets in her life, with firm resolve to remain standing. In this case, remaining standing meant, taking on a large farm enterprise and taking sole charge of an active family entirely on her own. "The kids understood that we were in this together, and that they needed to help out more than they had in the past, but I really didn't want them to lose out on a fun high school life because their dad had died, and I knew Vince wouldn't want that either ... so I had to do some serious reorganizing," she explains with understated emphasis.

Ben had been playing high school football since his freshman year, and after Vince died Kathy wasn't sure whether he would continue. "I told him it was entirely up to him and a week or so after the season began he decided he wanted to play, which meant Friday nights in the fall, which is harvest season, were football nights. I couldn't stand the thought of him out there playing his heart out and not being there to cheer him on, so no matter what needed to be done on the farm, I was in the stands every Friday night watching the high school football game."

During the same school year Bailey was in the school dance club, which competed on weekends. "Most Saturdays I took Bailey to dance, and stayed to watch her perform, which took another large chunk of my time ... even though I was the only parent the kids had, we were still a family and no matter how much farm work there was, I still had to be there for their games and other activities," Kathy stresses, adding that not everybody understood these decisions, which added yet another layer of doubt among those questioning her ability to successfully manage the farm. "I never questioned my commitment to keeping the family first, regardless," Kathy explains, adding that the amount of work during harvest/football season is entirely governed by the weather. "We have to work when the weather allows us to work," she explains, admitting that getting everything done on the farm while being a good mother to two teenagers who has suddenly lost their father became "a very big worry" that first year.

Kathy determined that the best solution was to hire a full time farm hand—another decision that raised some eyebrows. "With Vince gone, we were essentially one farm hand short, and it was pretty clear Ben and I couldn't keep up with everything on our own while he was still in high school, so I had to figure something else out," she says. John Seeger was a family friend who had helped Vince with some of the contract fieldwork, so Kathy approached him about working for her. "He didn't say yes right away, and I figured he was wondering what it would be like working for a woman, so I didn't push…. A few days later he called and said he'd do it. I explained that this would be a working partnership and I needed him to be forthright in telling me what he thought about my ideas, and to throw out ideas of his own…. It took a while, but eventually he got comfortable telling me when he believed I was wrong, and carefully explaining why. I didn't always agree with him, but I always listened to what he had to say, and sometimes I do go along with his ideas, when my gut tells me it will probably work … and he's never said 'I told you so' when my decision didn't turn out quite like I thought it would. Luckily, so far there haven't been too many of those times," she chuckles. "We work pretty well together, and I can't even begin to say how deeply grateful I am for that."

Kathy spent the winter of 2011–12 learning as much as she could about what, exactly, spring planting would involve. "Since I did the bookwork I knew what companies we used for various chemicals, fertilizer, seed, parts, and things like that—and I knew why Vince did some things, and why what he did on one field was different from what he did on another field. But he also carried a tremendous amount around in his head, so I didn't know, and couldn't figure out, when some fields had been fertilized, and why some needed more water than others did. I decided to take soil samples from them all and make planting decisions once I had that information, which was a good idea—but understanding the results was a real nightmare," she laughs. "I attended several soil science informational meetings, but I still need a lot more education about what goes best where … and I'm not alone in this—a lot of farmers don't understand all there is to know, or even what it is they need to know, about soils. It's amazingly complicated."

Kathy made several other big decisions that first winter, which was turning out to be exceptionally cold and dreary. "I added some outbuildings, including a large machine shed, which I felt we needed. And I traded our fairly new, but very temperamental New Holland combine for a brand new John Deere with a GPS system that actually worked. Other farmers notice things like new equipment, so I tried to keep that decision quiet for as long as I could, which was a surprisingly short period of time," she laughs. Turning serious, she adds that she has been amazed at how much money the GPS system saves. "The rows are straight so there's a lot less erosion and they don't overlap, so you don't waste seed—and it's all done by computer, so once you get it programmed for each particular field, you're all set to plant. It's hard the first time, but you can store the programs, so after that it's really very easy."

As an experiment, she also decided to strike a deal with a local dairy farmer to grow silage corn for him in exchange for manure to organically fertilize one of the small fields. Asked how she feels about organic farming methods, she laughs and repeats her point that there isn't enough cow manure in Wisconsin to fertilize all her acreage, not to mention the transportation costs she would incur bringing it in. "Seriously, though, I feel very strongly that we have to care for and replenish the land somehow, or we'll wear it out," she stresses. "But for an operation as large as mine is, there's really no way to replace soil nutrients other than to use chemicals. I try very hard to use as few as possible, but I have to use some ... and in reality nurturing and caring for the land is like nursing in some ways—you take care of it and try to keep it healthy, and make it well when it gets sick ... and right now we're still experimenting with several ways to do these things."

Kathy speaks of her land with deep affection. "I'm a believer in the Lord giving and the Lord taking away, and if we don't care for the land, it won't produce anything, and then we, as farmers, won't be able to keep it. We can't just rely upon nature to take care of it all—we have to use our own intelligence and technologies too.... You can't make more land, and once it's gone to development it's gone forever, so farmers absolutely have to take good care of what land we do have and do what it takes to keep it working for us." She acknowledges that accomplishing this is a tall order. "Farmers have to be everything—able to adapt to the weather, to land conditions, and variations in crop growth ... and achieving this is a lot like detective work—why did this work here and not there, and what made the difference? And once you think you've pretty well got that all figured out, the rest involves a lot of every-day TLC!"

Immediately after taking over the farm Kathy pursued obtaining the needed certifications to use farm chemicals, which she found was very similar to mixing up medications. "I had to learn how to mix, measure and combine the chemicals for fertilizing and spraying before they could legally sell me what I needed, so I had to take the classes and get certified—it's sort of like the in-service hours a nurse needs to keep her license," she explains.

When two smaller farms adjacent to hers came up for sale late that same winter, the first one after Vince died, Kathy decided to purchase them, adding acreage to the existing operation. Again, she raised eyebrows in the community and found herself on the receiving end of plenty of friendly, yet unsolicited advice that, somehow, always came around to being told she couldn't do whatever it was she was planning to do because Vince wouldn't have done it that way. She remained remarkably good-natured about all these freely offered opinions. "I explained that just like every patient is different, every farmer is different, every crop is different, and every piece of land is different, and you have to take care of different things in different ways … get as much information as you can and try new things, based upon what's best for your own individual operation," she says. "I was doing what I thought was best for our operation, and I never felt like Vince was looking down from above, watching me with a frown on his face."

From the moment she decided to take over the farm operation herself Kathy knew other farmers would be watching her pretty carefully and once she came to terms with this unwelcome, yet not surprising scrutiny she decided it was fun keeping everyone on their toes and guessing. "The thing is, if Vince were alive, he'd be changing how he does things, because all farmers do—just as with all businesses we have to be open to new things and new technologies in order to keep the operation going. Eventually people began to understand that I really can make the hard decisions a large farming operation requires, that I know what I'm doing, and I also know what I need to find out more about—and I'm not going to give up and go back to nursing. Once this sunk in all the free-flowing extra advice definitely slowed down."

One of the biggest ongoing challenges Kathy faces is navigating the grain markets, where the farm's profits and losses are ultimately determined.[5] "I don't know that anybody has the magic formula for that … and a lot of farmers struggle with it," she says. For now, she forward contracts about a third of the crop, meaning that before she plants in the spring she agrees to sell a certain number of bushels at a pre-set, per bushel price, to be delivered within an agreed-upon time frame. "I decide on the number of bushels I'll sell and when I'll deliver them to the co-op and they turn around and sell it on the grain market. I can sell more at market price at that time if the price is decent. Otherwise, I have the capacity to store up to 120,000 bushels, so I can hold back that much and sell later, when the market improves." On average she stores between one-half and two-thirds of the crop each year, banking on the market going up so she can sell later at higher prices.

Corn, wheat and soybean yields depend upon location, the weather in a given year and the percent of the planted crop that is actually harvested. Kathy's bushel per acre averages match fairly well with the national averages, so she expects to harvest 43 bushels of soybeans, 44.5 bushels of wheat, and between 150 and 174 bushels of corn per acre planted, making hers a high seven-figure farm operation. "Within weeks of Vince dying, Ben harvested nearly 5000 bushels of wheat, and by the end of the season we brought in just over 17,000 bushels of soybeans, and 150,000 bushels of corn—a little over 172,000 bushels total. I sold what was already contracted and stored as much as I could, and then played the market over the winter—and we survived," she smiles.

"Farming is a money in-money out game," Kathy explains, elaborating further on the finances. "Even though agricultural land is taxed at a lower rate than other commercial land, when you're farming this many acres, there's a hefty tax bill every year, plus paying back the annual operating loan, and the interest on that—those are costs I can always count on ... and I don't ever want to be in the position of not being able to pay back the operating loan and having to carry money owed over to the next year—if that happens I'd be borrowing money at a higher interest rate, and pretty soon it gets to be a vicious debt cycle that's hard to stop," she says. Annual operating costs include, among other things, fuel, seed, chemicals, equipment repairs, land taxes and salaries, all on the expense, money-out side of the ledger. The best years are when the operating loans are small or unnecessary, but this always depends upon the commodity markets and the prior year yields.

"Just when you think you've got it all balanced something breaks and you need to come up with a few thousand dollars to get it fixed ... you can always count on that happening," Kathy laughs. "That was the problem with our New Holland tractor—it wasn't very old but the computer wouldn't talk to the tractor. This wasn't something we could fix ourselves, and every time we paid to get it fixed it cost a couple thousand dollars ... pretty soon I felt like I was throwing good money after bad, so I told them to take it back." Reflecting her sharp business mind, Kathy adds that she would've loved to keep the tires for spares though, because replacing those aren't cheap either, but the dealer said the tires had to come back with the tractor.

When the ethanol boom crowned corn King of Cash Crops, and the price went up to $7 per bushel, the farm brought in over a million dollars just from the corn crop alone. "Everybody thought ethanol turned corn into a gold mine, so farmers started planting more and more of it. I never thought that price would last, but while it did, it gave us the chance to expand the operation and set something aside for a rainy day. I don't think we'll see $7 per bushel corn again any time soon, but when these price spikes do occur it's good to be able take advantage of them," Kathy points out.

Knowing how to make sound business decisions is vital to successful farming, and Kathy works very hard at doing that in a business environment where almost everything—the weather, the grain market, fuel costs, seed prices, fertilizer, per-acre yields and life generally, is wildly unpredictable. "I think it's definitely easier to make decisions about what to plant where than it is to cull a dairy herd and get rid of your favorite cows … nobody gets emotionally attached to a corn field in quite the same way they care about a live animal," she deadpans.

Kathy goes on to explain that she has to stay connected to more than just the grain markets. "Fertilizer contains petroleum, and is cheaper when oil prices are down, so in addition to paying attention to the grain market I have to watch oil prices to determine the best time to buy fertilizer and other chemicals. People have the notion that farming is a romantic, relaxed life riding around in the sunshine on a tractor all day, but the truth is farming is a business that depends on the financial markets, and that is definitely a 'you snooze-you lose' situation. You have to keep paying attention all the time, and can never relax for very long … nobody gets it right all the time, but in the long run it still pays to keep track of what the market is doing. There's just no way around that."

The need to pay attention to various world market fluctuations is one area where large farming operations like Kathy's depart from smaller, localized farm enterprises that focus on growing organic food and depend mostly on local sales. In local farmers' market settings, vendor prices vary only slightly, the customer base is much smaller, and the individual farmer has much greater control over direct sales. He or she doesn't have to worry about ups and downs in financial markets arising from politics or bad weather events on a continent half a world away. For the small farmer the dollars in-dollars out equation is much smaller, and business practices, in a practical sense are, in many ways, easier to manage.

Nevertheless, within their own context, the struggles to make ends meet small farmers face are just as great, if not greater, than those large farm operations like Kathy's must endure at the whim of multiple, worldwide financial markets. "I knew that the bigger we got, the bigger the decisions would be, and the higher the stakes, and the risks would be too, but I wasn't going to back away from it for that reason," Kathy says.

Adding acreage has meant Kathy has had to look harder at no-till planting methods and cover crops, an idea Vince was considering before he died. "My understanding is that cover crops really enhance soil quality by reaching down deep for added nutrients, so we're doing that on some of the fields now. The plan is to till them under in the spring, hoping those fields will need less fertilizer. I'm also thinking about planting wheat directly into the corn stubble, and right now am looking at the latest data on some new hybrids."

Meanwhile, four years have passed. Ben has finished high school and went on to earn an agricultural equipment service technician certificate at the local technical college. He has obtained a commercial driver's license to enable him to operate the grain trucks, and has moved into his own place. He's now farming full time, as his mother's business partner. "We're working well together—I trust his ideas and insights, and he trusts mine, so we've not run into any major problems," Kathy smiles proudly.

Bailey will be finishing high school in the spring, and is expressing an interest in nursing. However, both Kathy and Ben have stressed that she has the option of taking an active role in running the farm if she wants to. "Both Ben and Bailey have grown up knowing that the 'you can't do this because you're a girl, or can't do that because you're a boy' idea is stereotyping and that they can't let being a boy or a girl limit their choices," Kathy, who is a living example of this advice, says. "No matter what happens that knocks you down, you can't let life tell you that you can't do something—as far as I'm concerned you can do anything you put your mind to, and this is what I've always told the kids."

Kathy says that, besides playing the grain markets, her other great challenge is working with Mother Nature. "She's absolutely in charge—and no matter what I've planned to do on a particular day, if she wants me to do something else, she lets me know what it is and I do that instead," she laughs. "Farming's definitely not a profession for anyone who needs to have a lot of control over things, because we don't. A good example is that every spring I worry tremendously about whether that seed I paid a lot of money for, and we spent a lot of time and energy planting as carefully as we can, will grow and produce a good crop? I always believe it will, but the only one who really knows is Mother Nature, and once I've put the seed into the ground, the rest is basically up to her.... Farming is actually a very humbling profession, if you think about it."

In spite of the challenges, Kathy sees a bright future ahead. "Ben's goal is to farm 6000 acres, and we're adding land as we can. He believes several nearby farms in our area will come up for sale in the next few years as those farmers leave farming altogether, so the long range plan is to be in a position to purchase them as they become available. If prices fall and stay down for a long time we may have to rethink this, but I tell Ben that if we use good common sense we should be able to do it, because neither one of us is afraid of hard work," Kathy smiles confidently.

Driving away from Kathy's farm I measure two miles, which is the approximate side of 4.7 square miles, or 3000 acres of land. Standing by the side of the road, I realize this much land stretches as far as the eye can see. I add another mile, which gives me a sense of what 6000 acres of land looks like. Then I begin playing with numbers: 6000 acres of corn, producing an average of 160 bushels per acre, yields nearly one million bushels of corn. At current prices, this translates into a $4.8 million dollar cash crop, and a lot of hard work.

Like all the women farmers I know, Kathy possesses fearless determination, grit, and abundant horse sense. There's no question in my mind that she could run a nine square mile operation, and that a wise person would never bet against her.

Successful Dairy Farming Is the Ability to Think Like a Cow

> If you're a dairy farmer the most important members of your family are a bunch of temperamental lactating cows. Everybody else is a distant second.
>
> —Jeanie Lewis

"I truly believe women make better dairy farmers than men, because we can think like a cow," Sadie Zimmer smiles. An energetic, 39-year-old Wisconsin dairy farmer, she claims women intuitively understand dairy cows. "We have more empathy for them, and it's a proven fact that cows milked by women give more milk."

Sadie's organic dairy farm, located along Otter Creek, which runs through a broad, green valley alongside the lower Wisconsin River, sits in the shadow of the Taliesin compound, home of the famous "organic" architect Frank Lloyd Wright. Wright believed that inside and outside spaces should fit and function together organically, meaning that each compliments the other without interrupting the surrounding environment. Wright would approve of Sadie's use of her land and buildings, and would appreciate that the old house that serves as her office, the large

Sadie Zimmer stands in her barn on a very cold February morning, preparing to feed her 150 hungry Holsteins. During the winter feeding cycle, when they can't be in the pastures, the cows eat a carefully prepared and regulated food combination given to them inside the barn (photograph by the author).

barn that houses her cattle, and the outbuildings she uses for storage, all blend unobtrusively into the hills bordering Taliesin.

As we walk around her pristine 150 stall dairy barn on a sunny sub-zero winter morning, Sadie reveals the secret of her success running a large, non-commercial dairy operation. "I talk to my cows all the time," she laughs. "I tell them I've had two babies myself so I can sympathize with what they're going through when they've just calved and have to start nursing again.... I tell them I know how much it hurts at first, and almost before my eyes both the new mother and her calf start to relax. That conversation gets things headed in the right direction pretty quickly."

Sadie milks 150 Holsteins, the undisputed queens of milk cows, twice a day, 365 days per year, without fail, resulting in nearly three million pounds of organic milk produced annually. This equates to an average of about 65 pounds (7.5 gallons) of milk per cow, per day, over its 305 day lactation period, adding up to nearly 20,000 pounds of milk per year. She views this as "OK" output, and well above the 55.9 pounds (6.5 gallons) per cow, per day average, but it is still a figure she would like to nudge upward, with a view toward increasing profits.

While she realizes that cows aren't the only source of milk for human consumption, Sadie is also aware that traditional dairy farming is disappearing from the American agricultural scene. While she believes this will make her product more valuable, others disagree, and see alternatives to cows' milk as the wave of the future, particularly as more people, for whatever reason, become lactose intolerant or allergic to milk. There is also the matter of having to compete with commercial operations, which, nationwide, produce 85 percent of the milk consumed as a beverage, and making butter, cheese, ice cream, and other dairy products.

Whether raising dairy cattle is disappearing as a farming endeavor depends upon who you ask. However, nearly every state that keeps dairy farm statistics reports that the number of farms is getting smaller, the size of the farms is shrinking, and that, nationwide 99 percent of all dairy farms are owned and operated as family farms having an average herd size of 88 cows. Currently there are 51,000 dairy farms in the United States, with 74 percent of these milking less than 100 cows and, together, accounting for just 15 percent of the total milk production.[6]

The economic laws of supply and demand, as well as the structure of the marketplace where milk is sold, govern how it is priced, thus controls the profit margin. In simple economic terms, competitive market prices are set according to whether the product is made specifically for a customer, whether there are no other producers capable of manufacturing a similar item, how well a company can effectively differentiate its product from others, or how able a producer is able to distinguish his or her product from competing products. Milk has no intrinsic value, so a competitive marketplace is the best economic environment for the farmer, because this provides the best chance to sell at higher prices.

It can't be argued that milk can be made to particular specifications, or that there are no other cows capable of producing it. However, a case can be made that milk produced under certain circumstances can be distinguished from milk produced under other, different circumstances, and this is where organically produced milk currently has the economic edge. Currently Sadie is getting $33 per hundredweight for the organic milk her operation produces, which is considerably more than conventionally produced milk. Each year she negotiates this price with a local organic cheese making business that purchases her entire production load.

While the farm operation costs are about the same for both conventional and organic dairy farming, a conventional farmer would have to milk more than twice as many cows as an organic farmer to offset the expenses and match the income a smaller organic operation is able to generate. As an organic milk producer, Sadie receives about twice what a conventional dairy farmer receives for the same amount of milk.

The price Sadie is able to sell her milk for classifies Otter Creek Organic Farms as at least a $1 million per year dairy operation. Since her cows are the employees who generate this income, she doesn't want to risk anyone getting into a bad mood. "I need the cows to be lactating 305 days per year, which takes effort, and requires a whole lot of TLC ... it takes patience.... It's really no different from any nursing mother, who knows that she does better when she's happy. I get that, so it's in my best interests to keep my cows content, because they'll produce more and be less likely to get mastitis or some other infection," she smiles.

National organic milk standards require milk-producing cows be pastured at least 120 days per year, but Sadie prefers more. "The pasture season generally starts around mid–April and lasts until about mid–September, which allows the herd to derive roughly 40 percent of its dry matter feed from the farm's 500 acres of pasture land," Sadie explains, adding that she has to rotate pastures every 12 hours to keep them in the best condition for grazing.

Cows, which are very fond of eating, have several stomachs, and because of this they present unique nutrient management problems. "Cows are lazy and they'd be happy standing in the barn eating all day, but I don't want them to do that, and they like the pasture better once

In order to not overeat, which cows are prone to do, all 150 of Sadie Zimmer's cows at Otter Creek Organic Farm must take turns in the barn's cattle stanchions during the winter (courtesy Sadie Zimmer).

they move their butts to get out there, but sometimes I have to remind them of this, and coax them out of the barn. I don't allow them to drop much below 40 percent pasture grass, which means I have to very carefully control how much they eat in the barn and never put them out to pasture on a full stomach, otherwise, they'll bloat up and just eat themselves to death."

During a dry year pastures provide less nutrition. When this occurs Sadie supplements with feed pellets which neither she nor the cows like very well. "It gives them a bellyache, which gives me a big headache," she explains, adding that one hundred and fifty cows with stomachaches is a nightmare. "Think about how you feel when you have a stomachache," she says. "You're very uncomfortable and definitely not happy."

Sadie is not alone in believing contented cows are better milk producers. In her view, keeping the cows happy is a "best practices" issue, and the right way to dairy farm. Dr. Temple Grandin of Professor of Animal Science at Colorado State University[7] has dedicated her professional career to animal welfare, agrees. She firmly believes that animals are not things, and even though they are technically the property of their owners, they still have certain rights, and can suffer high degrees of anxiety if not properly cared for. Animal comfort and reduced anxiety is the driving force underpinning Sadie's relationship with her entire dairy herd. "I don't hesitate to fire someone if I don't like the way they treat the animals," she says.

Added onto Sadie's concerns for animal comfort is the fact that organic dairy farming is both more and less complicated than conventional dairy farming. "It's a highly regulated, one cow per stall, industry, and the paperwork really sucks," she sighs, explaining that one of her biggest challenges is keeping up with the bookwork. "I'm inspected every year, and I have to show all my records to prove I've only used organic fertilizer and natural medications ... it's on the honor system to some extent, but the inspectors look at your records pretty closely."

A central concern surrounding organically raised and maintained animals is antibiotic use. Sadie believes antibiotics have their place, and a lot more cows could be saved and retained in the herd if she could treat them with conventional antibiotics, but she can't do that and remain an organic operation. "One slip-up and it would take three or four years to become certified again, and that would really cost me financially. If a cow is really sick I'll isolate it and give it antibiotics to save its life, knowing that cow is permanently lost to the herd. As soon as the meat hold is lifted I move it off the farm."

Another concern is maintaining pristine, chemical-free pastures. This can be a challenge because on a windy day chemicals being applied to a neighboring farm can blow some distance across that farm onto the adjacent one, and if it is an organic farm operation, the organic farmer has to isolate that section of land and not use it until all the chemical residue is removed.

Conventional dairy farming is easier than maintaining an organic operation because antibiotic use is permitted, so fewer cows leave the herd and the farmer is not required to observe the cows as closely. Fewer regulations govern conventional feed and pastureland quality, so a conventional dairy farmer does not have to put in the time and effort required of an organic farmer who has to monitor the pastures constantly to ensure they are kept chemical-free.

Sadie grew up on Otter Creek Farm, which is owned by her father, Gary Zimmer, a pioneer in organic and biological farming methods. She began raising the farm's heifers when the operation converted to organic production in 2000. By this time, she had graduated from the University of Wisconsin–Whitewater with a degree in social work. "I did social work for a year and quickly figured out I like cows a whole lot more than I like people," she laughs. However, by then she had also married and managed to talk her husband into dairy farming, which they took up in Virginia. "Both the marriage and the farm lasted about four years, so I brought the kids back home and bought out my brother's dairy herd. The timing was good because he was tired of dealing with moody cows and kept complaining that dairy farming was no different from having 200 wives telling him what to do all the time—and he was getting pretty fed up with that," she laughs.

The timing was also risky, because the wider economy was faltering and many farmers (and others) were predicting an economic recession just over the horizon. This prediction came true, which meant that Sadie had to struggle to get, and then to keep, the operation on its feet. Right away she began making adjustments to the business plan, including getting rid of the crossbreds and going back to purebred Holsteins, who are better milk producers." She also found that milking 200 cows was difficult to effectively manage. "Each cow has its own way of doing things, so what I was actually dealing with was 200 immature kids, and that's way too many," she laughs. "We were overcrowded and the heifers were suffering because they weren't getting the space they needed to eat and grow, so I either had to cull the herd or add to the size of the stall barn ... and given the size of our pasture and how many cows it could support, culling the herd made more sense ... so the extra cows went to New York and Missouri." Asked if it was hard to decide which cows to keep and which to sell, given they all have unique personalities, she explained that it was a purely business decision, and emotional attachments can't enter into it. "I honestly didn't spend time thinking about whether I was going to miss the ones that left— I just patted them on their butts and wished them good luck as they were loaded into the truck, and then sent them on their way," she explains.

Sadie also modified the calving operation, downsizing it to raising just 50 heifers a year, which is enough to replace the herd as it ages. She will sell the rest, meaning the herd will go back to being bred for seasonal calving, and not all cows will be lactating at the same time. "This entire operation is on me—I'm a single mother and I've got two kids, so we can't be calving all year," Sadie explains. "In practical terms, it doesn't work well for us to be calving in the cold of January and February or the heat of June and July." This doesn't mean she entirely escapes spending some nights in the barn. "Usually cows prefer giving birth alone, but when they're calving it's hard not to check on them every couple hours, particularly if it's the first one.... I know first babies are the hardest, and I guess I feel their pain," she chuckles. She also knows that assisting a 1500 pound heifer to deliver her first calf, which will weigh about 90 pounds, in the middle of a cold night can be a real challenge. "Sometimes the vet can't get to her quickly, so I just take a deep breath, pull the plastic glove on up to my armpit, and do what has to be done to get the calf out, calming the mother at the same time.... I'd say there isn't an obstetrician anywhere who's any better at calming down prospective mothers than I am," Sadie, who doesn't weigh a lot more than the calf does, boasts with a wink.

The entire dairy operation encompasses 1400 acres, enabling Sadie to grow her own feed, which makes adhering to the stringent organic standards much easier. "I crop farm 900 acres of hay, soy, corn, peas and potatoes—and the rest is pasture land ... and when I'm growing the feed and maintaining the pasture I'm certain it isn't being somehow contaminated ... and I can control the animal nutrition better, which is really important." She also uses her father's bio-ag company as a consulting firm when questions of animal nutrition arise. "Nutritional levels in the feed come from the soil up, so in the end, it's all about the soil," Sadie explains. Key elements, such as calcium, sulfur, boron and nitrogen need to be balanced in the proper proportion to grow healthy plants, and to keep them that way, plus control the insects. Healthy soil needs to contain a ratio of 10 parts nitrogen to one-part sulfur, which is optimal for the plant digestibility. "Research has shown that increasing feed's digestibility by five percent results in 2.7 pounds more milk per cow, per day, and through our land fertility program we have been able to achieve that."

The other issue is the quality of corn silage, which improved dramatically after Sadie purchased a kernel processor, which grinds the corn into a consistent size thus improving its digestibility. "Feeding one ton of silage produced this way should result in 3550 pounds of milk, which is great results," Sadie says, stressing that, in the end, it's still all about healthy pastures and healthy cows. "We chose pasture-based dairying to fit our standards for feeding high forage rations, maintaining herd health, and providing cow comfort, and I believe pasture-based dairying produces a better quality of animal life and therefore better milk … and let's face it, there's no fun in losing money and no fun in having sick cows."

Chasing the cows when they escape isn't fun either. "I'll never forget the Thanksgiving we were just sitting down to eat and one of the cows ran right past the window … followed by about 100 others, headed straight across the road for the creek. We left a half-sliced, 22 pound turkey on the table and all 15 of us, including the kids, put on boots and coats, and started chasing them in a driving snowstorm. We barricaded the road in 2 directions so nobody would hit one of the cows, or one of us, coming around the curve, and started wading in the creek, trying to coax them back.… I really didn't want them drinking the creek water, and they were acting like a bunch of alcoholics who just found a case of beer," Sadie giggles. "We ended up eating cold turkey sandwiches at midnight, and were too tired to care."

The Otter Creek farm plan is based on two basic rules: Do everything you can to get soils healthy and mineralized and do everything you can to get the livestock healthy and keep them comfortable. This has been achievable, but not without glitches. Something goes wrong every day, and the key is to try to contain whatever that is, Sadie explains, quickly adding that some things are beyond her ability to manage. "The 2012 drought was devastating—the cows didn't give nearly as much milk, and I sustained huge losses … but the 2008 flood was probably harder mentally. The entire farm was a giant mud hole. I had a lot more sick animals and a lot less milk, so the books didn't look good that year either … it didn't help that I was just getting the operation going and the economy went into recession that same year." As a result of the economic hit brought about by the drought she decided to invest in an irrigation system to help maintain the pasture. "And ever since then, we've had enough rain, so I've hardly had to use it," she laughs.

Historically Wisconsin has been known worldwide as America's

Dairyland, a claim that endures as a verifiable truth appearing on the state's license plates. While Wisconsin is where the national pride surrounding dairy farming thrives, the industry itself is struggling. In the last several years California has surpassed the state in both milk and cheese production. In the last 60 years, the number of Wisconsin dairy farms has dropped from 121,800 to 9,900 at the same time that milk production has increased 26 percent. Most of the farm loss has occurred among the smaller, family owned operations, resulting in fewer small dairy farms and more large operations consisting of 1000 or more cows. The smallest dairy farmers are those milking 49 or fewer cows, and statewide there are only 3,000 of those left. Nevertheless, in 2014 the dairy industry generated a record $43 billion for the state's economy, more than ever before.[8] And because of California's ongoing, severe drought, many feel Wisconsin will quickly move back into that the state feels is its rightful place at the forefront of the dairy industry.

Regardless of the statistics, Sadie believes that owning a smaller farm is a good agricultural career. "I need one full time person per 75 cows, so the operation can run on minimal help, if it's good help." She acknowledges that finding that good help can be challenging because she feels that in addition to having good milking skills and knowing the ins and outs of dairy farming, the individual's personality has to mesh well with the herd. "I know I can get along with them when I see them getting along well with the cows, so when I do find someone good who fits into the operation, I try very hard to keep them with me."

Nevertheless, production costs for feed, electricity, repairs and farm worker salaries create a law of diminishing returns that is holding Wisconsin's small dairy farmers back. Rough estimates are that dairy farms with 33 or fewer cows have per-cow production costs that are 16 percent higher than farms with 300 cows, 29 percent higher than farms with 700 cows, and over twice as high as farms milking 2200 cows, which is an industrial-sized dairy operation.[9] Clearly, for conventional dairy farmers, which are what most dairy farmers are, the key to profit is in the ability to implement economies of scale.

However, Wisconsin pride in being America's Dairyland has kept the small dairy farmer from giving up without a fight. Over time pride, commitment and a positive attitude toward the industry has served the state's dairy farmers well. Many have created niches for themselves by manufacturing their own artisan cheese or selling milk directly to specialty cheese producers, which is what Sadie does. Others promote agri-tourism by converting their farms into bed and breakfasts, vacation on the farm destinations, working with animal and plant genetics, or by producing enough income to meet expense and generating additional, needed income some other way.

No matter how you look at it, dairy farming is endless hard work, and not too many jobs can boast having the level of commitment a dairy farmer has, particularly since it won't make you rich. Regardless, few dairy farmers actually go bankrupt; instead, they retire and sell out to their neighbor, who folds the two herds together to create a larger operation. Another reality is that the many smaller farms don't meet today's conventional or organic milking standards and those farmers feel like they are too old to modify their operation by taking advantage of the tax credits that would enable them to modernize and incorporate the latest technology into their dairy farm to keep it alive. "Cows don't go on vacation, or even take a day off, so it's an intensely focused, hard life, but it's a good life—most of the time," Sadie says.

Clearly, not everyone would agree with Sadie that farming is, in fact, a "good life." There are certain core economic inequalities and contradictions embedded in the food system, and farmers remain at the center of that system, thus are vulnerable to the whiplash created by supply-side economics that govern market variance. Weather; local tastes, interests, and cultural preferences, not to mention the myriad of farming conditions that are beyond a farmer's control all come together at the point where costs collide with sales. A good crop year can result in surpluses that drive prices down, and a poor year can result in shortages that drive prices back up when the farmer has less crop output to sell. Nevertheless, food has become one of the defining issues of the current generation, and the idea of buying local, and eating organically, has gained enough cultural traction to have staying power to keep operations like Sadie's alive.

Regardless of all these variables and how they come into play in on the agricultural stage in any given year, I've yet to meet a farmer, male or female, who's in it for the profit, or looking to build wealth, so contriving a counter argument to Logsdon's non-profitability perspective is difficult. No question all farmers want to stay in the black, but they love what they do too much to allow economics to be the sole driver of their decisions. Moreover, women farmers are proud beyond words of their ability to earn a living at farming, and it's impossible to put a monetary value on that kind of well earned, well deserved pride and deep personal satisfaction.

"Getting into farming's not easy—you've got to be tough, and be comfortable making tough business decisions ... but I don't see any distinction between who's doing it—a man or a woman ... we all work hard, and we love farming, so we don't want to do anything else. Besides, we need farm-

ers and women can farm just as well as men can, so why not women farmers," Sadie smiles.

Dan Dail, former chair of the Animal Sciences Department at Southern Utah University concurs that women make fine farmers, and has seen
a distinct shift in the population demographics of aspiring young farmers.
"For a long time it was rare to have a female in the program; now it's much
more common—and the girls who do go into agriculture are really good
at it. I'd even go so far as to say that women students are generally better
at things like artificial insemination procedures than guys are."

The most obvious explanation for women's exceptional command of
the all-important reproductive technologies that have overtaken the livestock industry is that women, not men, are the ones who get pregnant. This
simple fact gives them a unique understanding of the reproductive process.
Another explanation might be that women, because they raise children,
might significantly outdistance men in terms of the ability to understand
animal behavior, as Sadie's approach to dairy farming indicates, and Temple
Grandin's powerful observations about animal behavior proves.[10]

Dr. Grandin's work on the flight zone and other principles of grazing
animal behavior has helped many people to reduce stress on their animals.
Other areas of her research include cattle temperament, environmental
enrichment for pigs, reducing dark cutters and bruises, bull fertility, training procedures, and effective stunning methods for cattle and pigs at meat
plants. Driving all of her research efforts is a remarkably unique understanding of how animals behave under stress, coupled with a desire to
mitigate stress effects so the animals suffer less as they fulfill their assigned
roles in the food system.

It is impossible to know whether men would have seen the same
things Dr. Grandin saw as she observed cattle on their way to the slaugh-
terhouses, interpreted her findings in the same way she did, or made the
same enduring and very valuable contributions to animal welfare she has
made. And it doesn't matter, because the irrefutable fact is that she was
the first one to do all of these things. It is impossible to overstate, or to
overvalue her contributions to animal welfare, livestock agriculture, and
general understanding of animal behavior.

Sadie firmly embraces the need to understand the animals you are
working with, and strongly believes that women make good livestock
farmers. "Women are mothers, and mothers intuitively know how to read
their kids ... transferring that intuitive knowledge to animals is automatic—it just comes naturally," she laughs.

Five

Voting with a Fork
Farming as a Political Statement

Eating ends an annual agricultural drama that begins with planting a seed into the ground.
> —Wendell Berry

Eating is a moral act. It reflects a deeply personal, individual decision about how we are going to nourish our body. Eating also makes a political statement. Each time we eat, every piece of food we put into our mouth reflects our values, our health concerns, our eating habits and our lifestyle. What we choose to eat identifies us as either a passive or an active participant in the agricultural enterprise that produces the food of which we are about to partake. It also reveals our level of concern with the processes by which food is produced, and whether we select and purchase our food accordingly.

Do you, the consumer, choose to ignore, or to pay attention to how fresh your food is, how and where it is grown, and how far away that place is from your table? Do you wonder about whether your food is pure or genetically modified? Are you concerned about how clean and free of pesticides, herbicides and other dangerous chemicals your food is? Do you worry about how it gets from the place where it is grown to the place where it is cooked or processed, before it finally finds its way to your table? Do you consider how much your food grower's marketing efforts add to your cost?

Most people who endeavor to eat only, or mostly, organic and locally grown food would say yes, they are concerned about all of these issues, and they spend their food dollars accordingly. Those who give less thought to the mechanics of the food system are likely to answer these questions with a blank stare.

Confining food choices to only that which is organically produced involves a serious commitment to allowing food to become a big-ticket item in the household budget. Eating locally grown food almost always costs more than consuming large-scale, mass-produced food. There is also the issue of processed foods almost always including additives and preservatives that add to, or take away from, the food's quality and nutritional value. Small farmers who sell locally don't have to factor huge transportation costs into their prices, but they can't take advantage of the economies of scale available to large, industrial farming operations either, so their production costs are always higher. This is a lot to think about before sitting down to breakfast every morning, and the reality is that most people rarely, if ever, think about these questions at all.

How food is grown or produced, is also extremely political, particularly when the term "political" is defined as who gets what, how they get it, and who profits from the transaction? From this perspective, any discussion of food raises questions not just about quality, quantity, or value, but also about the farming infrastructure, specifically who controls it, and how it controls others? Other important questions concern who defines the dominant food culture, who is well fed, who is hungry, and who suffers from diet-related diseases such as diabetes, high cholesterol, hypertension and obesity? Most of the time government regulations and profit-motive agricultural economics set the parameters of the discussion around all of these questions—but not always.

The wild card in the food politics game is America's love affair with fast food. We are a highly driven, fast-paced nation whose behavior is controlled by competitive, free-enterprise, profit-motive capitalist economics. In behavioral terms, the first person out of the gate has the best chance of being the first one across the economic finish line, thereby winning the race to claim the biggest profit margin. In practical terms this means that, in order to compete in the economic game, we show up for work early, work long days, and stop off at a drive-through take-out for something quick and easy to eat in the car on the way home. Complicating mealtimes further is the fact that most families' need for two incomes means that, in most cases, both parents are employed long hours, so taking the kids through the fast food drive-up window on the way home from picking them up at day care is faster and easier than finding the time to grocery shop and prepare nutritious evening meals at home. There's also the comfort-food factor. After a long, stressful day, a broiled chicken breast, green salad and vegetable stir-fry really doesn't hit the spot in quite the same way a greasy cheeseburger and fries, washed down with a sugar and caffeine loaded soda and topped off with an ice cream cone, does.

These are the circumstances those who wish to change the current American food system are up against. Nevertheless, a growing number of small, independent farming operations, run mostly by women, are pushing up hard against the growing trend toward less nutritious food. These enterprising initiatives are placing Mother Nature's daughters front and center in a growing effort to take back the control of the food system they previously enjoyed, during the era when women planted gardens in order to feed their families fresh, wholesome food they prepared themselves, in their own kitchens, every day.

Several aspects of modern agriculture are coming together to pave the way for modern women farmers to succeed more than ever before. But attempting to change the food system and the rules of the food politics game involves much more than just addressing farming methods. Taking on this herculean task demands careful attention to the ethics of modern agriculture which govern how food is produced. Examination of consumer costs, environmental pollution assessment, sustainability, and concerns for both worker and animal rights all are equally important components of this conversation.

Tension arises when the industrial model of food production goes head to head with the agricultural ideals underpinning an agrarian social philosophy that views farming as a way of life that can shape right-thinking social values. Central to the agrarian philosophy is the belief that the simplicity of rural life is superior to the complexities of urban life. Accordingly, the independent farmer is highly valued, both as the chief participant in this way of life and as the backbone of food production, which is the economic mainstay of rural economics.

Agrarianism is also a political philosophy in that it proposes land redistribution from the rich to the poor or landless and views the agricultural enterprise as vitally important to establishing the base rhythms and character of society—a notion Thomas Jefferson profoundly agreed with. In the Democracy Jefferson envisioned, farmers make the best citizens because they do not live portable lives. Instead, they invest in land, which deepens their ties with and commitment to the communities in which they live and, ideally, will remain throughout their lives.

In today's world, building an agrarian society that is sensitive to the nature of the food production system requires women farmers to assume leadership positions at all levels of public engagement surrounding food, including food advocacy. Women are starting sustainable food businesses as well as urban agriculture projects that simultaneously flow in two directions—growing food for distribution to the urban poor and providing support to urban poor who want to grow their own food, in their own garden. "It's becoming more and more clear that we can't separate [food] production from social justice issues," says Danielle Nierenberg, cofounder of Food Tank, a food-policy think tank.[1] "Food needs to be safe, farmers, both women and men, need fair wages, and it needs to be environmentally sustainable."

However, there are other performers in this ongoing food drama. "Subsidy policies originally set in place to benefit conventional farmers are being criticized by consumer advocates who want food to be nutritious as well as cheap, by environmentalists who oppose conventional farming methods, and also by a new generation of alternative farmers promoting production systems that are small-scale, diversified, local, and organic. In this setting a new political dynamic emerges whereby food advocates push hard to bring their alternative preferences into the mainstream," explains food policy analyst Robert Paarlberg.[2] To the extent that "all politics is local" most food politics are focused locally, because purchasing locally grown food keeps money in local communities, Paarlberg stresses.

Not only is eating a moral act, purchasing food is a moral statement. The food we select and pay for is a reflection of the importance we assign to social justice as a personal value. "A person espouses their morals by the very act of purchasing food to eat," claims farmer and author Wendell Berry.[3] "Was it grown or 'manufactured,'" he asks. "Does the food producer employ fair labor practices, and is land, water or air potentially harmed to provide this food? In purchasing our food, are we keeping money in our own communities or sending it across this continent or either ocean?"

Berry contends that it is difficult to understand a local food economy without interacting with it at the most intimate level, the local farmers' market. This is where the farmer sells to the consumer, and they both get to know one another personally because they do business together week after week. Only then is it possible to really grasp the difference one sale makes to a family farm operating without paid staff and heavily dependent upon local buyers. This is, in Berry's view, the essence of a local farm economy.

By contrast, each time a local consumer purchases vegetables that are grown in far distant fields cultivated by unknown, low-wage laborers her or she is saying that worker justice is not an important personal value. Each time a consumer buys meat from animals that are reared thousands of miles away, under unknown conditions, that consumer is casting a vote against the livelihood of the local grower and in favor of mass-produced, less healthy food. And each time an individual chooses to eat in a chain restaurant rather than a locally owned one, he or she is voting in favor of an industrially-based food supply chain.

The current movement to change the food system represents not only a concern for social justice, it represents political action at its finest—and is proudly led by women who understand that "you are what you eat." Daily these women are acting heroically to ensure that consumers are given the opportunity to make healthy choices to eat trustworthy food, and are saving our health and local farm economies, all at the same time.

Hazzard-Free Farming: Idealism in Action

Whether the issue is ecological, environmental or economical, without sustainability we fail the future.
—Andrea Hazzard

"The state of our food system is a very passionate issue for me," 39-year-old heritage grain farmer Andrea Hazzard earnestly proclaims. We are sitting around a beat up oak table in her 100-year-old four-square farmhouse, drinking herbal tea. An old oil furnace blasts out much needed heat into the dining room, while a large white duck limps around, looking for a comfortable spot to get off her sore foot. The duck shoots off a couple loud quacks at me before mysteriously deciding her preferred resting place is under my chair, next to my left shoe.

Andrea was born and raised on this north-central Illinois farm, which has been in her family for 160 years, since Franklin Pierce was President of the United States. Less than 50 yards from the house, under a huge bur oak tree that reaches both upward to the heavens and outward to encompass the surrounding land, is the final resting for Andrea's grandparents and other family members, most recently, her mother. A wide creek near the back runs through the property, conveniently providing the animals with a natural drinking fountain.

Other than spending a few years in California, Andrea has never lived anywhere else. She grew up driving a tractor and mowing hay. Her mother taught her gardening and canning, her grandparents taught her the chicken business, and she helped with their fruit trees. Local 4H leaders taught her everything else about life on a farm. "The adults sent us outside all the time, no matter the weather. We were wiry kids who could climb anything and disappear into the fields and creeks for hours. It's in my blood to be in cahoots with Mother Nature," she smiles.

Andrea Hazzard hand hoes several acres of vegetables on Hazzard Free Farms during the growing season (courtesy Andrea Hazzard).

"I remember vividly as a child the wooden bins of grain in the barn and in the loft of the corn crib, the heavy, silken feeling of them as you thrust your arm in, the dust in the air as the sun streamed through the window. It's a smell I can't quite capture for you," she explains. "I guess it's a bit beyond words. I remember stuffing my pockets full to spirit some to the horses and chew them as I made my childhood rounds about the farm. I would go to the corn crib with my grandfather Earl Hazzard and choose a few ears of corn; we would shell them in the sunshine then trundle across the yard and down to the basement. Grandpa would get the hand crank grinder out and we would make cornmeal. Up the stairs we would go to deliver it to my grandmother, Marguerite, and she would make us corn cakes on her little iron skillet and later, for dinner, we would have cornbread. The cornbread recipe on my packaged cornmeal was adapted from her recipe, and her skillet is here in my kitchen as we speak. The lessons they taught me continue on through my beliefs and my work."

While she definitely has a strong connection with Mother Nature, Andrea has equally powerful feelings about what she believes is the dangerously sorry state of America's food system. "It is incredibly irresponsible of our society to burden our children with improper food and nutrition that will cause them a whole host of diseases and problems as they age ... it's not fair to kids and it really comes down to the fact that corporate food producers want to make money for their stockholders, and are sacrificing the health of an entire generation of children to do it," Andrea bristles.

Not only does she find the realization that corporate agriculture is being allowed to get away with their well-developed profit-motive approach to feeding the nation horrifying, Andrea also has a great deal of trouble understanding why this is happening in this country. She can't understand why people are not screaming in the streets over the issue. "Big business food production is a lie, and nobody cares enough to call them on it," she laments.

Problems with the food system have consumed Andrea's thinking for years, and it was the intensity of her desire to stop ignoring these issues and start doing something about them that drew her back to her family farm in 2007, eventually plunging her into actively farming—her way, and on her terms. "For me it has always been about so much more than growing food or farming," she explains earnestly. "Farming was a good place to start but it's expensive, so if I really wanted to do it, I had to leave California and come back home, where land was available to me." When she came to this decision Andrea was 31 years old, with a college degree in agriculture and considerable work-related experience. She acknowledges that, after nearly a decade of hard work on the farm, it remains surprisingly difficult for her to stay financially afloat.

"It is really hard because the price of food in our country is not real, and does not reflect the effort it takes to grow it organically on a small scale—at least it never has for me. I am still not financially solvent and it scares me to death ... and whether or not I succeed will depend not just on how good a business person and farmer I am, but also on whether or not human beings can learn to see the earth for what it is, a self-regulating system that is solar driven and exhaustible in its support of our species. I just hope that my life's work eventually leads to answers that can sustain us for the long term."

Andrea began her Hazzard Free Farm operation on eight acres of the home farm, raising vegetables she sold from a farm stand on her road, and at farmers' markets. "Vegetables are pretty labor intensive, making them expensive to grow," she says. "To keep up with everything the way I should I need five employees working full time in summer, at ten or eleven dollars per hour, and that adds up fast—so the logical business decision was to start phasing out most of the vegetables, which I'm just beginning to do, and start raising a less labor-intensive crop."

As she transitions away from raising garden vegetables Andrea's focus has shifted to raising 30 acres of heritage grains. This presents different challenges from purely organic vegetable farming, not the least of which is the issue of finding enough seed. "The seed is expensive and I need 20–30 pounds per acre, which is nearly a half ton total—and so far I haven't been able to buy it in bulk, which would be quite a lot cheaper than what I'm paying now."

Nevertheless, Andrea feels the expense associated with her enterprise is worth it. "Heritage grains are the most pure, and produce the best food, because they have higher nutrient content and aren't genetically modified," she explains. "We opt only for ancient, open-pollinated or heirloom varieties, and organic foundation seed is planted whenever it's available. I never use chemical pesticides, herbicides, insecticides or fungicides."

Andrea's resolve to grow ancient grains is remarkable. "I am deeply committed to adapting heirloom grains to our soils and our farming practices. It can take three to five years, or more, to do this, but these crops are incredibly adaptable over time and well worth the effort. Our invest-

After harvesting the grain fields on Hazzard Free Farm, they are carefully prepared for the winter. Some grains are planted in fall in order to be harvested in early spring (courtesy Andrea Hazzard).

ment in this process is definitely a risk but I believe it will pay off in the health and ecological benefits to our land, our products, the sustainable farming community and our customers' health."

It has turned out that raising grain is easier than growing vegetables in some ways and more complicated in others. "Vegetables have to go out as fresh as possible, and with grain you don't have to worry about that. But, there are storage issues with grain, plus the federal government carefully monitors the milling aspect of grain production ... the hard part there is that I have to be really careful not to mix the different varieties during the milling process—there's no going back and fixing it if I do make a mistake" Andrea explains. "For small farms, packaging and selling grain retail isn't terribly profitable because it's so labor-intensive ... everything has to be individually hand packaged and labeled in eight or sixteen ounce packages, Bulk grain sales are more profitable simply because bagging the grain reduces the production overhead costs," she adds, noting that she figured out the drying and milling processes herself.

Hazzard Free Farm places sustainability first and foremost. "We are proud to bring customers a wide variety of high-quality heirloom grains grown in the organic tradition and stone ground using age-old techniques," Andrea explains. "The beauty of the local foods movement is transparency. And as the movement continues to flourish, we encourage our customers to visit the farm with family and friends and see how we do what we do."

The whole grains are always stone milled to preserve taste and quality. This means avoiding the high-heat conditions that alter flavors and nutrients, and which are found in many industrial mills. Andrea's milled flours contain the germ and bran, and are unbromated, unbleached and unaltered by the addition of additives. "Our oats taste like no other, they are nutty, rich, and alive. Our rolled oats are never steamed, a process that removes nutritious flavorful natural oils in favor of longer shelf lives," she points out.

Because the flours, cornmeal, polenta, wheat, emmer, barley, berries, groats and rolled oats are fresh, they are also perishable. Like all naturally grown grains, they contain the germ, bran and natural oils that nature intended and, unless preservatives are added, which Andrea refuses to do, they must be refrigerated or, preferably, frozen for long-term storage, which adds to the production costs. The processing facility, located in a corner of the largest of several majestic old barns on the farm, is regularly inspected by the State of Illinois Department of Health. A Hazard Analysis and Critical Control Point Plan (HACCP) is in place. "We carry full product liability and are happy to provide a certificate upon request." She adds that she does not allow the grain products to be re-packaged or resold as seed for sprouting or planting

Wholesale grain prices range from $8 per pound for purple barley flour sold in 5 to 24 pound quantities to $1.75 per pound for triticum hard red wheat berries ($2.00 per pound ground) sold in quantities of 5 to 24 pounds. The prices drop as quantities increase, up to 100 pound sacks. Retail prices range from $7.50 for 14 ounces of purple barley flour to $2.74 for 12 ounces of triticum hard red wheat berries; 14 ounces of the traditional grind red wheat is $3.08.

Most of Andrea's retail sales occur in the three to five farmers' markets in the Chicago area that she frequents. Her market overhead includes transportation costs and a market participation fee that ranges from $160 to $200 per market day, for each market; anything over that amount, minus transportation cost, is profit. "I don't make much money at the farmers' markets, but they foster good connections to wholesalers and restaurants in the Chicago and Rockford areas."

Andrea acknowledges that her transportation costs are significant because Chicago is 110 miles east of the farm, and requires over two hours driving time on the heavily traveled, frequently backed-up Illinois Tollway. Rockford is about 25 miles from the farm and while getting there does not involve driving the tollway it does involve traveling slower roads with frequent stops that result in less efficient gas mileage. Nevertheless, both locations represent considerable travel distance to reach a retail market opportunity in a state where gas prices are always higher than the nationwide average, and the tollway is perpetually under construction. Despite the time and travel costs involved, Andrea feels the effort is worth every mile. "My customers are incredibly appreciative.... I get thank-you notes all the time, and plenty of kind words in public ... it's very satisfying ... and means a lot," she smiles.

"I love raising grains, but it's not easy ... soil amendments are an ongoing issue and sometimes I have to make hard business decisions because the operating costs are about $10,000 per acre, which is almost exactly what it costs to purchase an acre of farmland around here," she says. After eight years, she still isn't turning a profit and has lost any sense of romantic idealism about running her own farm operation. "I think it was my third year of farming, when the place was overflowing with weeds and I was putting in long, hard and tedious days and I was getting really discouraged. I was not winning and things looked really ugly on paper. My dad stopped by and we sat by the greenhouse and talked ... technically

I think he yelled about the weeds, but as we both calmed down and really started to talk in depth about what was going on with the fields and crops, sales, disease problems, and all the rest.... I admitted I was about to give up—but my dad said not to.... I hold that day dear in my heart because it was one of those days when you find yourself alone in your fields facing all of your mistakes, lack of knowledge, idealism and mostly your dreams are melting back into Mother Nature right before your eyes ... and my dad told me to keep going anyway ... it meant a lot."

Because she could not qualify for a bank loan, Andrea's father has bankrolled the operation from the outset, and he continues to be the financial backbone of the business. "It's always been hard working with Dad because conventional farming is so different from trying to grow many different crops, each having unique needs, which is what the vegetable operation has been. The conventional farming that Dad grew up with is like raising 5 children: two [corn and beans] require similar care and the other three [wheat, oats, and alfalfa] require almost none. Sales and marketing is simple—you call up the granary and you sell the crop, or feed it to your animals, which you will eventually sell, and the rest you'll eventually send to market."

Raising vegetables makes Andrea's farming model entirely different from her father's commodity crop farming operation. Vegetables involve seven to ten different families of plants (maybe more) with parent plants that need little care once established and start producing their children, which need much more care in the beginning, and much less as they mature. "Within each family is a set of plants which could have extremely different needs at different times," she explains.

"Alliums for example: Garlic needs to be planted in the fall and harvested midsummer. You have to sort and break your bulbs into cloves, mark your rows and plant, mulch, lay irrigation, weed usually twice lightly, if you mulched enough with straw that didn't still have grain seeds in it, and then remove the flowering heads. Then you harvest it, usually by forking it out and sorting the plants by bulb size and cleaning the mud and dirt off as best you can. You tie them into groups and hang them in a drying shed, carefully labeling them so as to not lose track of your varieties. As they dry you trim the roots, once dry you cut the tops, one by one with a pruning nips for hard neck or a garden scissors for soft neck and you strip the outer papers to make them as clean as possible. They are now ready for sale—and in terms of profit per pound, these are low maintenance vegetables."

Egyptian walking onions are another example of how complicated vegetable farming can be. "They are also in the allium family—a biannual onion that sets babies in the soil and on top of the plant, and you need to tend them seasonally usually two times a year, other than weeding and harvesting and watering," Andrea explains. "But the big onions need to be started from seed, typically in January, and planted outside in April, and they require a lot of weeding and watering. Then they have to be cured and cleaned, which we do all by hand ... and they can do well or not, depending on the weather ... and to insure we at least have some onions, there are also pearl, Cippolini and bunching onions, and the leeks, of which there are many annual and perennial varieties. That's a lot of crops in one small family ... and the Solanaceae family has all of the tomatoes, potatoes, eggplant and peppers plus some other, less common plants. It's incredibly overwhelming and yet it's also exhilarating ... but marketing and sales are all on me. There's nobody I can call and say 'Hey I have 200 pounds of Chinese cabbage to sell you.... I have to figure it all out myself.'"

Andrea says the money conversations with her dad continue periodically, and always get around to the same question: why does she keep doing what she is doing when she isn't making any money? "One day Dad asked me 'why do you keep doing this when you continue to lose money?' My response is always 'because you told me not to give up, and because this is the only thing in the world I want and because that's what you and Mom did ... and I'm a hands on person, not a desk person. I need to be outside getting my hands dirty."

Although the farm continues to struggle, Andrea puts tremendous energy into promoting healthy local food. Working with the University of Illinois Cooperative Extension Service Local Foods Program has brought her some successes. Her efforts resulted in Illinois food stamp recipients now being able to use their benefits to purchase fresh food from local farmers' markets throughout the state. Additionally, several urban gardening efforts have sprung up in her area. Her favorite is the Roots & Wings Network, which grows organic vegetables, while motivating, educating, and inspiring youth and adults to be leaders and role models in their communities. "I've been working with Roots and Wings in the city of Rockford, helping area kids grow organic vegetables ... what they did was create a free CSA [community supported agriculture market] in an urban neighborhood that allows seniors at the Booker T. Washington Senior Center to receive free vegetables every week during the summer. The kids learned how to keep records, meet with their customers to see if they were satisfied, and so on—it was a total win-win all around," she proudly explains. The kids agree. "We learn all kinds of things that will help us later in life, says Kolten Luvert, a Roots and Wings youth leader.[4] "I've been helping to sell our veggies at the farmer's market for a few years, and now I get to teach new youth leaders."

"If you take one thing away from our conversation, think about this," Andrea tells me as I prepare to leave. "To say that it doesn't matter whether or not your food is sprayed with chemicals is insane. The chemicals are still in your environment if not yours somebody else's. Sure they all have FDA [Food and Drug Administration] allowances but the FDA only tests one chemical at a time. Truth is that each crop can be sprayed with a whole host of different chemicals and they won't all be detected because the FDA isn't testing for them all. Now for the math: add those to all the chemicals in the air, water, your facial cream, cleaning supplies, the chemicals leaching off of the carpeting, paint, upholstery and on and on. Your body is teeming with all of those tiny or not so tiny amounts of seen, and unseen, chemicals. They come in through your nose, your mouth and your skin. Once in your body they can combine in any number of ways that we do not understand. No one is truly protecting you, certainly not your government … eventually it is the consumers who will have to change the food system." Clearly Andrea is working extremely hard to do her part to improve the food system.

Grassroots Organic Farm: Courage in Action

> *I've always had concerns about the food system, but I haven't always known what I could do about it.*
> —Gail Carpenter

"This farm looks like a Van Gogh painting," Gail Carpenter tells me while we are standing at the top of the hill overlooking her 40-acre plot of land. "Actually," I tell her, "to me it looks like something Grandma Moses, or maybe Norman Rockwell, would fall in love with."

Gail is obviously proud of the business she operates as the mother half of a mother-daughter farm business partnership and modestly dismisses the role raw courage has played in bringing Grassroots Farm to life. She doesn't dwell on the fact that she undertook this project in her mid–50s, without ever having farmed before in her life either. "It was something my daughter, Lindsey, really wanted to do, and it fit well with my interest in healthy food, so when she proposed the idea of a farm of our own, I listened to her ideas very carefully," she says.

While father-son farm operations are not too unusual, mother-daughter farm partnerships are rare. They are even rarer when, as in the Carpenters' case, farming is not an inherited business, neither partner comes from a rural farming community, and neither has ever owned, or managed, a small business. Instead, farming is a purposeful lifestyle choice Gail and Lindsey each has made. Gail jumped in feet first, without any prior experience or knowledge about living off the land to guide her. Lindsey, on the other hand, had some internship and farm job experience to guide her, which created an unusual power balance in their partnership. "Lindsey definitely knew more about what we were about to attempt than I did, and I had to listen to her advice ... usually it's the other way around and mothers are telling their daughters what to do," Gail admits with a shrug. "But we worked it out."

However, Lindsey's path to becoming a farmer took a circuitous route. "Lindsey started off pursuing an education in studio fine arts, and she's quite a talented artist, as well as a high achiever," Gail, 63, says of her 29-year-old daughter. "She attended two private art schools in Philadelphia before she moved back to the Midwest and 'stumbled' into a summer farm job in Stoughton, Wisconsin. That's when she fell in love with daily life as an organic vegetable farmer. She likes the rhythm of the seasons, and the endless supply of fresh veggies," Gail laughs. "Somewhere along the way she set her heart on owning her own farm someday."

Gail's back-story is different. Divorced for many years, she currently works as an administrative assistant in a downtown Chicago law firm, lives with her sister in a Chicago suburb during the week and farms on weekends. "It's just under 150 miles from Chicago to here, and I don't mind the drive at all—in fact, I love it ... except in a snowstorm," she explains, failing to mention that routine Chicago tollway traffic insures that this a nearly always a four-hour drive.

After five years of internships, apprenticeships, and eventually farm management training, Lindsey felt ready try her hand at running a farm operation on her own. She knew the time spent on farms located in south central Wisconsin, a northern suburb of Chicago, and on an urban farm on the south side of Chicago had taught her what she needed to know to begin farming on her own. Her stumbling block was she needed land to do it, and she didn't have any. "The more I thought about it, the more the idea of helping her get started appealed to me," Gail explains. "So we began looking for acreage, which was surprisingly expensive, particularly closer to Chicago."

In 2007 they found what they were looking for, snugly situated among

Lindsey (left) and Gail Carpenter proudly post the fence line along the boundaries of Grassroots Organic Farm, warning neighboring farmers to take care not to contaminate their land when spraying and fertilizing (courtesy Gail Carpenter).

the rolling hills of Green County, Wisconsin, an area of the state left untouched by the glaciers. The countryside is remarkably pristine, providing a setting for an organic farm operation so perfect that it would be hard to imagine anything else happening there. The influence of the original Swiss immigrants who settled the area in the 19th century because it reminded them of their native Switzerland is evident everywhere. A surprising number of the locals are quite adept at imitating Swiss goat herder by yodeling to call their animals back home, which is practice for the annual yodeling contest—the major highlight of the Green County fair every summer that brings thousands to the area. The number of Swiss-German restaurants in the closest town, famously known for its beer and cheese, outnumber most other businesses.

"I think when Lindsey came upon these 40 acres, somewhat accidentally as it turned out, and 'knew' this was the place she wanted, it was partly because it really appealed to her artistic sensibilities," Gail reflects. "I could see it too … it really reminds me of a place where, upon coming over this hill, Van Gogh would've sat down and painted what he saw, because it is so beautiful."

Eventually they found a way to buy the land, even though it wasn't located exactly where they'd hoped to be, and meant building the farm operation from the ground up—literally. "All we had to start with was the barn," Gail says, admitting that while it is a grand old barn in the finest Wisconsin tradition of stone foundations and painted wood siding, they weren't sure what to do with it. Often, it felt like they were flying blind, and in some ways they were. They lacked the security that comes with having an experienced farmer to reassure them and offer advice and counsel as they undertook the vast and complex decision-making processes that they were both counting on to eventually result in a successful farm operation.

Once they had developed an initial, working business plan, Gail and Lindsey's next goal was to observe and get to know the land and all its idiosyncrasies. In keeping with farmer Jerry Apps belief that observing the land is paramount in getting to know it, and to learning the lessons Mother nature has to teach, this period of observation was not only very important to the new land owners, it was also a very wise decision. "The land talks to us—tells us stories, and has a message it wants us to hear, but you have to know how to listen for the story," Apps says.[5] "Listen for the whispers and look in the shadows for a whole other world … soon you'll know that the right time to plant corn in spring is when the oak leaf is the size of a squirrel's ear, and that if geese aren't flying north and south, something's wrong somewhere nearby, and you need to stop and figure out what it is."

In May 2008, Lindsey moved a second-hand camping trailer onto the land, locating it right next to the barn, which had an electrical connection and a water source. This provided a roof over her head that first summer, but it was only a temporary solution to her housing problem and wasn't going to work once winter set in and the snow began to fly. Because this is rural farm country where houses are both few and far apart, finding a livable house nearby became both a pressing and a challenging problem. The "work in progress" farmhouse Gail and Lindsey eventually bought, four miles from the farm itself, was a significant add-on to the first-year farm operation expenses.

"The first year we rented the pasture to a herdsman raising Belted Galloway cattle, which gave us a little income while we planned improvements, mended fences, explored financial opportunities, and acquired equipment. In June 2008 we registered as Grassroots Farm, LLC, a Wisconsin limited liability company, and the rest is history, so they say," Gail smiles. She adds that the farm's agricultural goals are in concert with a small, diverse, closed circuit, full diet farm, similar to the farmsteads operated in the Green County area when the Swiss first settled. In Gail's mind, this farming style is the ideal method for managing and maintaining a healthy food system, and she derives great satisfaction from being an active participant in creating that food system.

By February 2009, Grassroots Farm's business plan was well enough developed that Lindsey felt ready to bring the farm into production. Although it was winter, she constructed a seedling greenhouse near the old barn. A serendipitous referral to a connection in Chicago led to an invitation to participate in the first year of a neighborhood Farmer's Market in Andersonville, IL, a metropolitan Chicago neighborhood located a few miles north of Wrigley Field, just west of Lake Michigan. "Our farmer's market business continued to grow with the Andersonville market, and became a multifaceted enterprise. We discussed food issues and politics, swapped recipes, and gave direction on preparation and use of the produce and herbs on the market table," Lindsey, who drove three hours each way to participate in this opportunity, explains.

A year later, in the spring of 2010, Grassroots Farm received a Frontera Farmer's Foundation grant that made it possible to construct a 24' × 30', two story aluminum pole barn that serves as a vegetable processing shed. This same year Lindsey added the first season of Community Supported Agriculture (CSA) program[6] to the business mix, bringing pre-paid share boxes to members in Chicago, which is southeast of the farm, and in Madison, Wisconsin, about 100 miles north. The CSA component adds considerable travel time and mileage costs onto the farm operation, but it is still financially viable, Gail explains. "People seem to really like knowing who grows their food, and they enjoy developing a relationship with that person, so are willing to go out of their way a little to support their farm."

Later that year the farm operation received a Natural Resource Conservation Service grant to build a high tunnel greenhouse, which Lindsey completed in November. This enabled the farm to increase its vegetable production substantially, as well as to plant earlier in the spring. As a result, CSA share members were able to start receiving spring vegetables sooner, which extended their season. "Throughout the year 2011, we added livestock to the diversity of products. Certified organic eggs were available to our customers from April through October, until our mature flock of laying hens made a trip to an 'old chicks' retirement home near Whitewater, Wisconsin. We made arrangements for acquiring a new flock for the upcoming season," Lindsey explains, adding that she also raised 8 Duroc-Hampshire cross pigs for market that year, which enabled the business to offer fresh, frozen and smoked pork cuts as part of its product mix.

Meanwhile, Gail and Lindsey both were quickly learning that raising hogs present unique, unexpected challenges, mostly because they each have distinct personalities and are smarter, and more stubborn, than most people give them credit for. "In the early spring Miss P, our very large Duroc-Hampshire sow, became the proud mother of 7 piglets, born in a makeshift sty adjacent to the house. They were cute as a button, of course, and, like all baby animals stuck close to their mother. It's close quarters and a week or two before it was time to wean the piglets and transport the entire family to the larger quarters down at the farm, we had a hard nighttime rainstorm that left us with deep mud everywhere. Early the next morning, Lindsey got a call from our neighbor Tom, asking if we might be missing some pigs? She didn't think so, but went out to the sty and discovered a hole in the corner of the fence, where the hog panels didn't quite meet. Apparently the piglets had escaped and when mamma discovered this, she corralled them into a very large mud puddle at the foot of Tom's driveway.

"Tom doesn't farm and had no clue how to solve this problem, so Lindsey called her friend Adam and asked him to come over and take a look at the situation and help make a plan. The solution they came up with involved Lindsey and Adam each picking up a slippery, squealing piglet, and running back up the hill, figuring Miss P would charge them and the other piglets would follow her. Pigs don't herd well—actually cats are easier to herd than pigs—and this idea just didn't work. Eventually they managed to get three of piglets back in the pen, but their mother wasn't budging, probably because trudging back up the hill would require her to exert her huge self well beyond her customary efforts. Lindsey was covered in mud and out of ideas. Then, at noon, which was near her usual mealtime, Miss P nudged the remaining piglets out of the mud hole, pulled herself out behind them, and began trotting back up the hill. The piglets all fell in behind her, and at that point they all willingly re-entered the sty.... I suppose if we'd left them alone, they'd probably have all come back on their own as soon as Miss P got hungry enough to want lunch," Gail laughs.

Before attempting to raise any more pigs Lindsey built a 12' × 16' hog pasture range house, which is larger and more comfortable than the sty near the house. She also constructed a multipurpose moveable livestock shelter she uses to house turkeys and added 12' onto the transplant production greenhouse. This greenhouse addition proved both fortuitous and wise, because the protections the greenhouse afforded the plants enabled the farm to successfully honor its CSA contracts for the entire

Lindsey Carpenter's goal is raising happy animals. She situated her chicken house facing a field of flowers she grows to include in the CSA share boxes her customers receive weekly, giving the chickens a pleasant environment (photograph by the author).

season despite the severe drought Wisconsin and the rest of the Upper Midwest experienced during that summer. "Our farmers' market revenue was affected the worst that year—the weather was too extreme to keep up with previous years' flow of customers. Consequently, after doing some math we made the tough decision to discontinue farmers' market sales this year and focus more on diversifying our farm operation. We began offering our fresh organic veggies exclusively to our CSA customers and minimally through wholesale arrangements with nearby grocers and restaurants," Gail notes.

That same year the farm was able to deliver whole, fresh and frozen turkey and goat's milk-fed pork to their CSA customers. After success with a pilot batch of 35 broad-breasted white turkeys, fed only organic feed, grazing in organic pastures, and raised from day-old poults, the farm was able to expand turkey production sufficiently to open sales to the public during the 2013 season. "Our pork production continues to expand and we have been able to keep back a female to breed in an effort to keep our costs down and create a more sustainable farm system," Gail explains. She withholds offering an opinion on Lindsey's habit of naming the animals and talking to them on a regular basis, making them all seem like they are household pets.

"During the 2013 season, the farm shifted into a new marketing plan that includes a single season summer CSA vegetable share, a fresh brown egg share, a cut-flower bouquet share, and a Thanksgiving share, with or without one of our own turkeys. Thanks to the help of a UW [University of Wisconsin]–Stevens Point intern Jacob, we constructed a permanent turkey shelter to house as many as 75 turkeys and also converted an old fashioned barge box wagon to a mobile chicken coop, which houses our mixed breed flock of rainbow egg layers," Gail says proudly, with business manager precision.

However, in practical terms the operation, which now includes a five and one half acre vegetable market garden, two and one half acres of prairie restoration, two orchards containing 20 apple trees each, and 30 acres of pasture, has grown larger and more diverse than this mother-daughter team can manage by themselves. They had to come up with a creative, low-cost solution to meet their need for additional farm labor. After considering several options, they decided the answer was to develop a cadre of volunteer workers they would pay in farm produce instead of dollars. "For every four to six-hour day a volunteer worker puts in he or she can take home as much produce as that week's CSA single share customer receives, and, so far, the plan has worked pretty well," Gail says.

What she doesn't point out is that simply being in the farm's peaceful work environment is its own attraction, even if volunteering didn't include receiving free food.

The other ingenious way Lindsey solved the farm's labor shortage problem was to offer hands-on farm internships to aspiring farmers. "A farming internship is an excellent way to learn many skills of the trade without enrolling in a formal education program," she explains. "Over the last few years it seems many farms have shifted away from the internship model and rely primarily on full and part time employees and/or formal work share agreements. As a past intern of small-scale, diversified and organic vegetable farming myself, I still believe it is an excellent step in the right direction for people who are very interested in pursuing dreams of starting a farm of their own."

Lindsey and Gail developed the internship program in such a way that it offers a wide variety of in-depth experiences in all aspects of the organic farming enterprise, and figured out a clever way to make it pay on both sides. "We are looking for self-motivated, weather-hardy, nature loving, curious individuals with good communication skills and a strong desire to learn by doing. Our interns must be interested in learning our methods of farming with some idea of starting an operation of their own someday. We find this to be an essential quality because much of the value of an internship is lost when the individual does not think the educational opportunity is important," Lindsey stresses. Anyone interested in working as a farm intern must apply for the program.

In addition to a full season of hands-on learning, intern compensation for a maximum of 30 hours per week of farm labor from April through October includes a monthly stipend, a large, furnished upstairs farmhouse room, a shared bathroom, free internet access and use of a large farm kitchen. A bicycle is available to travel the nearly four miles between the farmhouse and the farm fields. In financial terms, the total compensation package includes a $300 per month stipend, $180 per month food credit, a $350 per month housing credit and a "priceless, one-of-a-kind educational experience."

This plan has allowed the partnership to expand its operation, and in 2015 they will be offering over 75 varieties of vegetables, fruits, common and rare fresh herbs. They have also added humanely raised animal products, including naturally raised pork, free range rainbow eggs, pastured chicken, turkey and goose, grass-fed beef, and lamb, and honey to their product list.

From the outset Gail and Lindsey both have been clear in their own minds regarding their deeply-felt farming philosophy, values and goals. "We're all about food sovereignty—we want to provide safe, healthy, fresh and local food to our customers, utilize on-farm sourced fertility for a more closed-circuit operation, provide CSA membership options to a wide variety of customers regardless of economic background, raise animals for food by prioritizing a safe, healthy, natural and long life, support our neighboring vendors, farming operations, and businesses, share our accumulative farming experience with our interns and community, and provide a safe and friendly place for volunteers, employees and interns to improve their quality of life through healthy eating and hard outside work … and we've tried hard to remain true to all of these," Gail explains.

Grassroots Farm's current business plan focuses on crop and product diversity and divides the farm labor according to the individual strengths of the partners. Lindsey does the crop planning, operates equipment, manages the workforce, improves the farm infrastructure, keeps up with daily livestock chores, delivers product to their customers, and manages the website and CSA memberships. In addition to her full time weekday job in downtown Chicago, which helps provide steady off-farm income, Gail functions as the farm's weekend warrior handy-woman. She also manages the farm finances and takes care of the paperwork that comes with maintaining organic farm certification (the farm is now certified organic by Midwest Organic Services Association (MOSA) and the United States Department of Agriculture) searches out funding sources, manages the orchard, and acts as the value-added product chef and farm product recipe tester. "This works because I really trust Lindsey's decisions, and I think she trusts my financial advice … so between the two of us we've been able to figure things out as we go along," Gail proudly explains.

For Lindsey, her relationship to the land looms large. She sees it as the foundational underpinnings of a community to which all life belongs, and thus it must be treated with love and respect. In her view land is not a commodity humans own and can use for their own ends—it is something we are responsible for taking care of. Eventually she wants Grassroots Farm to be placed in a conservation trust that will prevent the land from ever being developed or used for anything other than what it is intended to be used for—organic farming. Ultimately the farm will become her legacy to her nieces, but that inheritance is a long way off.

Meanwhile, the farm's books have to balance, and the challenges to ensure that happens continue. So far, the farm is operating in the black, and Lindsey is able to draw a small, $1000 per month salary. Nevertheless, right now, the farm cannot survive without Gail's off-farm income. The long-term business plan calls for further expanding the CSA membership base, increasing the number of delivery locations, and enlarging the value-added product line, CSA offerings, and livestock enterprise. However, the basic goal of making local, fresh food and flowers available to an economically diverse customer base remains in place. Offering a variety of share choices at multiple price points, depending on proximity to the farm and customer preferences, is central to the entire operation.

"We have seven years to pay off the service debt, and it's hard knowing if we'll meet that deadline—it's a shadow hanging over us because right now we need my off-farm income, which I'm able to provide, but I'm nearing retirement age, so that's not secure forever," Gail explains. In terms of actual dollars in-dollars out, the farm brings in between $45,000 and $50,000 per year, before expenses. Both projecting costs and setting prices has proven very difficult because it is nearly impossible to estimate what producing a crop really costs a farmer, even in a closed-circuit, self-sufficient farming system like Grassroots Farm endeavors to be.

Gail and Lindsey have worked very hard to gain the technical knowledge needed to carry out their business plan, but this aspect of farming remains challenging. "Lindsey spends all winter figuring out what to plant where in the spring, how to rotate the crops, and how to carefully care for the land all at the same time," Gail explains, adding that, on a daily basis, something breaks and needs fixing. She says neither of them possesses the full range of mechanical skills that would come in very handy in solving these problems.

Lindsey is an exceptionally friendly, generously tattooed lesbian who is considerably less conventional than her more traditional mother. Even though she has won the prestigious Jon Kinsman Beginning Farmer Food Sovereignty Prize, she still faces particular challenges that come about simply because of her sexual orientation. "The religious right is prevalent in rural areas, where diversity is lacking, and I think it's taken a while for locals to feel entirely comfortable with Lindsey," Gail reflects. "There haven't been any incidents, but it has taken time for the gender role stuff to dissolve and go away—and I think most of it has…. Let's face it, we wouldn't be where we are today without the support of our neighbors and friends in the area, so it's all pretty much worked itself out now that they've gotten to know Lindsey…. She's a team player and wants everyone to succeed, so she shows up and helps out wherever she can, and that means a lot around here."

Grassroots Farm is, in many ways, a modern-day pioneer story of two women with the courage to embark upon a journey to a place neither

had ever been before, and where they didn't know anyone. Entirely on
their own they homesteaded a plot of land, and proceeded to transform
40 acres of Canadian thistle into a productive, diverse small family farm
that provides a fully organic, balanced and healthy diet to its customers.
Their farm operation has been amazingly successful in a relatively short
period of time, thanks to a manager with a good business sense, an operator who is passionate about her land, and a strong working partnership
between a mother and her daughter. Unquestionably, it helps that both
Gail and Lindsey are unwavering in their commitment to the values of
food sovereignty, work hard every day to do their part to make a better
food system a reality in American life, and truly love farming.

When Food Politics Get Tough Women Farmers Get Organized

> Farming's hard, hard work and the whole idea is to make it pos-
> sible for women who want to farm to do it successfully, which
> means helping each other out.
>
> —Lisa Kivirist

The decibel level of rural women's voices began rising rather dramatically in the late 19th century, with the dawn of the Progressive era in
American politics. The realization that most farms couldn't operate without women's active participation as part of the farm labor force was becoming firmly entrenched in the rural psyche at a time when most of America
was rural. So, grabbing opportunity where they saw it, women joined
together using their natural abilities as their husbands' helpmates, as
mothers to their own and sometimes their relatives, children, and as out-
standing multitaskers to make positive changes in farm life. "Midwestern
farm women began organizing auxiliaries and clubs on a large scale during
the Progressive era,, when women's activism was largely informed by social
feminism ... and engaging in activism on specific issues, such as public
health, maternal and infant care, education, or industrial safety, without
challenging male-dominated political systems," explains historian Jenny
Barker Devine.[7] The success of these efforts hinged on rural women's natural ability to build relationships with each other and then move forward
to bring about the changes they sought.

The end of World War II brought about another significant shift in
rural women's political influence. Many had been thrust into taking charge

of the farm when their husbands went off to war and, in his absence, they discovered they could keep the farm operation afloat entirely on their own. Upon their husband's return, many farm wives were more forceful in insisting that they farm alongside him, in a working partnership, rather than returning to their previous, less influential, more supportive farmwife role. Other women, whose husbands either did not return from the war, or came back severely, or permanently, impaired, continued farming on their own, without their husband's help. And, during the war some unmarried women had begun farming to help meet the acute national need for enough food to feed the fighting men. In every situation, women were afforded the opportunity to develop their own, unique understanding of large scale, conventional farming.

At about the same time farming itself began to change. What had been a relatively stable agricultural enterprise suddenly required much greater capital investment and knowledge of technology, as well as a willingness to use it. Many, mostly male, farmers weren't willing to make this transition to new farming methods and left farming altogether. Three things happened as a result: many women who owned farmland continued farming and women who wanted to farm but didn't have land bought the farms men were leaving. And while no one with any knowledge of the important and necessary role women have always played in farm life would ever argue that women haven't always had a voice in the rural agricultural enterprise, they might say it wasn't a particularly loud or obvious one. This assumption was proving untrue.

Fast forward to 2015, and women now own 50 percent of America's farmland. Some of this land has been passed down as a legacy from father to daughter, some has been inherited from husbands, brothers and other family members, and some has been purchased. "Women owning half the nation's farmland means women bear a huge responsibility for what happens to the food system," Lisa Kivirist, the Midwest Organic and Sustainable Education Service (MOSES) Rural Women's Project coordinator says. She works tirelessly within an organizational structure that is making heroic efforts to help women farmers succeed.[8]

Bearing Lisa's statement in mind, it is not at all surprising that, in post-feminist 2015, women farmers are actively seeking greater influence over the politics of agriculture and food production. This dramatic change in the rural landscape has given women unprecedented political influence, which they have had to figure out how to optimize. The most common, and obvious, response has been for rural farm women to organize once again, with a view toward ensuring that they can succeed in a new workplace environment where, not too many generations ago, women were rarely found, particularly as land owners, or in positions of leadership and influence. Rural, landowning women have had to figure out how to navigate their way around the demands and deeply entrenched cultural traditions of a rural patriarchy built around male-dominated land ownership. How better to do this than by drawing upon women's natural proclivity toward supporting each other?

"It's no different than if the three wise men would have been three wise women," Jeanie Lewis says. "They would've said to forget the gold, frankincense and myrrh and decided among themselves who was going to bring diapers, burp cloths and casseroles, and then stay to help clean up the manger," she laughs. "Men have probably been too busy to notice, but women have always gotten together to make things happen ... and it's foolish to think this hasn't been exactly what it takes to survive rural life."

Honoring their history of land acquisition, the Rural Women's Project[9] arose as a response to the United States Department of Agriculture's decision to classify women farmers as "socially disadvantaged." While this is not a label anyone likes, it has had the benefit of enabling women farmers to qualify for special funding programs through the Farm Service Agency, which is the local point of entry for administering federal farm programs. These specifically designated funds have allowed women farmers to purchase land and secure farm operation loans. Eventually, easier access to farm loans became a mandate for women to organize and dive deeper into the relationship between women and the food system.

The Rural Women's Project is based on the model that women farmers learn best from each other in a peer-led format," Lisa explains. "Since 2008 we've been trying to develop programs and workshops collaboratively and by building local connections ... we want to bring together women who are really passionate about transforming our food systems on all levels and especially try to offer support to beginning female farmers. More than half of workshop attendees have not yet launched businesses and another 30 percent have been in business one to three years ... and nearly all are passionately committed to long-term sustainability." In other words, these women are serious about writing their own success stories as farmers, and are in for the long haul in terms of making that happen.

One of the Rural Women's Project's primary programs is In Her Boots, a hands-on, experience-oriented farming education initiative. "These full-day workshops take place on women-owned farms throughout the Midwest," Lisa stresses. Farm tours center on topics and themes that include business diversification, family integration/balance and challenges of specific groups of women farmers (single women, seniors/retirees, etc.).

Women Caring for the Land: Conservation Learning Circles is a collaboration between the Women's Food and Agriculture Network (WFAN)[10] and MOSES that acknowledges the significant impact of the growing percentage of rural land owned or co-owned by women, many of whom are single, widowed or have inherited their family farm. Workshops designed to connect these women with female conservation professionals who teach them about conservation resources and principles, and take them to visit farms where these practices are in place, and popular and well attended.

WFAN, although centered in Iowa, has members in more than 25 states and several foreign countries. The organization's membership is diverse in ages (ranging from teens to seventies) and backgrounds, and includes farmers, urban gardeners, environmental educators, community activists, academics, and others who care about food and the environment. While similar to the MOSES and Rural Women's Projects, and using similar means to reach their goals, WFAN's efforts include:

- Promoting sustainable agricultural and community structures.
- Insisting on social and ecological justice for current and future human and non-human communities.
- Providing opportunities for education on economics and environment that articulate a holistic view of agriculture, instill a sense of place, and draw forward useful experiences from the past.
- Creating networks that support communities of growers, consumers, workers and others who strive for sustainability, increase effective access to and use of existing resources, engage participants in experiential learning, provide safe places for self-expression, and respect the spirituality of the land and people.
- Advocating for change by exploring alternatives and challenge the globalization of economies, cultures of domination and institutionalized discrimination, the disintegration of landscapes, and oppressive conceptual frameworks.

Soil Sisters: Wisconsin Women in Sustainable Agriculture Farm Tours is another MOSES-WFAN collaboration that highlights a cross section of women farmers in south central Wisconsin who prioritize small-scale, diversified, community-focused agriculture. Kinkoona Farm and Grassroots Organic Farm have both been part of this initiative for several years. Suellen, Gail and Lindsey all say showing off their farm to the wider community is a highlight of the farm's growing season.

Wisely, the Rural Women's Project grabs at every media opportunity it can find to share the inspiring stories of women farmers who practice sustainable and organic agriculture. The project also works collaboratively to support national efforts aimed at enhancing women's efforts to work for food system change, as well as provide education and training on policy issues and grassroots organizing.

However, in reality, active concern about the health of the food system as an integral part of the agricultural enterprise is a relatively recent political phenomenon. While women have always been in charge of feeding their families, thus have always been concerned for the quality of the food their families eat, it was not until men like Michael Pollan and Wendell Berry, who have written extensively on food and agricultural issues, took up the food quality concern that it began to gain political traction. However, given women's natural ability to organize and their willingness to step up and support one another, it's neither a surprise nor an accident that WFAN, founded in 1997 in Iowa, the heartland of American farming, is one of the strongest food advocacy organizations in agriculture today. "WFAN exists so that women can give each other the information, connections and encouragement they need to be effective practitioners and supporters of sustainable agriculture and healthy localized food systems," Lisa, a long-time supporter of WFAN efforts, explains. "WFAN and the Rural Women's Project work closely together to link and empower women to build food systems and communities that are healthy, just, sustainable, and that promote environmental integrity," she says, adding that both organizations "are all about providing women farmers with opportunities to do what women have always done, which is to develop helping relationships with each other."

Utilizing the time-honored principle of strength in numbers, both organizations have developed several ways for rural women to come together. These women are connecting with each other and, as a group, have begun garnering significant influence in the previously male-dominated rural political and social arenas, and using very simple means to do it. "Potlucks never fail to bring women together," Lisa chuckles, "so we rely heavily upon the potluck method to provide all kinds of networking opportunities … women love to make and share food with each other, and are very willing to collaborate and share information, so the potlucks are always very well attended." Jeanie Lewis adds that the while the surest way to get men to a meeting is to have something for them to eat when they get there, she's never, in more than 75 years on the farm, ever seen a man actually bring anything to a potluck.

Lisa and WFAN both strongly believe women learn best through connecting with each other, and to this end, are oriented toward building upon women's abilities to develop and maintain a far-reaching web of relationships across all sectors of agriculture—mechanics, veterinarians, seed and feed suppliers, fencers, neighbors, local and state governments. The women team up to share equipment, chores, farm hands, and information, and this is part of the reason women in farming are succeeding. The other reason is women's willingness to seek out, and eagerly learn, what they need to know to carry on. "It's like asking for directions—men won't do it, and women never hesitate," says Jeanie, referring to the large numbers of women, and many fewer men, who attend local university agricultural extension service farm education programs on topics such as how to take and read soil samples. "Men solve their problems and get their questions answered over at the grain elevator—women take a class from an expert," she laughs.

One of the newer collaborations between WFAN and MOSES directly aimed at educating women about political processes is the Plate to Politics initiative. "Plate to Politics is a nationwide effort to support and strengthen the national leadership role of women transforming our nation's food system, from the federal agriculture policy agenda to what's on our family's supper plate," Lisa explains. To this end, the key projects include:

- Developing a national database of the many inspiring stories of women farmers and food activists across the country and connecting these women with leadership opportunities.
- Educating Congressional leaders on policy issues of importance to women in sustainable agriculture.
- Creating an informational toolkit and resources to educate and inspire voters on food issues.
- Supporting and further developing an authentic, positive message about the importance of prioritizing the relationship between health, the economy, and food in the media.

Women have also been the voice of reason when agricultural food policies have gone berserk, as reflected by the infamous "Oleo Wars" which erupted over the use of this healthy, hydrogenated vegetable oil-based substitute for decidedly unhealthy, animal fat-laden butter. This, often volatile, conflict went on for more than 75 years until, by 1902, 32 states had outlawed the use of Oleo.

In order to differentiate Oleo from butter, it was required to be white rather than yellow. To enforce this requirement, lawmakers drafted a federal law that made coloring Oleo to closely resemble butter a federal crime, punishable by fines and/or imprisonment. In response, women strenuously objected to the ban on Oleo and convinced former first lady Eleanor Roosevelt to step up to the cause. Mrs. Roosevelt made a television commercial in which she stated that she put Oleo on her toast every morning.

Meanwhile, margarine smuggling had become rampant, and a very lucrative black market for Oleo that rivaled sales of bootleg whisky during prohibition sprung up, particularly in Illinois, a strategically located border state just south of Wisconsin. This act of aggression placed Wisconsin, America's Dairyland and the country's largest producer of butter, front and center in a national food fight.

However, thousands of health-conscious Wisconsin consumers were regularly crossing the state line into Illinois to purchase bootleg Oleo. "Margarine villages" sprung up alongside the Illinois-Wisconsin border, hiding in plain sight in gas stations and roadside restaurants. Enterprising Wisconsinites were bringing carloads of illegal Oleo across the state line where it was being sold in the back rooms of local grocery stores and meat markets.

Learning of this assault on the dairy state, Wisconsin State Senator Gordon Roseleip voiced loud objections. A boisterous, dedicated Wisconsin dairy farmer given to dramatic displays of political theatre when advantageous to making his point, Senator Roseleip hoisted his rotund body to its feet and stood before the state legislature to declare an all-out war on the neighboring state of Illinois. His war strategy included introducing legislation that made crossing the Wisconsin-Illinois state line for purposes of purchasing Oleo a criminal act. Roseleip saw himself as the charging general bravely stepping up to fire the first shot in the butter versus Oleo conflict, and proudly vowed to lead his beloved Wisconsin's charge against its neighbor to the south.

Opponents of his legislation challenged the vociferously pro-butter Senator Roseleip to a butter-Oleo dual. A blind taste test between Oleo supporters and their enemies was arranged, with each side choosing its representative. Roseleip had no choice other than to accept this challenge to his integrity. In what ultimately proved to be the Butter Battle that ended the war, Roseleip went with margarine—an acutely embarrassing choice that haunted him for the rest of his political career.

Roseleip's legislation failed, but not because the margarine supporters prevailed. His legislative failure was that no one could figure out how to enforce the law if it was put into effect. Roseleip realized that creating (and funding) a new state law enforcement agency to train and administer a corps of butter police would cost Wisconsin taxpayers an exorbitant amount of money and cost him re-election, so he dropped the entire idea. As a result, Wisconsin finally did something legislatively sensible by decriminalized purchasing, coloring, and using Oleo margarine.

After his death, Roseleip's wife revealed that she had been serving him Illinois Oleo for years. She believed margarine was much healthier than Wisconsin butter and knew he needed to lose weight. She admitted she had purchased and colored the Oleo herself, and never worried too much about whether, by doing this, she was committing a federal crime. Senator Roseleip's enduring legacy is that both his supporters and detractors feel he would have been a much more effective politician if he had picked his battles more carefully and listened to his wife more often.

Women also stepped up to argue for sensible action when the bottom fell out of Wisconsin milk prices. Seeing no relief in sight, the male-dominated dairy industry organized a milk dump. Their hope was that if all dairy farmers dumped milk on the same day they would be making a dramatic political statement as well as creating a milk shortage that would force prices back up.

As Jeanie explains it, dairy farmers' wives and other women working in the industry didn't disagree with the notion of withholding milk from the marketplace in an attempt to regulate pricing, but strongly objected to just dumping it in the streets. "Most of us felt that there were a lot of poor and hungry people out there who could've used that milk so it would've been better to donate somewhere rather than completely wasting it and I know some farmers who did that on the sly, without telling anybody."

The court of public opinion issued a strongly worded ruling against the milk dump in editorials appearing in newspapers across the state. Nevertheless, as show of public solidarity and support for the multi-billion dollar dairy industry, which is vital to Wisconsin's economy, it has become traditional to serve milk at every public event. There is no legislative mandate to do this; it is a voluntary effort on the part of the Wisconsin food service industry to create an additional, ongoing market for milk, and had been in practice since the milk dump—as clear proof that there is more than one way to score an important political victory.

Today, it is very clear that women farmers don't want to speak truth to power so much as they want to be the truth that is part of the ongoing power struggle agriculture in general faces. Accordingly, women are working hard, together, to reach the goal of being at the center of the food system, and having more than one, merely token seat at the table where agricultural policy decisions that directly affect them are made.

Six

Farming for the Love of Farming

Farming is all I ever really wanted to do.... I can't imagine doing anything else.

—Mary Dunn

Farmers don't complain much. They will grouse over the weather or feed prices, but no matter how tough the going gets, rather than wasting time lamenting their misfortune, most farmers just keep going.

Farmers aren't quitters either. To the contrary, I've never met one who wasn't both a good-humored optimist at heart and stubborn as a mule in their resolve to continue farming, no matter what misfortune befalls them.

Every farmer I've ever known loves farming a lot more than most city folk I've ever met love their desk jobs. No farmer will ever claim theirs is an easy life, but it takes a lot more than a bad crop year, bad knees, bad floods, or a bad drought to convince a farmer to give up farming. "I'd sooner cut off both arms than give up driving my tractor," one of my farmer friends once told me when I asked him what kept him going during a bad drought. Mary Dunn would have a similar answer.

I first encountered Mary about twenty years ago, when all Wisconsin counties were developing legislatively mandated Smart Growth Land Use Development Plans.[1] Both rural and urban counties were charged with figuring out a local plan framework that met the legal specifications the state legislature had set forth and that was palatable to most, if not all, landowners. Rural folks in particular were very skeptical of Smart Growth, generally referring to it as Dumb Growth. No one I'd spoken with about the idea thought any long-term good could come from this state directive and most bristled at yet another instance of government telling them what to do, and then expecting them to actually do it.

194

Emotions around the concept of establishing policies that govern how farmland is sold off or developed were reaching a boiling point. Nevertheless, I wasn't happy when my editor at the local newspaper asked me to cover this evolving story because I knew the assignment was going to require sitting through endless, usually boring public meetings extending throughout the summer. Worse, I wasn't particularly interested in the issue and didn't care about regulating land division or development. However, I soon discovered that I was probably the only person among the more than 22,000 county residents who didn't have an opinion on regulating land use.

The first public hearing I attended was neither a pleasant nor a particularly interesting experience. Mostly, people yelled back and forth at each other while the county board chair banged his gavel calling for order. The outcome was that the county's draft plan was sent back to the ad hoc board committee for further revisions. My report of the meeting wasn't the most compelling news story I'd ever written.

A month later, the public hearing on the revised plan was scheduled. Word was out that the plan was going forward one way or the other, so the county board meeting room, located on the second floor of the oldest courthouse in the state, was packed beyond capacity. The maintenance person had yet to turn off the boilers for the season, so even though it was 85 degrees outside, the heat was on. No one had thought to set up a pick-a-number system for those who wished to speak at the meeting, and based upon what I could determine, everyone who had made the effort to attend the hearing felt they had something to say, so what promised to be a very long evening had a high potential for erupting in chaos before the meeting ever began. Worse, latecomers were forced to stand in the back of the long, narrow room or out in the hallway, where they gathered near the door, in an effort to hear what was being said, which was then passed along to the folks standing on the stairs downward to the first floor and all the way out the door. The information chain resembled a game of Gossip; what the person at the end of the line heard generally bore no resemblance whatever to what was actually said inside the room.

A few minutes before the scheduled hearing time, a robust woman entered the room through the front side door. She was wearing blue work clothes selected for their practicality rather than their style, and sporting an approximately two-inch haircut she probably styled with a shower nozzle and a broad smile. Using a cane in each hand to steady herself, she surveyed the room for an empty seat. Several people in the front stood up to offer her theirs. "Just like in church, nobody wants to be in front where it's hard to make a fast getaway," she observed. As she settled in people began coming over to greet her, shaking hands, patting her on the back, and chatting her up. She was a large presence in the room, and everyone was glad to see her. The person in front of me turned to the person next to him and whispered that Mary Dunn had just arrived.

Mary held court among her fellow farmers, giving as good as she got until the 21 county board members, most of whom were farmers themselves, entered the room by the same side door she had used and sat down around their elevated table. Some nodded to her, some offered her the universal farmer's salute, and several acknowledged her by name. Seeing this, and since she had also entered the room by the same door, it occurred to me that Mary might have had a private meeting with the board ahead of this public one and I made a note to ask her about it later.

The chairman finally called the meeting to order. Because the board secretary had failed to show up, the first order of business involved the chairman asking me to take the minutes, since I'd be reporting on the story anyway. In return for this favor, he offered me a seat next to him, and gave me the use of the official county board tape recorder which he instructed me to hit with my fist if it stopped recording.

The first, deadly boring, hour was spent explaining the proposed revisions to the earlier Smart Growth Plan that the ad hoc committee had "worked very, very hard" to configure. When the time for public comments finally came, the board chair asked that everyone use the microphone at the front of the room, speak clearly, state their name and township of residence, and confine their remarks to five minutes. He also instructed speakers not to repeat a point someone else had already made. Because there are only so many comments to be made on any given topic, and the room was severely overcrowded and hot, I figured testimony wouldn't last very long. I could not have been more wrong.

Soon it was evident that the time-limit constraints on comments were meaningless because the chairman, despite repeated warnings, lacked any effective means of enforcement. Everyone ignored him and his gavel, and he, in turn, ignored repeated requests for a bathroom break. I thought he was probably hoping full bladders would accomplish what he could not do himself, which was to adjourn the meeting sooner rather than later, and spent several minutes trying to configure this idea into a headline for the report I would be writing later.

Mary listened to what others were saying for nearly two hours before standing up to be recognized. Someone handed the microphone over to her and she introduced herself as Mary Dunn. The chairman immediately interrupted her. "There isn't a person in this room who doesn't know who you are, Mary, so just go ahead with what you have to say." I noted that he did not, as he had with the others, admonish her to keep it short. Mary's demeanor commanded serious respect, and the deference he showed her suggested that the chairman knew better than to take her on over something as trivial as time limits.

Within her allotted five minutes, and without notes, Mary presented a soft-spoken, clearly articulated argument for her opposition to the county's proposed Smart Growth plan. When she finished speaking, she smiled, thanked the board for their time, and sat back down. The room was silent. Everyone present had just witnessed Mary Dunn very politely, and supremely effectively, take down the entire 21-member county board for presenting what she obviously felt was a stupid draft plan—and they knew there really wasn't anything left to say. I was wordless myself, and had no idea how I was going to report on this meeting in a way that would convey what I'd just witnessed, which was a remarkably articulate, highly respected woman in action. I was sitting at the table with my arms crossed, wishing my editorials were half that powerful, when the chairman rose to his feet to declare the meeting adjourned.

I walked over to Mary, introduced myself, and asked if she'd care to elaborate on her statement for the news article reporting on the meeting that I would be pulling together? "Not really," she said. "These guys are all farmers and they know a farmers' land is their 401(k)^2 and they also know they have no business trying to mess around with land use, because it could really hurt farmers. They already know good neighbor policy trumps public policy every time—all I did was offer a friendly reminder." She smiled at me, stood up, nodded to the board chairman, who remained standing and appeared as though he was expecting Mary to come over and discuss her point with him one-on-one. I started to ask her whether she had met with board members prior to the meeting, but Mary gathered her canes, and slowly walked out the door. "She's really good," I thought to myself, wishing I had the ability to set men straight half as effectively and efficiently as I'd just seen her do it. And while it might've been my imagination, I thought I heard the chairman exhale a deep sigh of relief as Mary left.

Over the next several years, Mary and I occasionally crossed paths. Most often I ran into her when she was in her old, faded blue pick-up, either loaded up with some kind of equipment or overloaded with hay, and pulling into the courthouse parking lot across from my office at the newspaper. She obviously loved driving that truck, because she always had a huge grin on her face while she cruised the lot looking for a hand-icapped space.

Each time I encountered Mary it became more evident that her ability to get around on her own was diminishing. I knew she still farmed, and wondered how she managed to keep going? I had the opportunity to ask her this question once, in the Farm and Fleet parking lot while I helped her lift her walker out of the back of the truck, where she'd wedged it between a couple bales of hay. She told me she loves shopping at the farm implement store too much to quit, and without the farm, there'd be no reason to keep doing it. Reflecting on this answer later, I concluded her answer was probably more truth than teasing. Yet, after every chat with her, I still wondered why, and how, she persisted in doing such physically difficult work at the same time she was becoming more and more disabled. When she agreed to talk with me about this book, I was thrilled at the chance to spend more time with her and hear her story in greater detail.

When our agreed upon interview day finally arrived it was snowing steadily, with a blustery wind blowing hard out of the west, offering up a wind chill far below zero. To get to Mary's farm, I had to drive several miles across the rolling back-country hills, through wind-whipped snow drifts, and down a long, icy gravel road peppered with potholes and sharp switchbacks. Despite increasing my four-letter word vocabulary considerably as I crept along on this perilous journey, I was also congratulating myself for deciding to drive my old junker. The tires aren't the best, but it is heavier in the back end than my pickup, thus more likely to stay on the road. Nevertheless, with each curve it became increasingly obvious that the likelihood of sliding off the road into the ditch loomed large—and would do a fair amount of damage to whatever I was driving. This wouldn't matter too much to the junker, whose best days are behind it, but it is definitely something I preferred to avoid having to explain, especially to Mary.

The danger I'm not prepared for, as I round the last curve, is a large cattle trailer parked about 75 yards straight down the hill, across the road, back end pointed toward the barn door. It takes all the courage I have not to slam on the brakes, which would be guaranteed to send me skidding into the side of the trailer at the perfect angle to roll it. Instead, I hold my breath, stiff-arm the steering wheel, and manage to let the car slowdown of its own accord—hoping it won't hit the trailer, slide right on through the barn, or perform some other weird, not immediately evident combination of maneuvers that could do even more damage. I miss both the barn and trailer by inches, finally stopping right next to Mary's beloved truck. Obviously I had been going a little too fast for conditions.

I exhale a huge sigh of relief. Two seconds later, I suck all that air back in because I hear Mary hollering something unintelligible at me. I have a pretty good idea what she's saying and don't feel compelled to ask her to repeat herself. She is sitting about 20 feet in front of me, in her wheelchair, next to the cattle gate, unloading 22 Brown Swiss baby bull calves from the cattle trailer which had arrived a few minutes ahead of me. The truck driver is standing off to the side observing the situation. I'm sure it hasn't escaped his notice that neither Mary nor the calves are occupying a position of safety within my personally designed traffic pattern. I can't blame him, or Mary, for being a little irritated about my unnecessarily dramatic arrival, which I didn't particularly enjoy either.

However, not wanting to reveal my fright, which has not yet fully subsided, I decide to pretend that nothing unusual has just occurred, or that, five minutes ago, I nearly killed her, and her baby bull calves. Instead, I offer to help her finish unloading. I walk over toward the barn, calling out the standard farmer greeting, which always pertains to the current state of the weather. "It's bitter cold out here," I announce cheerfully. "You should've worn a warmer coat," Mary answers, pulling a wool cap further down over her ears and then asking me to hold the barn door open. I don't feel it is in my overall best interests to admit I'm not wearing warm enough mittens to stand there hanging onto a metal cattle gate, so I do as she asks.

An hour later, after we have settled the calves safely in the barn, Mary turns her wheelchair around and motions for me to follow her into the house. By now I am so cold I figure I've done adequate penance for the earlier excitement I'd caused and feel much less compelled to apologize for my rude arrival. Nevertheless, I do believe good manners dictate that I offer to push her wheelchair up the hill toward the old farmhouse, so I place the package of cookies I'd brought for her in her lap and start pushing. She waves me off without any suggestion that I might've just insulted her by implying that she can't manage this herself, and proceeds on her own, at a pretty good clip, using both arms to roll the wheels forward and her leg to help pull her along through the snow. I go up ahead, looking for a snow shovel to clear her path, but by the time I eventually find one she has already arrived at the back door of the old farmhouse.

Wrapped entirely in plastic to ward off the cold winter winds, the chipped, gray asbestos-shingles are holding together an old house that looks like it is bursting with stories to tell. But at this moment I am just too cold to spend much time wondering what they might be. Meanwhile, Mary has pulled the storm door open without letting the wind catch it, and motions me into an air-locked mud room where we shed our coats, hats and boots. While I struggle to convince my frozen fingers to get a grip on my jacket's zipper tab Mary already has her hat, coat, boot and mittens off, and is tightening the knot in her empty pant leg. She transfers to an indoor wheel chair, explaining that this avoids tracking cow manure through the house. She deftly maneuvers her way around several pairs of crutches, a wooden milk crate containing various styles of walking canes, and an electric scooter. Two artificial left legs, with shoes attached, are standing upright in the middle of the room. "Two left legs is a bad visual," Mary laughs. She uses her leg to pull herself through the door into the kitchen that is too narrow for her to use her arms to maneuver through. She avoids scraping any paint off the door jam.

While I continue the zipper struggle Mary heads for the stove. She fumbles around looking for matches to manually light the front burner on the old gas range, saying that her helper doesn't always put things back where they belong. "Do you want coffee or tea?" she asks me, adding that

Because it is the warmest room in the farmhouse during the winter, Mary Dunn's kitchen also functions as her office. The kitchen table, which doubles as a desk, has been placed on bricks to raise it up high enough to accommodate her wheelchair (photograph by the author).

she also has some home baked chocolate cake. I am too focused on my numb, useless fingers to make a decision about either offering. It's doubtful I could hold onto a fork or a coffee mug.

Eventually we sit down across from each other at an oblong, 1950s style red Formica and chrome table. Someone has been thoughtful enough to placed two bricks under each table leg to elevate it enough for Mary's wheelchair arms to fit underneath, allowing her to sit close into the table. A space heater is strategically placed near the outside kitchen door, which was covered with indoor plastic insulation to cut down on the cold air leaks, but it's obvious that the old table has occupied the place of honor in this large drafty kitchen for a very long time

"In 2018 this will be designated a century farm—it'll have been in the Dunn family 100 years by then," Mary tells me, adding that the house is even older. "I've not done much updating," she laughs, gesturing toward a chipped, blue metal dry sink against the far wall that would be a coveted find in any antique store. In this kitchen it doubles as counter space as well as a shelf for dishes. "I don't see much sense in replacing things that still work, and everything in here still works," she tells me, adding that the linoleum's pretty worn. "My dad put this floor down for my mother just before I was born, and I'm 64, so I'd say it's lasted pretty well.... Besides, I'm not much on throwing fancy dinner parties, so who cares what the kitchen floor looks like.... It's not like anybody besides the dog eats off it, and I haven't heard him complain!" She nods toward a large dog of undetermined ancestry sleeping soundly in front of the warm stove, without a complaint in the world.

Mary's goes on to explain that her grandfather moved his family into this house when her father was two years old. At no time during the rest of her father's life did he live anywhere else. All three of his daughters were born and raised under this roof and Mary has never lived anywhere else either, even while she was attending a four-year college. "Platteville[3] isn't that far, so I commuted—that way I was home to help with chores," she recalls. In today's world where people move from place to place often, living in the house one was born and has been raised in is unusual, and I ask Mary what it feels like? "It's not Buckingham Palace, and won't be featured in *Better Homes and Gardens* any time soon, but other than that, it's fine," she quips. A moment later she adds that she never thinks much about the house, which has four downstairs rooms, if the adjoining living and dining rooms are counted separately. "I'm not into fancy decorating—obviously," she teases.

Recently one of Mary's brothers-in-law widened the bathroom door to accommodate her wheelchair. Other than the addition of some assistive equipment, no other modifications to make the house more handicapped accessible have occurred. Undoubtedly Mary could have added a ramp, and made other structural modifications that would make her life easier, added to the house, which would be paid for through her health insurance or a disability assistance program. But my sense is that she would view this as an insult to an old house that has served her faithfully and well across her entire lifetime. So, instead of accommodating the house to her needs, Mary continues to accommodate to the house. "I sleep in what used to be the dining room so I don't have to go up and down stairs—I guess that's kind of weird, but it works ... the front room has my piano, a couch and a TV, and my office is in the little room we came through into the kitchen. That's really all I need," she shrugs.

Mary's practical nature and the ability to live within her modest means are evident everywhere, bringing to mind something I've observed about her since the first time I ever saw her: she's always the same. She has two basic sets of clothing. In winter she wears blue cotton pants and long-sleeved turtleneck shirts, and in summer she wears blue cotton pants and short sleeved polo shirts. She never lets her hair get much longer than approximately two inches in any direction. A broad, beautiful smile completes her. When I comment that she looks better than the last time I saw her, she takes me literally. "I aim for a timeless style, so you could write that I'm not a victim of the latest fashion trends and be correct," she laughs, smoothing down the cowlick that springs up in the back of her head.

Realizing how crippled Mary has become over the years, I ask her the big question that always comes to mind whenever I see her, which is how she manages to keep farming? "I've never wanted to do anything else," she explains, looking me squarely in the eye. She goes on to tell me that her freshman adviser at the local agriculture college was not particularly supportive when she told him she wanted to major in music and minor in animal husbandry. "He seriously questioned my decision, but eventually he realized I'd already made up my mind that farming was what I wanted to do, and wasn't really asking for his advice, so I think he sensed that I wouldn't be easily deterred," she says. Her advisor pushed her to explain what she planned do with this unusual academic combination. "Tell me, Mary Kathleen, are you thinking you'll sing 'Old MacDonald had a farm...' while you milk the cows every morning?" she repeats, setting her jaw in just the right way to be sure I understand that she's never forgotten the sarcasm behind the remark.

Mary says she wasn't amused, or particularly bothered, by this response. "I loved music, and I really wanted to farm, so it made sense to me to study both," she explained. "I figured if my adviser didn't understand this, it was his problem ... but I was a little worried that it could become my problem too since there was only one other woman enrolled in agricultural sciences, making me one of just two women among 78 guys.... I figured the best thing to do was to dig in my heels and just do it, so I did ... that was almost 50 years ago, and I've never been sorry ... not even for one single minute have I ever been sorry."

As young adults, Mary and her two sisters went into a farming partnership with their parents. In the late 1970s the three girls entered into a seven-year land contract with their dad to buy the farm outright. By the time the final payment was due both parents had died, and both of Mary's sisters had married. One sister moved to upstate New York, while the other sister stayed closer, moving into a house a few miles farther down the blacktop road from the home farm.

By 1985 Mary was 34 years old, farming entirely on her own and loving every minute of it. But a dark cloud, in the form of significant symptoms of early-onset, crippling rheumatoid arthritis, was forming overhead. "I knew something was wrong, but I wasn't eager to find out what it was. I guess I was afraid it would change things I didn't want to change. I'd grown up on this farm—it's the only place I've ever lived, and I love everything about it—the smell, the view, even the dirt, and I didn't want to give any of that up," she explains.

"Over the years I'd learned a lot from my dad, who was a good farmer. He taught me more than I ever learned in college, so I knew I was a good farmer too. Even though my body wasn't working nearly as well as the old tractor was, it never occurred to me that I couldn't find some way to carry on," Mary says, with mix of much deserved pride, sprinkled with a hint of remarkable tenacity. "I can problem solve as good as any other farmer, and I've had a lot of hands-on experience with dairy cattle, pigs, a beef herd, and crop farming our entire 220 acres ... and I guess I just didn't want to worry about the limitations arthritis might impose on me until I absolutely had to. The doctors told me that sometimes the symptoms come and go for several years, and there was no way to predict how fast or slow the disease might progress, or how long a remission would last, so I made up my mind to just carry on and not worry about it."

Unfortunately, in Mary's case the stiffness and pain arthritis caused her didn't come and go. Instead, it quickly settled into a chronic condition, giving her almost no respite as it progressed more quickly than is typical of the disease. Step by step, she was forced to face the ugly consequences of a painful and crippling degenerative disorder that eventually destroys both the small and large joints of those who suffer from it. "It hit my legs particularly hard ... those were the first joints to go and it got to the point I wasn't able to use them much, so I was having a pretty hard time getting around," she explains. "Farm equipment is made for men, and men quit farming when they become disabled, so none of the equipment comes handicap accessible. I had to figure out how to make the tractor fit me, and then eventually jerry-rig some hand controls, which wasn't too hard after I got them put on my truck," she says, leaving me to wonder exactly how someone could make a tractor handicap accessible. She waved me off when I ask her to explain how she did it. "It was so long ago I don't remember exactly how I did it—I just did," she said.

Other issues that accompany Mary's condition include fatigue, low-grade fevers from joint inflammation, stiffness, flu-like symptoms, and perpetual weakness—and Mary has had them all. Nevertheless, she refuses to allow the disease to win, or to force her off her beloved farm, even as her limitations continued to multiply. "It's not like I've had any choice—I wasn't going to let arthritis force me to give up something I loved doing, so I had to figure out how to keep going, and direct my energy there ... I know a lot of farmers would quit farming under my circumstances, but I just didn't think about the situation that way. I just never seriously considered giving up."

While gritty determination has helped Mary carry on, so has a larger than life, dry sense of humor that sees hilarity everywhere and focuses on funny side of every disaster that would dissolve most people into tears. She is blessed with abundant, rock-solid common sense, and delightful personality, and is beloved, and profoundly respected, among her fellow farmers. These qualities say everything there is to say about the remarkable life she has crafted for herself. She's a lot of fun to talk with, work with, and spend time with, so finding hired hands to work for her, and other people willing to assist her has never been an insurmountable problem. "I'm on good terms with my neighbors, and we help each other out all the time," she explains. "Just the other day I fell out of my wheelchair getting into the truck and had to call my neighbor, who pulled on her snow pants and came right over. Let's face it, I'm not a lightweight, so she decided to call her partner to bring their skid steer over and they scooped me into the bucket and got me back up." Seeing me grimace at this image, she adds that she "wouldn't want that picture on the front page of the newspaper, but we got the job done ... and let's face it, it's not an experience everybody gets to have."

She asks me if I've ever ridden in a skid steer bucket. I acknowledge that I have not had that pleasure. "You should try it sometime—it's fun, as long as you don't fall out," she chuckles. Maybe her remarkable ability to laugh at herself and not let embarrassment get the best of her is what saves Mary every single day, I think to myself, knowing that I'd never want to remember, much less admit to, a situation where I was so helpless someone had to use a skid steer to get me up off the ground after I'd fallen.

RAISING BESSIE: DAIRY FARMING IS EXPENSIVE

Just like raising a child, it takes a lot of money to raise a dairy heifer.

—Larry Tranel

Mary's "it's better to laugh than to cry" attitude, regardless of how "unfunny" a problem or situation is, has proven to be one of the many traits that has made her an effective leader in the local dairy cattle industry. She is president of the county Dairy Promotion Committee, which sponsors several large events each year that are intended to support local dairy farmers both directly and indirectly. Most of the money raised goes toward promoting local dairy products, with a view toward increasing sales. The county where Mary resides includes several cheese factories making artisan as well as conventional cheeses, and is the site of a grilled cheese cook-off each year, sponsored by Wisconsin Public Television. This means dairy farming is a very significant player in the local economy.

Each spring the committee organizes a breakfast hosted by a different area dairy farm each year and served to over a thousand people. They also partner with the local farmers' organization to publicize and organize an annual Farmer's Appreciation Day each July that includes a steak feed serving between 1200 and 1800 people. Each August they also serve another 2000 guests at a cook-out on a near-by beef cattle farm.

Through her leadership in the organization over several years, Mary has helped guide the conversation around the emergence of organic dairy farming as an alternative to conventional milk production. "No farmer wants to produce a bad product. We're consumers too, and all of us want what's best for everybody ... so I've basically decided that the organic farming notion is using a lot of new words for the same stuff ... it's a marketing gimmick that gives the impression organic products will solve everything from bug bites to relationship problems, and that's just not true," she says.

As Mary explains it the core of the organic farming versus conventional farming controversy centers on antibiotic use to treat cows that develop mastitis. This is a serious infection of the milk ducts in the udder. I ask her for her opinion on this. "Would you rather drink milk from a conventional dairy farm that withholds milk, treats the infection until it's cleared up and the somatic cell count[4] is down, or from an organic cow that has been treated without antibiotics and whose cell count remains higher than the antibiotic-treated cow?" Mary asks me. I certainly don't want to admit to a former dairy farmer that I don't drink milk, so I feign cell count ignorance and shrug. Mary stares out the window deep in thought and drumming her fingers on the table for several minutes before continuing.

"I don't think it helps anybody for farmers to argue among themselves about organic versus non-organic farming methods, or to imply that non-organic farming is somehow immoral, or that organic farmers are saving the food supply, which will go to ruin otherwise," she says. "Deciding how to farm is a choice every farmer is entitled to make, and whatever choice he, or she, makes should be respected. There are a lot of people in the world who need to eat, and are totally dependent upon farmers to feed them ... and the facts are that conventional farming produces better yields, at lower cost, than organic farming ... and this can't be ignored. Conventional and organic farming need to co-exist because both produce a good product." She stops speaking and sets her mouth in such a way that signals she doesn't want to discuss this issue further, thereby refusing to reveal her own opinion on the matter.

Getting back to the subject of dairy promotion activities, Mary tells me that the committee members are also active in both the logistics and the judging activities at the county and state fairs. "We're really a family," Mary explains. "We help each other out, and support each other's efforts— and for the most part we're all on the same page, so it works out pretty well for everyone who makes the effort to be involved."

Currently Mary's dairy farming efforts focus almost exclusively on raising Brown Swiss bull calves, which she purchases as newborns and remain under her care until they reach about one third of their adult weight, at which time she sells them. "Brown Swiss are great dairy cows— they're my passion," she says. "Tell me honestly—have you ever seen anything cuter than a newborn Brown Swiss calf?" she asks. I'm hesitant to admit to my personal belief that if you've seen one cow, you've seen them all, or to acknowledge that I probably wouldn't know a Brown Swiss calf from any other 80 to 90 pound animal that moos. I'm also thinking that those cute calves weren't that cute a couple hours ago when it I was standing in a driving snowstorm coaxing them out of the back end of a cattle truck.

Attempting to shift the conversation, I ask about how the operation works, in practical terms. "I had to quit milking about five years ago, after my ankle joint completely disintegrated and the only thing left for me was a below the knee amputation of my left leg. Once I got back on my feet, so to speak, I decided to start raising baby bulls, which, logistically is a little easier, as long as they don't get out and take a walk someplace … it's pretty hard for me to catch them when that happens," Mary smiles. "I get them as soon as they're born—if they're born in the morning, I have them that afternoon. The ones we just unloaded were born last night," she explains.

"I buy them through a network and pay between $200 and $300 each, raise them as feeders, until they hit around 500 pounds, which takes about six months. Then they go out to the feedlot as steers, and when they reach about 1500 pounds they're sold for meat. In a good market I'll get $2 per pound, or about $1000 per animal. When they're ready to go I have three or four regular buyers always interested in buying from me, so I don't generally go to auction." The feeder-to-steer process is labor intensive in the beginning, because the calves are bottle-fed for the first two months. "I don't personally bottle feed them, but we have to mix formula and be sure to keep their feeding apparatus full at all times … and they eat a lot, so it's a last thing at night—first thing in the morning situation."

PAYING IT FORWARD: RAISING THE NEXT GENERATION OF FARMERS

4-H taught me a lot of things I've never forgotten.
—Andrea Hazzard

While dairy promotion is important to her, Mary's deeper passion has been working as a volunteer leader with the county 4-H program, which she has been doing for the past 42 years. As the nation's largest youth development organization, 4-H is a free program that functions as the youth arm of the Cooperative Extension Service, which brings research-based information to agriculture through the land-grant universities across the country. While it is best known for its outreach into rural areas, 4-H is also a presence in urban settings, beginning in elementary school and continuing through high school graduation. Estimates are that 4-H programs, which aim to teach youth how to respond to the everyday challenges they meet in their communities, and learn valuable skills in their interest areas, reach several million children each year, allowing them to engage in hands-on learning activities in the areas of science, citizenship and healthy living.

"Mary is one of the last members of a dying breed of volunteers—not many have ever stayed with 4-H as long as she has," says Deb Ivey, the local 4-H County Program Leader. "She keeps attuned to change and is always open to new ways of doing things, which makes my job much easier." Mary's Pleasant View 4-H Club has consistently been one of the larger ones in the county, averaging 20 to 30 members, and is the same club she belonged to growing up as a 4-H member herself. She has been both an individual club leader and a general leader who helps organize programs for several clubs to participate in, both individually and by bringing several clubs together.

"I think Mary really loves seeing the kids get excited about raising their animals, and watching those same kids learn and grow into agriculture," Ivey says. "She's there when they show at the county fair, and she brings kids out to her farm where she teaches them all about the hands-on, practical aspects of a cattle operation. She's been a great mentor to generations of 4-H'ers who have followed in her footsteps and gone into farming. You can safely say she's been an important influence on several hundred kids, and I don't hesitate to say that Mary's 4-H work has been an important local contribution to the future of farming in our county."

Heritage grain farmer Andrea Hazzard credits 4-H for helping to make her the farmer she is. "I learned a lot from my dad and grandparents, but also from 4-H, where I got to try new things and learn about the science behind why we, as farmers, do what we do."

4-H volunteers endeavor to both teach skills and lead by example. "The caring support of adult volunteers and mentors inspires young people in 4-H to work collaboratively, take the lead on their own projects and set and achieve goals with confidence," Ivey explains. "4-Hers, from kindergarten through high school, chart their own course, explore important issues and define their place in the world ... and none of this could happen without volunteers like Mary ... she's stayed with it even as her health has deteriorated, and I'm sure the kids learn as much from her tenacious spirit and 'do what you love' example as they actually learn from her in the formal sense."

PRAISE THE LORD AND PLAY THE ORGAN

The tradition of Sunday afternoon hymn sings in the Wyoming Valley will continue as long as we have people who want to sing, and Mary Dunn can play the organ for us.

—John Hess

Mary picks up extra money playing the organ at Sunday church services in her local church. She is in high demand throughout the area, often being asked to provide the music for weddings and funerals. She's also a popular addition to the old-fashioned summer Sunday hymn-sings that have been an ongoing and continuous event for more than 160 years in an old country church a few miles from her farm. "I'm not a rock star, but I do enjoy it, and am lucky I can still do it," she tells me. "Rheumatoid arthritis is so strange—it is completely destroying my major joints, but has left my hands basically alone, so I can still play the piano, and the organ.... I don't know what I'd do if I couldn't."

Sponsored by the Rural Musicians Forum, the hymn sings are a lively

Mary Dunn plays a keyboard as the instrumental accompaniment for a community sing-along during the summer. In addition to farming, she sight-reads music and plays the organ (photograph by the author).

experience. Several years ago I heard Mary accompany local farmer Paul Ranum, who had one of the most beautiful bass baritone voices I've ever heard, as he sang "How Great Thou Art." I don't know what the faithful hymn-sing lovers would do without her either.

"Mary's everybody's favorite accompanist," says Jack Hall, a hymn-sing participant. "She laughs the loudest when she messes up or misses notes, which helps the people who want to participate not to feel shy about singing along with the group, even if they don't think they're good at it. They figure out pretty quickly that even if they don't have particularly good voices, or can't read music, they can still have a good time. Mary's message is that you don't have to be perfect to join in the singing. And when her sister Marilyn comes along with her, it's a real treat, because Marilyn has an awesome singing voice … they're quite a pair … and I remember when Mary accompanied Marilyn and Paul Ranum in a duet— you'd not hear better in any church, anywhere. We're lucky to have them all."

Mary also volunteers to provide the music for the weekly religious service at the county nursing home and rehabilitation center, where she has been a patient several times. "It's a way to give back," she says of those she calls her "other family" that includes both the facility staff and the long-term residents.

At the present time, Mary's life includes a patchwork of various people and needed resources available for her to access on a continual basis, in a variety of ways, to help her out. "They took the rest of my left leg six months ago, after the knee joint had completely deteriorated to the point I couldn't do anything with an artificial leg. They also placed an artificial knee in the other leg, in an effort for me to hang on to it. But since the last amputation I've been much more dependent on outside help," she explains, resting her chin on her fist, and looking at the floor, obviously unhappy about what she has been forced to admit. "I'm used to being independent and I've had a hard time using an above-the-knee artificial leg, so this adjustment has been hard. I spent months in rehab learning how to manage without one leg and being pretty gimp on the other one." She tells me there aren't any occupational or physical therapy programs that help farmers accommodate to livestock farming. "They don't help you figure out a different way to milk a cow, because there isn't any, so you have to figure that balancing act out yourself, by trial and error, and it's mostly error," she chuckles.

Mary's disability assistance and resource availability learning curve has been steep. Currently she receives 25 hours per week of general help with personal care, household chores, meals, and tending the animals. Her helpers come from a local agency that provides Medicare and Medicaid funded services aimed at keeping the elderly and disabled living in their own homes. Unfortunately, this is not enough. "I'm cutting back on the number of calves next time, which will cut back on my income, but I don't see any way around it ... and I'm not happy about it ... but I'm getting older, so maybe I'd be cutting back anyway—who knows?" she shrugs.

Mary no longer crop farms. Instead she rents out most of the 220 acres she owns as pasture or for growing feed corn, which brings in additional income. She's optimistic about the trends in cattle futures because there are fewer cattle available nationwide, and scarcity is always good for prices. Nevertheless, she doesn't expect to get rich. "Because of my health situation I've had some atypical years recently, so while a fair amount of money passes through the operation, I don't clear a lot, but my current goal is still to wing it without taking out operating loans, and continue to keep my head above water," she explains. "So far—so good ... which I'm glad about, because a few years ago the loan officer at the bank made an issue about me being disabled and a woman, and questioned whether I'd be able to repay the loan.... It made me mad, but at the time I was too busy to complain, so I just decided to avoid doing any more business with that bank."

Another remarkable reality in Mary's life is that she is an astute businesswoman who manages to live nearly debt-free. The farm is paid for and, having avoided taking on debt in the form of farm operating loans, she has a lot of freedom in her decision-making. But the picture is not all rosy. She faces significant practical constraints. "My health is too unpredictable to think about enlarging the operation, so it's more a matter of staying afloat until Prince Charming shows up, and since lately I haven't been working much on solving that problem, it's probably not going to happen anytime soon," she laughs.

I ask her what the hardest thing about continuing to farm has been as she has become more disabled. "It's pretty frustrating to wake up every morning and find out my leg didn't grow back overnight," she says, without cracking a smile. "My personal life's not the greatest either. There's no Prince Harry knocking on my door," she adds, more wistfully than I anticipated. "My love life is at the bottom of the barrel ... and I just haven't had time to go looking for Mister Right—but I'm thinking I'll probably get around to that next week, after I catch up on the books," she grins, using both hands to fluff up all two inches of her hair. "You never know who's around the corner and might be worth a second look."

By the time the interview is finished and I prepare to leave the farm, it has finally stopped snowing. The storm clouds have broken up, revealing a blinding western sun sitting low on the horizon, reflecting off the glare of fresh snow. As I slowly maneuver along the slick, hilly gravel road I came in on, it occurs to me how embarrassing it would be to slide off into the ditch and have to walk back and admit what I'd just done to someone as capable and self-sufficient as Mary. No doubt she'd point me in the direction of the tractor and tell me to pull the car out myself. I suppose I could do this, I think, but I'm very sure I don't want find myself in the position of having to try.

The other thing I'm quite certain of is that beneath Mary's cheerful demeanor is an unusually sensitive, lonely woman who has worked extraordinarily hard to create the life she wants for herself. Despite very trying and much more physically difficult circumstances than most people ever have to face and deal with, she's singlehandedly forged ahead, catching every curve ball thrown her way, pitching it right back. Somehow, she has never lost sight of her desire to farm, and has carried on doing what she loves in spite of the obstacles that keep falling across her path.

Mary could have quit farming after arthritis stole away her physical capabilities, but she didn't quit, because she wanted to continue farming. She's always had other options, and could have made different choices, but she didn't want to explore any of those possibilities because she didn't want to stop doing what she is doing and, so far, she has found a way to avoid that. In this regard, she's a very lucky woman.

I've never had a sense that Mary has given much thought—ever –to the depth of personal courage, determination and conviction her decision to continue farming takes. My guess is that she believes, but would never admit, that it's her God-given right to do what she wants to do so she does it, and that's as far as her analysis goes. This logic seems a little like being hit by a truck and not being upset about it, because you love trucks so much. It's an unusual approach to life, but for some people, Mary included, it works just fine.

I've not met many women as inspirational as Mary Dunn. She has faced down challenges most people would find insurmountable and gone on to create the life she wants and then proceeded to live it her way, and on her terms. Every woman should be so courageous, and so fortunate. Bravo, Mary. Bravo!

Conclusion:
Cultivating the Dirty Life
Feminism at Its Finest

No matter what people say, farming is the oldest profession in the world, because the need to eat is much greater than the need for sex—and women are involved in both.
—Unknown

I loved writing this book. I even learned to live with the acute attack of pitiful inadequacy I knew would overtake me following every interview with these amazing women farmers. I learned to ignore being repeatedly and forcefully reminded that a university education only gets you so far, and rarely guarantees the satisfaction that comes from grinding out solutions to the real-life challenges associated with working on the land—and this is where the women farmers I met have it all. They know everything there is to know about the decidedly unglamorous realities of backbreaking farm work and they don't romanticize any of it, nor do they express any interest whatever in doing something else with their lives. They are fortunate enough to have discovered what, for them, has deep personal meaning and they are living out this imperative every day. I can't imagine a more privileged and satisfying life, and insofar as I could determine, neither can they.

The beauty of it all is that their life's work is not about the money. In fact, in terms of cash in their pockets after all the bills are paid, these women farmers don't generate much discretionary income. In fact, when considering the number of hours the average farmer puts into farming, together with the whiplash created by agricultural price variations, most farmers are earning considerably less than half the minimum wage.

One of the most interesting things the women farmers described in this book taught me concerns the broad-based politics that govern farming and the food system—startling things that had never occurred to me. I was not aware of how broken many farmers and most foodies believe the food system is. I was not conversant in the arguments surrounding genetically modified corn, high fructose corn syrup, antibiotic use in meat and dairy animals, or the complex issues associated with fertilizer, herbicide and pesticide use. I wasn't aware that there are good, not so good, and very bad farming practices.

Whether the prevailing claims that the food system is dangerously dysfunctional on several levels are true, or are merely political theatre contrived to create a new food industry is, in my current view, a question without a definitive answer. Nevertheless, I became aware that the concern is out there, and is so real for some people that it bears more serious consideration.

After many conversations on the subject, my takeaway on any hope for fixing the food system and guaranteeing its quality depends entirely on empowering women to do the hard work that will achieve this goal. But, more than that, repairing the broken food system involves the agricultural industry getting out of their way so women can empower themselves, and there is abundant evidence that women farmers nationwide are doing exactly that. They know that when the volume of women's voices in the arena where farm and food policies are made, rises, more sustainable farm and food policies will result. And, just maybe, the big hulking Farm Bill, which has traditionally focused almost exclusively on subsidizing high-yield commodity crops over promoting and enhancing sustainable food systems, will eventually be modified to better support small farmers, thereby benefiting women farmers in particular.

While increasing numbers of women are going into farming, this doesn't mean women who operate farms are enjoying as much financial success as their male counterparts. Most farms run by women have slim profit margins and the money in-money out ratio is often perilously close to 1:1. As a result, most women farmers consistently fall below the poverty level. One reason for this disturbing fact is that most women seek to fill a smaller niche market, such as Suellen Thomson-Link's sprout growing business, Andrea Hazzard's heritage grains, and a recently discovered project I encountered that produces 16 specialized varieties of garlic to sell at local farmers' markets located within a small geographic area. The risk in such an enterprise is great in that only those people who take food and its preparation very seriously are aware that there are 16 or more different varieties of garlic and have the time to pursue finding the kind they want.

Because fresh garlic is perishable, it can't be stored, making the market for the more esoteric kinds even smaller.

All of these are very labor-intensive farming efforts and the return often barely covers costs, so the profit margin, if there is one, is very slim. Nevertheless, women farmers' attraction to these small crop enterprises makes sense when considering that traditionally women have grown the foods that families eat (vegetables, fruits, protein rich grains and poultry) while men have typically grown commodity crops or raised livestock for market, which is where the profit in farming more often resides. In terms of percentages, in addition to tending toward specialty crops women farmers run more equine facilities and poultry operations than men do, and are much less likely to be found on large-scale crop farms, cattle feedlots or large dairies, where there is more money to be made.

However, Kathy Nickel, Sadie Zimmer and the Cistercian nuns are three powerful examples of the exception that proves the rule. All manage large farm operations and prove that there is no obvious reason why women farmers who want to do large scale farming can't do it; it's more a matter of most electing not to.

Women's unique ability to organize themselves around professional farming is, in equal measure, both inspiring and truly remarkable, but not too surprising. The one certainty about women is that they know how to get organized, and they will always pull together around something they care about. This is how suffrage succeeded, how the modern feminist movement was born and how, most recently, women's reproductive rights have been protected in the face of assaults from every direction. And this is how women will succeed in farming and agricultural enterprises far into the future.

Among the many organizational resources available to women farmers, the Women's Food and Agriculture Network (WFAN) is among the most phenomenal. Led entirely by women, the initiative provides rural women with abundant opportunities to connect with each other, and to learn how to farm, to sustain good conservation practices, to run for political office to change agricultural policies, and how to impact the food system. The organization uses social media to connect with women farmers across the nation, offering workshops and go-to conferences where they can connect with and learn from each other, as well as engage in hands-on learning experiences. These meetings occur through teleconferencing, video conferencing, Skype, YouTube videos, and kitchen table potlucks, making it possible for women farmers all across the country to get to know each other, and then go forward together.

WFAN also acts as a clearinghouse for new information about the latest in farming's best practices first hand, as well as promoting related initiatives, such as the Slow Money movement designed to help identify new sources of capital investments for developing small food enterprises, organic farms and local food systems.

My personal favorite, however, is WFAN's Plate to Politics initiative, which is a rogue effort within the organization that specifically targets the gender inequality in the halls of agricultural power and prepares women farmers to speak truth to that power. By cleverly naming the effort Plate to Politics instead of Politics to Plate, women have used their power to take control of the food production process, pointing out that the food that appears on any individual plate is the result of political decisions, not the other way around. The initiative directs training resources toward women and girls, with a view toward helping them ramp up their leadership skills at all levels of public involvement, and empowering them to use their voices as agents of change.

On one hand, I find this an interesting initiative to throw both dollars and personal energy toward because I've yet to encounter a woman farmer who wasn't already politically savvy and a force to be reckoned with. Consequently, I have a hard time imagining how any one of them could be any more politically astute and capable than they already are. On the other hand, every generation needs to recognize how important public and political engagements around issues that matter to them is, and learn how to do this effectively.

In addition to creating stronger women, the common core undergirding all of WFAN's efforts is a heartfelt commitment to health, social justice, and environmental sustainability. It's hard to argue against food needing to be safe and nutritious, or that farmers are entitled to earn a fair wage and that the land must somehow be sustained and nurtured in order to remain productive. All three concerns are obvious no-brainers, but it is women farmers who are tackling them head-on, doing whatever it takes make their voices heard, and working to create an environment that promotes greater social and economic justice for both large and small-scale agricultural enterprises.

I Don't Know Whether I'm a Feminist or Not: I Just Like to Farm

> I'm not sure what being a feminist means ... but I do know I'm doing what I want to do and living the life I want to live—and doing it on my terms.
>
> —Kathy Nickel

When I set out to write this book, I was seeking the answer to one question: Why do some women choose farming as their life's work? I was expecting to discover that women who embrace farming as a lifestyle or a livelihood possess, because of their natural nurturing abilities, a unique spiritual connection to the land that somehow sets them apart from other women. I hypothesized that this spiritual quest is what draws them into farming and sustains them through the good and bad times, and I wanted to explore this idea further.

I still believe this may be true, but I was unable to get very far in terms of uncovering it. The closest I came was in my conversations with Sonia Kendrick and with Sister Gail Fitzpatrick. Sonia is very articulate in explaining that she is trying to do God's work here on earth and she knows the land is central to this desire. But she does not speak of land in spiritual terms. The Cistercian nuns, on the other hand, spend their lives on a perpetual spiritual journey that leads them down the sacred path working the land provides. They don't separate work and prayer, so everything they do, including farming, is tied into their desire to lead a spiritual life. They view the land and every other living thing on the planet, as God's creation and focus their lives on caring for what God has created. Not surprisingly, theirs is a more developed sense of spirituality of the land and of farming than the other women farmers I met indicated.

There are several possible explanations for my failure to get at the spiritual component of working on the land among the other women farmers. The simplest is that I wasn't asking the right questions. Although I tried several different approaches, the answers I received always came up short. Another possibility is that because farmers are very busy people they generally aren't given to spending a lot of time thinking about spiritual journeys or searching for life's deeper meaning, so they've never given the topic serious thought. Ultimately I concluded that the most likely reason for not finding a uniquely spiritual component to women farmers' lives is that women farmers do feel an unusually deep spiritually sustaining connection with the land, but this is so much a part of who they are that they can't, or don't want to articulate it, and I couldn't find a way to help them out. Eventually, I found that asking these women about the spirituality of farming was no different than asking them why they like the color blue better than the color red—they don't know why, they just do.

What I did not start out looking for yet was delighted to find, is that all of these women, including the Cistercian nuns, are an awesome group of the strongest feminists I've ever met. However, if I told any one of them this they'd probably have no idea what I was talking about. Neither the term "feminist" nor the concept of feminism commonly flows through most conversations rural folks have.

WHAT IN THE WORLD IS A FEMINIST?

I myself have never been able to find out precisely what feminism is: I only know that people call me a feminist whenever I express sentiments that differentiate me from a doormat.
—Rebecca West

There are as many definitions of feminism as there are recipes in a Betty Crocker cookbook. Feminism can be as simple as the radical notion that women are, like men, human beings, thus in all ways equal to them, or as illuminating as the realization that women are too intelligent, too demanding, and too resourceful for anyone other than themselves to be in charge of their lives. Everyone from Karl Marx, who has a surprisingly positive view of women's rights, to the Pope, who praises women's equality but won't let women enter into the exclusively male, no-women-allowed priesthood, probably has a personal definition of feminism and holds an opinion on the subject.

The modern notion of feminism has emerged out of the lives of middle-class urban women and encompasses a range of ideologies that share a common goal: defining, establishing, and achieving equal political, economic, cultural, personal, and social rights for women in all spheres of society, including equal opportunities in education and employment. Feminism as a social movement arose in response to what urban, middle class women, living mostly in the northeastern corridor states, viewed as their oppressive lives. They felt men dominated them and stood in the way of their right to make personal choices for themselves, based upon what they wanted rather than what society expected of them. These women felt that a deeply entrenched, male-centered culture driven by male expectations of who women should be, and how women should behave, defined their lives as wives and mothers. They protested women's economic dependence upon their husbands and lack of personal freedom to make their own decisions and choices. Married women believed that, as wives without independent means of financial support, they had no power in their marriages, held no sway over their husbands, and must defer to him. Single women who, absent a husband, had to support themselves lacked the earning power their male counterparts enjoyed, and were unable to access most of the same social and economic opportunities.

To a large extent all of these beliefs were correct, as far as they went, and with two caveats: one was that most poor women have always needed to find a way earn money, thus have always had some measure of economic independence and power in their relationships with men. The other, partial exception is that wealthy, upper class women surrounded by servants who did the hands and knees work of maintaining a household and caring for the children had the time, but not always the means, to pursue their own interests apart from their obligations as wives and mothers. However, for these women, wealth did not entirely guarantee their personal freedom because their husbands controlled the money, thereby also controlling their wives.

When a few brassy, articulate women got behind the notion of women's full social equality, the idea quickly gained traction and a full-scale feminist revolution began. Women writers began saying women existed as human beings apart from their roles as wives and mothers, and they were entitled to live their own lives, on their own terms. English author Virginia Woolf claimed every woman needed a room of her own in which to develop her thoughts. French feminist Simone de Beauvoir declared that women were the "second sex"[1] and coined the classic phrase "One is not born a woman—one becomes one." Simone argued that a woman's biological gender should not define her destiny and that a woman should be able to define womanhood any way she wished.

In 1963, just as the sexual revolution[2] was getting up a full head of steam, fire-breathing feminist and gifted journalist Gloria Steinem took a job as a Playboy Bunny and then wrote a scathing exposé of the experience. She concluded that Playboy Clubs, which were springing up all over the country, were nothing more than institutionalized exploitation of women.[3] At the core of Steinem's essay was her belief that the sexual revolution was doomed to failure if men were the only ones allowed to define it. To make her point, she argued that both women and men would benefit from women having greater sexual freedom.

Most men, including Playboy Magazine founder Hugh Hefner, did not agree. Earlier Hefner, one of the pre-eminent media moguls of the day, had attempted to define the terms of the sexual revolution solely from the male standpoint, all of which Steinem ultimately defined as "bunk" because Hefner viewed women as objects for male sexual gratification. "A woman reading *Playboy* feels a little like a Jew reading a Nazi instruction manual," she said.[4]

After years of research on the nuances of marriage and family life, prominent scholar and sociologist Jessie Bernard concluded that marriage between men and women was an unequal relationship that was more beneficial to men and was thus an overall "better deal" for them.[5] She pointed out that women work just as hard as men do but because all of this occurs within the sphere of home and family life, it is expected of them and they receive no direct financial reward for their labor. Conversely, men hold down paying jobs outside the home, are in a position to advance themselves as members of a paid workforce. Jessie also pointed out that men, who are able to earn more money, are held in higher esteem and are viewed as "more valuable" members of society than are women, and women's work, merely because it is performed by women, as part of the social expectations that surround being a wife and mother, is never as highly valued.

Ultimately Jessie concluded that it was in men's best interest to limit women's options outside marriage and keep their wives "barefoot and pregnant" because, lacking other options, these women would remain in their homes cooking their husband's meals, washing his dirty underwear and raising his progeny. She stressed that while this arrangement left women wanting it served men's interests very well, and was at the core of men's resistance to the feminist movement

Expressing concerns about the future of family life took on considerable political significance after the birth control pill became widely available to help women control their own sexual and reproductive lives. Then the U.S. Supreme Court determined that abortion was legal and women had the right to have one if they desired, thus giving them control over their decisions regarding motherhood. Suddenly urban, middle-class women had choices they merely dreamed of previously. They were no longer doomed to lives as unpaid household servants and baby machines. Instead, they were full-fledged human beings who were quickly gaining control over their own destiny. When men began to realize they were losing control of and power over women, and that all their free household benefits were at risk, they became more frightened than they had ever been before.

Meanwhile, Back on the Farm

If I'd spent time worrying about whether I was being treated equally with men, I'd have never gotten a damned thing done. Truth is, the thought never crossed my mind.

—Bytha Naderer

Rural women and men, many of whom were descended from early pioneer stock, viewed this national soap opera with amusement, peppered with considerable curiosity about what, exactly, these so-called feminists wanted? They were busy people, and couldn't help wondering what all the uproar was about?

My first glimpse of the wide rural-urban divide arose during the late 1960s, when the women's movement was gaining a full head of steam and a lot of press. It came during Christmas vacation from college when my great-aunt Bytha, a feisty woman of unacknowledged age with a flaming red wig she claimed was her natural hair color and a genetic inability to withhold her opinion about anything, invited me to lunch. She said she wanted to talk about "all this feminist stuff" she was hearing about, which she neither understood nor had much patience with—and neither did any of her friends. She was hoping I could explain it to her. For various reasons, including wide age spans among brothers and sisters, Bytha and her sister Kora were the only older female relatives I'd ever known. And, as the only girl born into my generation of the family, they felt both a particular responsibility toward and special affection for me, especially since I was growing up as the only girl among so many boys. I genuinely enjoyed spending time with them.

Bytha was one of 13 children, and like all of her siblings, had been born in a covered wagon. She first saw the light of day sometime between the end of the Civil War and the turn of the 20th century, during a fierce ice storm in what was then the Missouri Territory. The reason for the wig, to hear her tell it, was that, as a young bride in the Oklahoma Territory, she had an unfortunate encounter with an Indian raiding party that had left her mostly bald. I never believed this, but it made a good family story.

By the time she was 35, Bytha had buried two husbands, both of whom were cattle ranchers, out on the plains of eastern Colorado. After her second husband, Karl, died, she continued living on the ranch, running the operation on her own while she finished raising their children. Eventually the catastrophic winds accompanying the Dust Bowl years drove her into town.

Bytha's claim to fame was that she started voting in public elections when William McKinley ran for president, many years before suffrage became the law of the land. When I asked her how she managed this, she said she just did it. Nobody who knew her questioned the possibility that she might be telling the truth. She also believed, in her bones, that Franklin Delano Roosevelt, rather than Jesus Christ, was the savior of the world. A robust, outspoken woman, Bytha was not given to entertaining opinions or beliefs that ran contrary to her own. Many of these evolved out of her personal re-interpretation of the Bible, which she read on a daily basis, and believed she could've done a much better job of writing. She was also certain she could substantially improve upon it. Family was everything to her, because family loyalty is what guaranteed survival in the early days of the frontier life she was born into.

Bytha had invited her supposedly older sister Kora to join us for lunch. Tall, slender, and, as proof of her claim that she'd never met a horse she couldn't ride, Kora was as bow legged as a rodeo cowboy. She had never married, and was, for her age (which no one had a clue about) very fashion conscious. She continued to dye her abundant head of hair jet black, and always wore just a little too much make-up and jewelry. Bytha believed Kora's excessive concern for her appearance was because she still looking for a husband. Kora vehemently and without humor, denied this notion whenever it came up, which was often.

A persistent rumor about Kora, which she seemed to encourage, was that the one true love of her life had died in the Great War, and that she'd never gotten over it. My armchair calculations suggested that, at the present, she was closer to 90 than to 80 and therefore a little too old for this claim to be precisely true. But Aunt Kora could be somewhat intimidating so I was reluctant to pursue the facts of this story with her.

True or not, after World War I ended she spent most of the rest of her nursing career, which began when she was a teenager, as a midwife out on the plains of eastern Colorado, where a few of her sisters had also settled. She carried a revolver, made house calls on horseback and, among other things, attended her youngest sister at the time of my father's birth. Later she became the Otero County public health nurse, which forced her to learn to drive the car that came with that job. I knew she kept her nursing license current over the years, but wasn't sure about whether she still carried a gun. My dad thought she probably did, but neither of us was willing to ask her.

According to my aunts, and everyone else in the family, a "real woman" was one who was able to ride a horse, rope a calf, shoot a rifle well enough to take out a coyote at 50 yards, and render lard. Rendering lard was particularly important because it had multiple uses, including being the key ingredient for making soap to wash everything, including people, floors, horses, and clothes. More importantly, lard was the most vital ingredient in a decent piecrust, and on the frontier, pies were the social mainstay of family and community life. Any female unable to do this all of these things, and do them well, was somehow failing to uphold the sacred honor of womanhood.

I could ride a horse, but that was as much frontier womanhood as I could honestly own up to. Everything else seemed to me to be irrelevant. However, my aunts disagreed and believed these failures cast grave doubts on my future.

I was looking forward to lunch, but was a little worried about the menu. It didn't surprise me to find that Bytha had set out the good china, which, many years ago, she had promised me would be mine someday. She had gone to a lot of effort to make a hearty meat and potatoes noon meal that would appeal to ranch hands, but definitely was not the first choice of a college girl who enjoyed spending her summers tanning on the beaches of southern California.

Nevertheless, I always felt at home in Aunt Bytha's four-square, prairie-style bungalow in the Mission Hills section of San Diego. She had reluctantly moved to the area several years ago, at my father's insistence, because it had fallen to him to keep a watchful eye on both of his mother's older sisters. Her chief decorating mode consisted of large pictures of the women in the family who came before me, which she hung strategically on every wall of nearly every room of the house. After each visit to this multi-room portrait gallery, I went down on my knees and begged God to save me from what I deeply feared was my inevitable destiny. I prayed to keep all my own teeth and that wearing the weather-beaten ravages of a long life out on the Great Plains on my face was not a genetic trait I would inherit.

After we sat down at the table and returned thanks for the food, Bytha passed me the meat, which I passed on to Aunt Kora untouched. It did not escape Aunt Bytha's notice that I was picking at my food, and she asked me why I wasn't eating? I explained that I was a vegetarian now. "Rabbits eat vegetables—the rest of us need meat," Bytha proclaimed decisively.

"You'll never have strong, healthy babies if you don't eat meat," Kora added.

"Paul [my father] says she's not getting married and having babies," Bytha leaned across the table to tell Kora, effectively excluding me from the conversation.

"Is that right?" both turned to ask me at the same time, each taking off their identical, round, black-rimmed glasses, enabling them to better stare their listener down. This happens frequently with them, but the dramatic effect is often ruined because their eyeglass prescriptions are not identical, and they usually choose the wrong pair when they finally put them back on.

I tried to explain that women have lots of options they've never had before, and are getting more, so they don't have to get married and have babies and that sometimes being a wife and mother holds women back. I added that women don't necessarily need husbands anymore either. Bytha turned toward Kora and whispered that maybe I was "one of those feminists" she's been hearing about on TV. Kora whispered back that she heard feminists were communists and wondered whether, if Paul knew what universities were teaching these days, he'd be quite so willing to pay for sending me to one.

I decided not to try explaining that, in fact, there was a healthy dose of Marxism, which I found very attractive, underpinning the basic principles of the feminist movement and instead decided to play with my mashed potatoes while I waited them both out. Finally, Kora picked up the conversation again.

"I had a career of my own and never needed a husband.... I don't think not having one is a new idea," she said. "If that's what college is teaching you, Paul's wasting a lot of money," she added as an afterthought.

"I ran the ranch all on my own, for over 20 years after Karl died. A husband is handy, but not absolutely necessary," Bytha declared, with such conviction that she was compelled to put down her fork and fold her hands in her lap. "I couldn't go running for Karl every time I saw a rattle snake— I had to carry my own gun and shoot that snake myself, right then. That's what he expected me to do—he didn't want a wife who depended on him so much she couldn't take care of herself and manage on her own, for God's sake ... she would've been way too much of a bother," Bytha continued, with obvious pride in her contribution to the conversation. "He expected me to do just about everything he could do, and at least as well ... and I could have babies, which he couldn't." She chuckled at having scored one for honor and glory of womanhood and then took another bite of food.

"Nursing wasn't any different," Kora pointed out. "I had to make decisions every day, and know how to do what any doctor, or veterinarian, for that matter, could do—if I couldn't, the patient might die. I never worked with a doctor who wasn't grateful to me for all I was capable of ... there weren't that many doctors out there, and they couldn't be everywhere they were needed, so they depended upon me more than I depended upon them, truth be told.... It didn't make sense for me not to know as much as the doctor did, and we both knew it," she added, with uncharacteristic humility. "I knew a whole lot more about female issues than any doctor could hope to know—and I saved more than a few mothers and babies, as well as calves and colts that the vet couldn't get there in time to deliver," she pointed out, mixing her typical arrogance with a healthy dose of pride. "Sure, I learned by experience, and doctors went to school … but book learning isn't always the best way … sometimes just jumping in and doing it is better," she exclaimed.

I happened to know that the "just jump in and do it" method was exactly how Kora had learned nursing, and that she had never seen the inside of a classroom after eighth grade. I figured she probably learned how to deliver babies from watching the farm animals drop their young. I wanted to ask her about it, but she wanted to talk about modern marriage instead, particularly why I was opposed to it.

I offered that a marriage to the right man is a wonderful concept and that marriage to the wrong man, simply for the sake is getting married, is far worse than remaining unmarried. I also explained that sometimes marriage stifles a woman—keeps her tied up raising kids and cooking meals, and as a result, she doesn't have the chance to develop her own interests and her own life, and is oppressed.

"Well, you can't cook, so that won't be a problem for you!" Bytha quickly pointed out, a little more harshly than I felt was necessary to make her point. "I told Paul a long time ago that if you don't learn to cook you'll never keep a husband. He said he wasn't sure you even wanted one. I thought he was kidding, but you make it sound like that might be true."

"It might be," I admitted, nervously rolling my green beans around the plate, feeling like this conversation was getting out of hand and I'd been cornered into making a bigger confession about my future than I had intended.

"I don't understand why women have begun thinking that men and marriage hold them back … a man can only hold a woman back if she lets him … and most men are at least smart enough to know better than to try…. If they aren't, then they're too dumb to be trainable and you wouldn't want them anyway. No woman has to get married, she just has to be brave enough not to," Kora declared, in a tone suggesting most women are smart enough to figure this out without having to march in the streets and make speeches on TV to prove their point.

"Men need women to help them out, and smart women know it. I don't understand about men oppressing women, whatever that means? I always ran things the way I wanted them run, and when Karl didn't agree, I set him straight, and after that things were just fine. I took charge and just let him think he was in charge," Bytha said, obviously getting bored with the direction the conversation was taking.

"Women should quit talking about being held back and just start doing what they want to do—men will go along to get along, just like they do when they think nobody's going to stick around and cook them a hot meal. Frankly, I don't know what the hell women are waiting for?" Kora pointed out, with monumental conviction, particularly for someone who had never actually been married. While I was still pondering a response Bytha admonished her sister that here was no swearing at the table while we were eating food the Lord had provided. Kora ignored her and continued.

"Remember when Mama got mad about Papa drinking and drove the wagon into town and shot up the hotel bar? Scared the crap right out of him." I grimaced at the image of my great-grandmother, obviously a follower of Carrie Nation and her Women's Christian Temperance Union, taking out a saloon with a shotgun.

"I don't think she spent any time wondering what anybody would think. She had a problem to solve, so she solved it—and I don't recall that Papa ever drank again," Kora added decisively. I can't say I'd blame him for that, I thought.

Bytha nodded in agreement, adding that the sheriff did say that if my great grandmother ever pulled that again, he'd arrest her—a prospect my great grandfather probably did not find amusing. While I could not personally even begin to imagine this scenario, neither woman seemed to see anything particularly negative or unusual about the way their mother had behaved, and my guess is neither one would've hesitated to do the same thing if the situation warranted.

"As I see it, the only thing holding women back are women themselves. If you young girls want choices for her life, she should just start making them. Who's going to stop you, really?" Kora asked me, reaching for my hand. That was when I knew she was expecting me to quit blathering about women's equality, and simply pick up the "strong, independent woman" family tradition and run with it. I also began to understand that women's equality cuts more than one way, and that place and circumstances really matter in women's lives.

My great aunts and I never really got on the same page about the feminist agenda, and soon they were bored with the whole idea of women's equality. They didn't understand social movements, certainly didn't grasp the notion that, for women, the personal is political, or that freeing women from social and cultural male domination and allowing them to make their own decisions and choices required mass action on a national scale. This had not been their life experience, and they had a hard time envisioning it for others.

As the daughters of a frontier woman, and as frontier women themselves, my aunts, like all rural women, had been living with and working alongside men on an equal basis for their entire lives, as had their mother before them. They truly did not comprehend what I was talking about when I said not all women could live their own lives, on their own terms. They did not see being born female as a pre-determined destiny; instead, they learned to do whatever needed doing to survive, crafted their lives accordingly, and made no apologies for any of it. It never occurred to them that not all women had that same opportunity or that some women were unable to do what they, themselves, had done. Like most rural women, they were far too busy tending the animals, raising the children, cooking for the farm and ranch hands, and bringing in the crops to be tuned in to urban women's lives, problems or personal struggles.

Most important of all, particularly in the context of feminism, rural women didn't see men as the enemy. They knew they had power in their marriages and in the wider community, and weren't likely to let anyone take that from them. They also knew, in their bones, that women and men needed each other. As a result, men trusted them and weren't so reluctant to stand in the way of women having the freedom to live their own lives. This isn't to say there weren't times when rural women found themselves holding the short straw when it came to equal partnerships, but in the realities of everyday life, rural men and women got along together because it was in in the best interests of both to do so. They were strong, independent women, and these qualities benefited the men in their lives, and benefited themselves as individuals, and both knew it, so there was no reason to do anything differently.

The same is true of the women I met while writing this book. To a person, none saw what they were doing as independent women farmers as unique, unusual, or something they weren't entirely capable of being successful at if they set their mind to it. Farming is what they want to do, have chosen to do, like doing and feel good about doing, so they are doing it. They are active, rather than passive, participants in their own lives. Their daily routine is packed with abundant, never-ending hard work, but they aren't afraid of hard work and don't run from it. And while farming is a difficult and risky way to make a living, they aren't afraid of challenges or risk either. They believe in their own ability to problem solve, and this self-confidence carries the day for them—every day.

In other words, in today's world women who choose to farm have claimed their right to make their own choices, on their own terms, just like frontier pioneer women before them did, and they don't care what others think of this choice. They have rejected workplace politics in favor of personal freedom and independence. They aren't worried about crashing through the glass ceiling, because, for them, there isn't one. They aren't interested in chasing wealth, acquiring material goods for the sake of accumulating things, or pursuing the conventional definitions of success, because their wealth comes from the satisfaction they gain every day as farmers. They prefer a modest lifestyle and personal freedom over being tied to the expectations of a job with a regular paycheck … and whether they farm for the glory of God, to care for the earth, to heal themselves, to impact the food system, to make a political statement or to earn a living doesn't matter. They are doing what they want to do, which reflects the deep and essential core of feminism that began with the courageous pioneer women who helped advance the western frontier and continues today among the equally strong, courageous women who choose to raise the animals and farm the land that grows our food.

Chapter Notes

Introduction

1. Alice in Dairyland is a spokesperson for Wisconsin agriculture and a public relations professional working for the Wisconsin Department of Agriculture, Trade and Consumer Protection. After undergoing a lengthy and intense selection to determine the best representative for Wisconsin agricultural initiatives, each year's Alice travels throughout the state, nation and world to promote Wisconsin products to audiences of all ages, educating the media, youth and civic groups about the many facets of the state's agricultural industry. It is a highly competitive and widely sought position among young women interested in Wisconsin agriculture.

2. Women's Food and Agriculture Network, http://www.wfan.org.

3. Virginia Harris, Report on 2012 Agriculture Census Findings on Women Farmers. Webinar: Women in Agriculture Learning Network, December 2, 2014.

4. *Ibid.*

5. Carolyn Sachs, Report on 2012 Agriculture Census Findings on Women Farmers. Webinar: Women in Agriculture Learning Network, December 2, 2014.

6. Lyn Garling, Report on 2012 Agriculture Census Findings on Women Farmers. Webinar: Women in Agriculture Learning Network, December 2, 2014.

7. Carolyn Sachs, *Gendered Fields: Rural Women, Agriculture and Environment* (Boulder, CO: Westview 1996).

8. Sonya Salamon, *Prairie Patrimony: Family, Farming and Community in the Midwest* (Chapel Hill: University of North Carolina Press 1992).

9. Including farms that produce as little as $1000 annually, even if there are not very many of them, in the calculation of the average farm income women farmers earn can artificially skew the income figure downward.

10. How Women are Changing Board Rooms and Rural Landscapes. Webinar: Women in Agriculture Learning Network, November 18, 2014.

11. *Ibid.*

12. *Ibid.*

13. Jenny Barker Devine, *On Behalf of the Family Farm: Iowa Farm Women's Activism Since 1945* (Iowa City: University of Iowa Press 2013).

14. $430 in 2014 dollars.

15. Using $6000 per acre as the average 2014 price of one acre of Midwestern farmland (where most homesteading occurred), today these 160 acres would be worth $960,000.

16. Margaret Mitchell, *Gone With the Wind* (New York: Scribner and Sons, 1936).

17. *Ibid.*

18. Deborah Fink, *Agrarian Women: Wives and Mothers in Rural Nebraska* (Chapel Hill: University of North Carolina Press, 1992).

19. *Ibid.*, 4.

20. www.ctlibrary.com.

21. There is anecdotal evidence, found in the diaries of some pioneer women that, unlike their male counterparts, homesteading women, by adopting a "Live and Let Live" attitude, were able to forge cooperative relationships with the Native Americans upon whose land they were homesteading.

22. Relative to the total body of work on pioneer women, considerably less has been written about African American women farmers in the Reconstruction-era south. These women did not have the benefit of large land grants, but they did obtain small land parcels they farmed to support themselves.

23. Virginia Crocheron Gildersleeve, *Many a Good Crusade* (New York: Macmillan, 1954), 118.

24. *Ibid.*

25. Rose Hayden-Smith, *The Victory Growers* (Jefferson, NC: McFarland, 2014).

26. During World War II my mother was a volunteer nurse at the largest naval hospital on the West Coast. She answered a call for qualified nursing personnel that went out after all navy nurses were sent to base hospitals in the South Pacific following the Japanese attack on Pearl Harbor . My father's niece stepped up to raise several infants and young children alongside her own son, through the end of the war. Included were three of my cousins, whose mothers also joined the active war effort. One mother went to the Port Hueneme Navy language school to assist with efforts to break the Japanese war code; the other went to work in a steel mill in Colorado.

27. *Ibid.*

28. Originally the U.S. Crop Corps was a men-only organization whose wartime goal was to recruit non-farm men to spend a few hours each week volunteering as farm hands.

29. *Ibid.*

30. Cecilia Gowdy-Wygant, *Cultivating Victory: The Women's Land Army and the Victory Garden Movement* (Pittsburgh, PA: University of Pittsburgh Press, 2013).

31. Devine.

32. *Ibid.*, 3.

33. *Ibid.*, 2.

34. *Ibid.*, 139.

35. *Ibid.*

36. Betty Friedan, *The Feminine Mystique* (New York: Dell, 1964).

37. *Women on the Land: Creating Conscious Community in a Forty Year Journey Back to the Land in Search of a Sustainable Future* (Mendocino Coast Films).

38. Rhian Sasseen, "Where Have All the Women Farmers Gone?" *Modern Farmer,* January 14, 2015.

Chapter One

1. Ben Logan, *The Land Remembers.* (Minneapolis, MN: Creative, 1999).

2. The term permaculture was first coined by Australians Bill Mollison and David Holmgren in 1978 and originally referred to permanent agriculture. As the notion of permaculture as a farming ecology that stresses regenerative, self-maintained habitat and agricultural systems caught on, the definition was expanded to stand also for permanent culture. Permaculture is a philosophy of working with, rather than against, nature; and of protracted and thoughtful observation of the land and of looking at plants and animals in all their functions, rather than treating any area of the total growing system as an independent, singularly functioning entity.

3. According to Bill Jacobs, founder and president of Saint Kateri Tekakwitha Conservation Center, Catholics today promote "creation spirituality," "creation theology," "Earth spirituality," or a "new cosmology" of the Universe, parts of which are variously called the "new story," "Earth story," or Universe story. Generally speaking, the creation theology movement seeks to integrate the wisdom of Western and Eastern religions and the traditions of global indigenous cultures with the emerging scientific understanding of the Universe. Creation spirituality emphasizes the relationship between humankind and nature and the protection of nature is considered a sacrament and an expression of God and the "Cosmic Christ." This approach is promoted by former Catholic priest Matthew Fox and was endorsed by "ecotheologian" Thomas Berry, among others.

4. bell hooks, *Belonging: A Culture of Place* (New York: Routledge, 2009), 67.

5. Margaret Roach, *And I Shall Have Some Peace There* (New York: Grand Central, 2011).

6. *Ibid.,* 17.

7. www.philosophy.rutgers.edu.

8. Lori Rotenberk, "Raise the Flag High: Queer Farming in Rural America," *Modern Farmer,* January 22, 2015.

9. www.feediowafirst.org.

10. Excerpt from the Official Slow Food Manifesto, as published in *Slow Food: The Case for Taste* in 2001.

11. *Women on the Land: Creating Conscious Community* (Mendocino Coast Films, 2012).

12. *Ibid.*

13. *Ibid.*

Chapter Two

1. www.rabbisforhumanrights.org.

2. Abbot is a term meaning father, and is an ecclesiastical title given to the head of a monastery or an abbey.

3. The Order of Cistercians of the Strict Observance, also known as Trappists, is a Roman Catholic contemplative religious order consisting of both monks and nuns. Together, the Trappists (male members) and Trappestines (female members) belong to the larger Cistercian family, which traces its origin to 1098. Cistercians follow the *Rule of St. Benedict* and dedicate their lives to seeking union with God through Jesus Christ while living in community with other nuns or fellow monks. Presently there are 1800 Trappestines worldwide and five abbeys housing members of the order in the United States.

4. Mother Rebecca's, Sister Louise's and Sister Kathleen's comments are taken from a video they made for young women who are considering entering the Cistercian community at Our Lady of the Mississippi Abbey.

5. Address of Pope Francis to Cloistered Nuns, Chapel of the Choir of the Chapel of St. Clare, Assisi, October 4, 2013.

6. From ancient times the Church has had the custom of celebrating the liturgy of the hours each day. In this way the Church fulfills the precept to pray without ceasing, at once offering its praise to God the Father and interceding for the salvation of the world.

7. Many orders of religious women are shrinking, and because their land is their only true asset, they are turning to some form of farming to support themselves, even if this has not been the part of their historic tradition.

8. *Rule of St. Benedict*, Chapter 48, On the Daily Manual Labor. March 30, July 30, November 29.

9. www.feediowafirst.com.

10. *Ibid.*

11. Joe Clark, Dave Martin, Martin Dwyer, Chris Formanek and Elizabeth Blood's comments are all taken from www.feediowafirst. com.

Chapter Three

1. Post-traumatic stress disorder (PTSD) is a psychological war casualty disorder affecting soldiers upon return from combat. It manifests itself in several ways, including shock, anger, nervousness, fear, helplessness and guilt. Often these feelings continue and even escalate over time, becoming so strong that they keep the person from living a normal life.

2. See Chapter Two.

3. Anna Mann, Sonia Kendrick, and Althea Raiford all appeared in the documentary film *Terra Firma* produced by Anthony-Masterson Productions, 2014. Their stories are also found at www.farmvetco.org, a coalition of veteran farmers.

4. The post-9/11 GI Bill is an education benefit program for individuals who served on active duty after September 10, 2001. Individuals are eligible for these benefits if they served at least 90 aggregate days on active duty after September 10, 2001 (40 percent of educational costs benefit level); if they were honorably discharged from active duty for a service-connected disability after serving 30 continuous days following September 10, 2001, or served 36 months of active duty, they are eligible for 100 percent of the allowable benefits.

5. Master at Arms is the Navy's police force. They provide waterborne and land security, aircraft and flight line security, strategic weapons and cargo security, maritime security and platform protection. They also conduct customs operations, corrections operations, detainee operations, and protective service operations. MAs perform force protection, physical security and law enforcement, physical security, law enforcement, and develop plans for physical security and force protection enhancement of Navy bases, installations, property, and personnel. They assist commands in conducting terrorist threat analysis and, when necessary, implementing defensive measures.

6. This policy remained officially in place until 2013, when Defense Secretary Leon Panetta removed the military's ban on women serving in combat.

7. Harlan K. Ullman and James P. Wade, *Shock and Awe: Achieving Rapid Dominance* (National Defense University, 1996), XXIV; *CBS Evening News* broadcast, 24 January 2004.

8. www.feediowafirst.com.

9. Veterans Administration is the federal agency charged with providing immediate and lifetime medical care to veterans.

10. Nada's story was presented in the documentary *A Powerful Noise,* produced by Unity Films, LLC (2008).

Chapter Four

1. Gene Logsdon, www.landinstitute.org.

2. www.newyorktimes.Com, August 8, 2014.

3. Michael Pollan, "Wendell Berry's Wisdom," *The Nation*, September 2, 2009.

4. Aspects of Kathy's story appeared in Sara Bredesen, "Continued Legacy," *The Country Today*, November 12, 2014.

5. For a full explanation of the grain markets and how they function see Paula vW. Dáil, *Hard Living in America's Heartland: Rural Poverty in the 21st Century Midwest* (Jefferson, NC: McFarland, 2015).

6. United States Department of Agriculture, www.nass.usda.gov.

7. www.templegrandin.com.

8. Midwest Dairy Association, www.midwestdairy.com.

9. National Milk Producers Federation, www.nmpf.org.

10. Temple Grandin and Catherine Johnson, *Animals in Translation: Using the Mysteries of Autism to Decode Animal Behavior* (Ft. Washington, PA: Harvest, 2006).

Chapter Five

1. www.foodtank.org.

2. Robert Paarlberg, *Food Politics: What Everyone Needs to Know*, 2d ed. (New York: Oxford University Press, 2013).

3. www.poemhunter.com.

4. www.rootsandwings.org.

5. Jerry Apps, *The Land* (Wisconsin Public Television, December 2015).

6. CSAs are Community Supported Agriculture farm memberships whereby individuals purchase a seasonal membership in a local farm operation that guarantees the purchaser a certain amount of fresh, seasonal produce each week during the growing season. Presold CSA memberships are a significant source of income for small, usually organic farmers.

7. Devine.

8. The Midwest Organic and Sustainable Education Service (MOSES) is a nonprofit organization designed to promote organic and sustainable agriculture through providing the education, resources and expertise farmers need for a successful, certified organic farm operation.

9. www.mosesorganic.org/rural-womens-project.

10. www.wfan.org.

Chapter Six

1. Smart Growth was a public policy attempt to control land use, particularly in rural areas, with a view toward restricting certain types of development and preserving wide, open spaces, particularly around public land areas.

2. Mary was using this term loosely to refer to retirement plans farmers, who are self-employed, configure for themselves. Farmers who own land frequently use it as their "retirement plan" by planning on selling a portion of it when they quit farming and then living off the proceeds. Because of this, farmers are heavily opposed to any restrictions on how their land can be divided, who can purchase it, and what can be done with it when it is no longer used as farmland.

3. The University of Wisconsin-Platteville is located about 25 miles south of the Dunn farm and is a common destination for area students after they complete high school.

4. Somatic cell count is an indicator of milk quality. The number of somatic cells increases in response to bacterial infections in the cows and is a means for establishing milk safety. Counts greater that 250,000 cells/ml indicate significant pathology and a reason declare the milk unsafe.

Conclusion

1. Simone de Beauvoir, *The Second Sex* (New York: Alfred A. Knopf, 1971).

2. The sexual revolution arose as an unexpected and unintended consequence when the birth control pill removed the fear of pregnancy, thus allowing women much greater sexual freedom.

3. Gloria Steinem, "A Bunny's Tale," *Show Magazine*, May and June 1963.

4. *Ibid.*

5. Jessie Bernard, *The Future of Marriage* (New Haven: Yale University Press, 1982).

Bibliography

Bernard, Jessie. *The Future of Marriage.* New Haven: Yale University Press, 1982.

Bray, Nan. Interview, July 7, 2014.

Brooks, Zoey. Interview, March 16, 2014.

Carpenter, Gail. Interview, August 30, 2014.

Dáil, Dan. Interview, May 16, 2015.

Dáil, Paula vW. *Hard Living in America's Heartland: Rural Poverty in the 21st Century Midwest.* Jefferson, NC: McFarland, 2015.

De Beauvoir, Simone. *The Second Sex.* New York: Alfred A. Knopf, 1949, 1971.

Devine, Jenny Barker. *On Behalf of the Family Farm: Iowa Farm Women's Activism Since 1945.* Iowa City: University of Iowa Press, 2013.

Dunn, Mary. Interview, February 13, 2015.

Fink, Deborah. *Agrarian Women: Wives and Mothers in Rural Nebraska.* Chapel Hill: University of North Carolina Press, 1992.

Fitzpatrick, Sister Gail. Interview, August 13, 2014.

Friedan, Betty. *The Feminine Mystique.* New York: Dell, 1964.

Garling, Lyn. Report on 2012 Agriculture Census Findings on Women Farmers. Webinar: Women in Agriculture Learning Network, December 2, 2014.

Gildersleeve, Virginia Crocheron. *Many a Good Crusade.* New York: Macmillan, 1954.

Gowdy-Wygant, Cecelia. *Cultivating Victory: The Women's Land Army and the Victory Garden Movement.* Pittsburgh, PA: University of Pittsburgh Press, 2013.

Grandin, Temple, and Catherine Johnson. *Animals in Translation: Using the Mysteries of Autism to Decode Animal Behavior.* Ft. Washington, PA: Harvest, 2006.

Harris, Virginia. Report on 2012 Agriculture Census Findings on Women Farmers. Webinar: Women in Agriculture Learning Network, December 2, 2014.

Hayden-Smith, Rose. *The Victory Growers.* Jefferson, NC: McFarland, 2014.

Hazzard, Andrea. Interview, October 24, 2014.

Hill, Sister Myra. Interview, August 13, 2014.

hooks, belle. *Belonging: A Culture of Place.* New York: Routledge, 2009.

Kendrick, Sonia. Interview, August 10, 2014.

Logan, Ben. *The Land Remembers.* Minneapolis, MN: Creative, 1999.

Mitchell, Margaret. *Gone With the Wind.* New York: Scribner and Sons, 1936.

Nickel, Kathy. Interview, January 13, 2105.

Norman, Corrie. Interview, July 14, 2014.

Paarlberg, Robert. *Food Politics: What Everyone Needs to Know,* 2d ed. New York: Oxford University Press, 2013.

Pollan, Michael. *The Omnivore's Dilemma.* New York: Penguin, 2007.

Pollan, Michael. "Wendell Berry's Wisdom" *The Nation,* September 2, 2009.

A Powerful Noise. Unity Films, 2008.

Reinhart, Peter. Presentation to 2014 University of Wisconsin Summer Forum on Food and Spirituality. Madison, July 18, 2014.

Roach, Margaret. *And I Shall Have Some Peace There.* New York: Grand Central, 2011.

Rotenberk, Lori. "Raise the Flag High: Queer Farming in Rural America." *Modern Farmer,* January 22, 2015.

Sachs, Caroline. *Gendered Fields: Rural Women, Agriculture and Environment.* Boulder, CO: Westview, 1996.

Sachs, Carolyn. Report on 2012 Agriculture Census Findings on Women Farmers. Webinar: Women in Agriculture Learning Network, December 2, 2014

Salamon, Sonya. *Prairie Patrimony: Family, Farming and Community in the Midwest.* Chapel Hill: University of North Carolina Press, 1992.

Sasseen, Rhian. "Where Have All the Women Farmers Gone?" *Modern Farmer,* January 14, 2015.

Steinem, Gloria. "A Bunny's Tale." *Show* magazine, May and June 1963.

Terra Firma. Anthony-Masterson Productions, 2014.

Thomson-Link, Suellen. Interview, August 16, 2014.

Ullman, Harlan K., and James P. Wade. *Shock and Awe: Achieving Rapid Dominance.* National Defense University, 1996, xxiv.

Women on the Land: Creating Conscious Community in a Forty Year Journey Back to the Land in Search of a Sustainable Future. Mendocino Coast Films, 2013.

Zimmer, Sadie. Interview, February 4, 2015.

Index

Numbers in **_bold italics_** refer to pages with photographs.